I0422454

RED STATE, BLUE STATE

RED STATE, BLUE STATE

DEFENDING THE LIBERAL JESUS AND BLUE STATE MORALITY FROM RED STATE RELIGION AND HYPOCRISY

John Grevstad

iUniverse, Inc.
New York Lincoln Shanghai

Red State, Blue State
Defending the Liberal Jesus and Blue State Morality from Red State Religion
and Hypocrisy

Copyright © 2005 by John Grevstad

All rights reserved. No part of this book may be used or reproduced by any
means, graphic, electronic, or mechanical, including photocopying,
recording, taping or by any information storage retrieval system without the
written permission of the publisher except in the case of brief quotations
embodied in critical articles and reviews.

iUniverse books may be ordered through booksellers or by contacting:

iUniverse
2021 Pine Lake Road, Suite 100
Lincoln, NE 68512
www.iuniverse.com
1-800-Authors (1-800-288-4677)

ISBN-13: 978-0-595-34484-0 (pbk)
ISBN-13: 978-0-595-79242-9 (ebk)
ISBN-10: 0-595-34484-4 (pbk)
ISBN-10: 0-595-79242-1 (ebk)

Printed in the United States of America

For
JUDITH M. GREVSTAD (1942–1989)
and
LARRY L. GREVSTAD
My parents provided me with my liberal roots and showed me the liberal
Jesus.
For some reason, I still became a sarcastic jerk.

Acknowledgments

I would like to thank the Blue State liberal's true nemesis, Ralph Nader, and his group of supporters in the 2000 election. Without his selfish diligence and the mental retardation of his flock of trust-fund hippies, George W. Bush would have never won the 2000 presidential election, and I would have never been motivated to document the differences between Red States and Blue States.

My warmest regards to evangelical Christians for destroying the message of the liberal Christ: may they burn in a lake of fire.

Finally, on behalf of Blue State liberals everywhere, I would like to extend my appreciation and thanks to Red State conservatives for their continued efforts of putting American democracy and individual freedom at risk.

I hope all of these A-holes get what they deserve.

Contents

PART I

The Plight of a Blue State Liberal

1

Blue State Horror

Why Did God Have to Get Involved?

Liberals have greeted the results of the 2004 national election, which gave George Bush another four years in office, with despair. It is hard for many of us to believe that George W. Bush will serve four more years as the president of the United States. Furthermore, the Republican gains in both the House of Representatives and the Senate continue to be a cause of concern and worry by all members of liberal America.

What is of further concern to liberals and their leaders is the idea that something called "moral values" was one of the deciding factors in the 2004 election. After the loss of the presidency, the House of Representatives, and the Senate, liberal heroes like Bill Clinton and Ted Kennedy have been claiming that the liberal left must reach out to Americans interested in morality, ethics, and religion.

Not only are liberals scratching their heads in disbelief, but there is also an overwhelming sense of depression and even outrage that all of this could have happened—despite a war in Iraq that looks increasingly impossible to win, an economy that is in decline, and America's archenemy, Osama Bin Laden, still on the loose and more threatening than ever almost four years after the attacks on the World Trade Center. These problems—combined with other issues such as millions of Americans losing or paying more for health care, the mounting need for education reform, and an out-of-control national debt—seemed to indicate that there was the potential for a political landslide—not in favor of the Republicans, who got us in this mess, but for the Democrats, who could have pointed the country in a new, more positive direction.

President Bush was in office for four years, and during this time it is obvious to millions of Americans that just about everything got worse. I was one of the very naïve people who believed, right up until the last vote was cast on election night, that our great nation would not only send George W. Bush back to Texas, but also deliver liberals to the House and Senate on the way to a majority for the Democrats. It would be the liberal Democrats who would set the country straight after four years of bad international policies and an equally oppressive domestic agenda.

But God got involved…

According to many conservatives, George W. Bush won the 2004 election with divine assistance. Conversely, according to many liberals, George W. Bush may be the Antichrist. How could one man inspire such conflicting religious inferences?

This presidential election of 2004 showed that the United States is divided in numerous ways. Obviously, there was always division between conservatives and liberals, and between Republicans and Democrats. But now that religion has been invoked into presidential politics, there is an ever-widening chasm between conservative and liberal Christians.

Also, we saw a new trend sweep the country after this election. Suddenly, we saw a reminder of an old classification of the states that make up our Union. Now and forever hence, we will have Red States and Blue States. The Red States that voted for Bush lean towards the conservative side of things, whereas the Blue States that voted for John Kerry having strong liberal tendencies. The divide in the country and the division between these two classifications of states are more than political. The division is religious and cultural as well. There is a huge difference between life in a Red State and life in a Blue State. I, for one, am very thankful that I live in a Blue State.

Voting against Myself

It was not lost on me and many other liberals that, when we cast our vote for a Blue State liberal (John Kerry), we were voting entirely against our own self-interest. Life for a professional, college-educated liberal in a Blue State is pretty good. I have a great life, and I really don't have all that much to complain about.

I am a middle-class white male with a BA in English and an MA in Social Sciences. Since I am a high school English teacher, I have a very stable job, with zero prospects of being fired or otherwise relieved of my duties. I have rationalized all of the political insanity by selfishly asserting, and rightly so, that my life will not change very much because of a second presidential term from George W. Bush and a Republican—controlled House of Representatives and Senate. Because I am an educated, middle-class white male, my personal situation might even get better with Republicans controlling everything.

I am not, nor was I ever, in the military, so I won't get called up for active duty. I am not gay, so I don't have any plans of marrying another man and being denied what ought to be a legal right. I am not a woman, so I won't be going to Planned Parenthood seeking consultation regarding a potential abortion. A continued poor economy does not outsource my job to another country. Nothing really changes for me. I seemed to have voted entirely against my own self-interest when I voted for every single Democrat on the ballot.

The never-ending and numerous exit polls confirm that God influenced this election. The general ideas, if not the specific results, of these different polls are pretty much common knowledge by now. However, for those of us who question George W. Bush's unethical presidency in light of his constant preaching about his faith, it remains startling and disturbing that so many people have been hoodwinked by his devotion to a God that seems completely foreign to millions of Americans.

For example, according to cnn.com, of all of the voters who chose "moral values" as their number one issue, over 80% voted for President Bush. My vote is always guided by my moral values, but apparently many of us "liberals" don't classify our vote as a "moral value" in an exit poll. My vote for John Kerry and against George W. Bush was completely based on moral and ethical concerns. Participation in the war in Iraq is not just a political issue, or a national security issue, or an economic issue—it is a moral issue as well.

So when someone running an exit poll asks the question, "What was the most important issue that guided your vote?" most liberals have a different answer because, to a liberal, *all* issues involving an election are moral ones. Concern for the environment is a moral issue. Allowing two gay, law-abiding taxpayers the protection from the government to get married is a moral issue. Involvement in a war is a moral issue. It seems that Republicans vote with their morality on their sleeves, and everyone else doesn't.

There are some other interesting results from the cnn.com exit poll data.1 Amazingly, President Bush was also able to garner 56% of the white Catholic vote, with John Kerry getting only 43%. John Kerry is a white Catholic, for crying out loud! Additionally, 61% of churchgoers voted for Bush.

But one of the things that was particularly disturbing to me was that 8% of the voting population believes that a "strong religious faith" is the most important quality in a president. Out of this group, a whopping 91% voted for President Bush. Equally disturbing was the fact that only 7% of voters chose "being intelligent" as the most important presidential quality; 91% of these people voted for John Kerry. Putting intelligence aside, the vague concept of religious beliefs and attitudes became one of the dominant personality characteristics in a nation with a religious diversity that is unheard of in other countries.

Likewise, I voted entirely against my own socioeconomic group: 55% of males voted for Bush, I am male; 58% of white people voted for Bush, I am white; 53% pf people between the ages of 30 and 44 voted for Bush, I am 38 years old; 55% of people with incomes between 50,000 and $100,000 voted for Bush, I earn about $70,000 a year; 59% of Protestants voted for Bush, I am a confirmed Lutheran; 57% of married people voted for Bush, I have been married for three years. The list goes on and on. The one classification that I belong to in which the majority voted for Kerry comes in the area of education, where there was a tie: 49% of college graduates voted for both George W. Bush and John Kerry. However, 55% of people completing post-graduate work voted for Kerry. I have a master's degree—this was one of the few areas in which I voted with my group.

All of the questions and answers indicate a pretty significant divide in the United States. The divisions are in a variety of different areas, including political parties, religious affiliations, values, and, yes, even the dreaded Red States and Blue States. To me, a Blue State liberal, it all represents a war of cultures: us against them.

Reclaiming Jesus

The citizens of the United States of America elected George W. Bush and his conservative friends, in spite of most Americans believing on Election Day that the country was headed in the wrong direction. All told, there was some horrible news as the election returns were ratified. Here's the bad news: 62,040,606 Americans cast their vote for President Bush. Here's the good news: 59,028,109 voted against him.

There is more bad news: George W. Bush thinks he earned "political capital" and now he wants to use it. Again, I must selfishly repeat; I am still a heterosexual, middle-class, married white male with a stable job, and his "political capital" isn't going to affect me.

This is still more bad news: the continuation of George Bush's policies are going to harm millions of American, most of whom voted for him. This is even more good news: his policies will barely, if at all, have an impact on my life. The notion that this shift in American politics is based on religion is more than a little disturbing, especially since I am certain that Jesus was a liberal. Furthermore, as some states continue to struggle with an uncertain economy and war hanging over their heads, I remain very thankful that I am a liberal living in a Blue State.

On a very serious and extremely bitter note, liberals need to stop being such wimps. We need to take back what is and will always be rightfully ours, and we need to be aggressive about it. Conservatives "conserve" the old way. Liberals "liberate" to the new way. And as the Red State conservatives pontificate about religion and "God", we must remind them that Jesus did not conserve the old ways and customs: He liberated to the new. Simply put, liberals need to reclaim Jesus.

Conservative Christians started this whole argument about morality and ethics, and Jesus was never a conservative. Jesus was and will always be a liberal. More than that, He was a radical liberal: perhaps, as Martin Luther King indicated, "the most radical liberal of all time." He was so radical that the conservative Sanhedrin wanted him dead. He was so radical that the ultra-conservative Roman state obliged and had him crucified without a trial. He really didn't do anything wrong, He just had a bit of a revolutionary, liberal message. Yep, conservatives crucified a liberal. Imagine that.

By looking at the words of Jesus, it is obvious that the modern day Christian is obligated by the nature of his or her religion to be a liberal. To prove this point, it is necessary to see where it all went wrong. In order to accomplish this, we must go to the Old Testament to get some of the old rules and regulations of the past. Likewise, it is important to "open Paul's mail" and get his view on things, since he wrote most of the New Testament. How did the message of a radical liberal become the judgmental morality of the Red State religious conservative?

Also, we must do something that conservative Christianity does not do very often. It is imperative that we go straight to the source: the Gospels. That's right, the justification for Jesus being a liberal and advocating the policies and lifestyle of the Blue State liberals lies in the books of Matthew, Mark, Luke, and John. We are going to look at what Jesus said to see what He would think of the state of the moral issues of our day. The intended result is to expose Red State religion as the mindless, selfish hypocrisy that it is.

Since Red State conservatives have made religion an issue, it is time to take all of the little pet ideals of the conservative right, led by their champion George W. Bush, and see how they hold up to the words and philosophies of our Lord and Savior Jesus Christ. What does Jesus say about homosexuals? What does He say about invading other countries whether they threaten us or not? Would Jesus be a willing taxpayer, understanding the need for taxation with representation, or would he cry like a baby if the government raised His taxes two hundred dollars a year?

Along the way, we must keep in mind that the conservative movement in any culture, religion, or philosophy seeks to conserve antiquated doctrine, whether it is right or wrong. We should not forget that liberal religions, philosophy and culture seeks to liberate from the old and progress to the new. As a result, it will become obvious that Jesus was a crazy liberal and that it is in the Blue States of America that His philosophies and ideals are emphasized and valued. It is in the Red States that His message is either ignored, or worse, turned completely upside down.

We are going to discover the answer to these questions and more, and, for the conservative Christian right in the good ol' U.S. of A., it ain't gonna be pretty. Red State conservative, Republicans do not have a monopoly on moral issues. Make no mistake about it—it is the Blue State liberal who values the teachings of Christ.

But first, we need to find out where it all went wrong. How in the hell did half of The United States of America, the most powerful nation in the history of the world, turn the message of a radical liberal into the political philosophy of the angry white man and the sheltered white woman?

What Happened to Christianity?

Before I move on with my Red State diatribe, I must give some justification for my belief that it is the heathen liberal—not the arrogant, preachy liberal—that needs to do the slimy job of stooping to the level of the Red State conservative Christians in the effort to expose them for the self-centered blasphemers that they are. First of all, I am a negative, sarcastic jerk. I can't stand conservatives, and I have no problem letting the world know. I do not have the desire to take the high road of dialogue and acceptance of others. The tendency of the Ivy League, Northeast liberal to talk down to the Red State conservative has got us in this mess. Now that the Red State conservative has taken over the country, the silence from the Left is deafening, especially on the combined issues of politics and Christianity.

I have always found it a bit fascinating that so many people with conservative leanings have been able to permanently designate Jesus as some sort of conservative hero. While I am no biblical scholar, there is little doubt that Jesus was one of the most radical liberals in human history. This has been completely lost on American culture. It is because of the bad theology practiced by the Red State Christians.

For this reason, declaring myself a Christian becomes a little bit of a problem for me. The Christian Right in the United States consists of a wild pack of very odd people. I am embarrassed to call myself a Christian because of what Christianity has become. I don't think I am the only liberal to feel this way. Conservatives have driven liberals away from a liberal God.

I have no problem saying this, because I believe it. The modern-day American Christians are kind of dumb. Plus, they are so goddamn vocal and obnoxious about everything, it is upsetting. Whenever there is a Bible study at school or a prayer group, it is usually dominated by a lunatic fringe of society. We all know who they are, those people who love to talk about God and parade around like they are better than everyone else. To be perfectly honest, the God of the conservative-minded Bible study group is not the God that I want to worship. I would rather go to Hell.

Unfortunately, it is this group that has covered Jesus in conservative slime. I feel bad for the guy. His modern-day American followers are both strange and very selfish. I would be embarrassed to aggressively call myself a Christian, because the boisterous Christians currently occupying evangelical pews all over the country are dorks.

Tragedy Strikes

Religion has a different impact on each person's life. Currently, it does not have much of an impact on mine, and I can't see much of this changing. There was a time when religion was a little bit more important. Those days are gone and probably will never return. While I am familiar with the liberal message of Christ, being a religious zealot isn't in my future.

I was confirmed a Lutheran when I was a teenager. Don't blame me; my parents made me do it. Because I was forced to do it, my confirmation has little importance. As a child, I would go to church and I hated every minute of it. It was boring, and I was a kid who either wanted to be out playing or watching a football game on television. Steve Martin once said in one of his comedy routines that he goes to church every Sunday that there isn't a game on television. I felt that way as a kid and I feel that way now. My wife drags me to church every now and then and I am obsessed with my watch and with my boredom. Time stands still when I am in the House of the Lord.

However, sometimes things happen in life that eventually forces each individual to ask some of the more important questions in life. Tragedy struck. My mom died in my early twenties and the members of my immediate family went on a quest for "the meaning of life."

People die and it is depressing. My family situation was no different than any other situation in which a family loses a loved one, and I am not begging for pity. The members of my family missed our mother. My sisters and I watched our father struggle with loneliness. It was difficult. Eventually, we all worked our way back to being a normal, healthy family.

People mourn loss in different ways. I think that every member of my immediate family went through some similar experiences on the road to recovery. We experienced times when we were obsessed with work; I launched a career as a dedicated, idealistic teacher who believed every kid wanted to learn (boy, was I wrong on that one!).We all entered semi-dysfunctional relationships; I dated some strippers—they were all very hot and all very crazy—and all occupied a lot of time. On a side note, even though I can be a sanctimonious liberal, I am also disturbingly shallow. These extremes make me charming.

Finally, we all started to try to find the liberal religion of our mother, the religion that gave her the strength to fight a losing battle against cancer for five years. I read the Gospels, different liberal theologians, and came to understand that people can be religious and be smart at the same time. Imagine that. A message not yet learned by Red State "Bible thumpers."

Before I started on my quest for a liberal theology, I contemplated a conversation that I had with my mom a few months before her death. It was this conversation that best summarizes the strength of her humble and liberal religious convictions.

One day, when she was about two weeks or so from taking her last breath, she told me that she knew she was going to die soon and that she wasn't sure if she was going to get into Heaven. She didn't think she was good enough. This from a woman who read the Bible daily, went to church weekly, started Bible studies with friends, helped those who were in need, all while going through years of chemotherapy. To me, her entrance into Heaven was a certainty, not only because her life was filled with good works and love, but because she was humble in her faith. I told her this as she fought back tears.

Essentially, she cemented the liberal leanings of her husband and three of her four children for the rest of their lives. To my family, Jesus was a liberal. There was no question about it. The liberal leanings of my mother and the liberal teachings of Jesus influenced my ideals, morals, and life in many ways.

I would like to claim Christianity, but unfortunately a bunch of sanctimonious, boring nerds have hijacked the liberal faith and teachings of Jesus. Now, I can't stand "Christians" because these people are always proselytizing about convictions that are much different than mine. It certainly isn't very Christian, but I literally can barely stomach being in the same room with them.

The other problem with my claiming Christianity is that I am far from a saint. I get drunk. I smoke occasionally. I use foul language all the time. I lust after women. I listen to Nirvana and Howard Stern. I watch *The Sopranos*. I am surrounded by sin, and I love absolutely every minute of it. I have a very fun and a very enjoyable life.

I am not going to change that any time soon just to become a boring goody-two-shoes Christian. I would kill myself first. My Hell would be sitting in a Bible study with a bunch of geeks singing "Jesus is my Rock." What a nightmare! If that is Heaven, I don't want to go there. If that is Hell, I might have to repent.

I also know from the teachings of Jesus that we are not supposed to boast about our faith or brag about our relationship with God. I have Biblical justification for this one. "Beware of practicing your piety before men in order to be seen by them; for then you will have no reward from your Father who is in heaven." (Matthew 6:1) There is more, "And when you pray, you must not be like the hypocrites; for they love to stand and pray in the synagogues and at the street corners, that they may be seen by men." (Matthew 6:5) These directives, straight from the mouth of Jesus are much different than the practices of the evangelical Christian. It is my understanding that we are supposed to be humble in our faith, and my humility accepts Hell as my probable destination.

In spite of my waywardness, it is true that I wouldn't mind classifying myself as a Christian. But I don't. I am not evil nor am I embarrassed of Jesus. Being part of that simple-minded, arrogant group called "Christians" is of no interest to me.

The message of Christ, not the Bible, not God, not Paul, but the message of Christ has been ignored, or worse, has been totally hijacked by the American Christian conservative. It is troubling that all of us liberals have let them do it.

Red State Rant

It is about time somebody aggressively defends the philosophy of the liberal Jesus and the values and culture of Blue States. I am totally against the idea that liberals need to reach out to Red State religion and their voters. Screw that. Liberals need to expose the theological shortcomings of the modern-day American conservatives who live in Red States or have Red State ideology.

Liberals need to express pride at the lifestyle and values of the liberal Blue States. It is here that the nonjudgmental, liberating message of Christ is lived to its fullest.

While I am a liberal, I am not a wimp. In the past, I used to try to reason with religious conservatives. What a waste of time that was! Now I laugh at them. I make fun of them. There is no way to change them, so why not have a little fun at their expense? More liberals should try calling a Red State, rightwing, Christian fundamentalist a moron. It is quite liberating, even if it is extraordinarily childish.

I continue to be stunned by the silence of Blue State liberals and their inability to aggressively defend a liberal God and ridicule conservative religious ideas. I just can't believe that there has never been an aggressive defense of the liberal Jesus combined with the politics of Blue States. It doesn't make sense.

In many ways, I believe that I am the perfect person to write a book that defends the liberal religion of Jesus and asserts the dignified culture of Blue States that traditionally elect liberal political candidates. Because I am a heathen who has some familiarity with the Bible, I can analyze the contradictions contained in the Bible and even laugh at all of the downright insane material contained in the holiest of books. It is these holy contradictions that confuse hoards of religious conservatives. Because I am a sarcastic and judgmental liberal, I don't have to take "the high road" in my condemnation of the conservative Christian Right and their clueless minions.

Because I am protected by the lifestyle and freedoms of a progressive Blue State, I can laugh at the backasswardness of the Red States. Because I am self-deprecating, I can criticize others without restraint. Because I do not want to be a politically correct, wimpy liberal, I can stoop to the level of the conservative windbag. And, finally, because I have actually read the Gospels and I have noted the liberal leanings of Jesus, I can expose Red State Christianity for what it really is—a doctrine filled with misinterpretation, lies, blasphemy, ignorance, and hypocrisy.

But first I must address the vast differences between Blue States and Red States. Just so you know, Blue States are better.

2

Red State, Blue State, Part I

A Geography Lesson

The buzz about Red States and Blue States accelerated during the 2004 presidential election. We have had national elections for years. We have been counting electoral votes for years. We have been monitoring how different states vote for years. It is only recently that we have begun harping on the idea that the cultural, moral, and geographical differences between Red States and Blue States are significant.

Looking at an electoral-college map from the 2004 presidential election indicates that one of the primary differences between Red States and Blue States is simple geography. First of all, most of the country is Red. If we move from left to right, we see that the entire West Coast (Washington, Oregon, and California) is Blue. Then, the proverbial "Sea of Red" begins. It starts with some Western states (Wyoming, Nevada, Montana, and the Dakotas) and moves on into the Southwest (Texas) and the Heartland (Oklahoma, Nebraska, Missouri, and Kansas) before we see another Blue State. After the "Sea of Red" that dominates the middle of the country, there are a few industrial states in the Midwest that voted Blue (Minnesota, Michigan, and Illinois). Moving east, the entire Northeast voted Blue also. Just south of this area, there is another "Sea of Red," this one, the South.

The country is divided geographically—with the Far West, Midwest, and Northeast voting Blue and the West, Southwest, Heartland, and the South voting Red. All told, 31 states voted Red and 19 states and the District of Colombia voted Blue. In spite of a lopsided state total, 62% of all states cast their electoral votes for George W. Bush; he only garnered 51% of the popular vote. So, even though the "Sea of Red" that dominates the electoral map indicates slaughter in favor of Red State politics, the election was much closer than the electoral map would indicate. The truth is that out of 100 people, 51 people voted for Bush, 48 people voted for Kerry, and 1 idiot threw his or her vote in the garbage. It was a Republican victory, but it was hardly a landslide.

Reinforcing Stereotypes

There are significant differences between Red State and Blue State culture and lifestyle. Before I move on to discuss the stereotypes of these areas, I do know that all of this is a generalization. I fully understand that there are Blue State liberals living in Red States. I pity them. Likewise, there are Red State conservatives living in Blue States. These people will never move to a Red State because they enjoy mooching off the freedoms provided to them by the liberal and tolerant culture of the average Blue State.

I actually think that, while some of the stereotypes are funny and perhaps even a little disrespectful, many of them have some truth. For example, I drink beer. My Blue State favorites are Heineken, Pilsner Urquell, or a snobby, Northwest Microbrew. Red Staters decide between Budweiser and Miller Genuine Draft or Bud Light and Miller Light.

If it is hard liquor that the local drunk desires, it is Vodka, Scotch, or a Martini in the Blue States. Bourbon, Bourbon, or Bourbon is the preferred booze of the Red State alcoholic. Wine sucks, but it is also popular amongst the hoity-toity Blue State drinker. Wine in a Red State is called moonshine.

I am proud of the music from my Blue State of Washington (Jimi Hendrix, Nirvana). Other Blue States gave us some pretty good music as well: Motown (Michigan), two talented goofballs, Bob Dylan and Prince (Minnesota). The South gave us the Blues, Elvis the rip-off artist (Mississippi), Lynyrd Skynyrd (Florida), Brittney Spears (Louisiana), and a slew of country music, which I know nothing about since I am a "Generation X" Blue State liberal.

Because I don't drink coffee, I understand the pomposity of ordering a "double tall carmel machiatto" (a Blue State favorite), while the Red State caffeine addicts like their coffee black, unless latent homosexuality appears and they order it with "a splash of cream." Hike up your skirts, ladies!

Red State shoppers love Wal-Mart and Sam's Club; Blue Staters roam the aisles of Target, Nordstrom, and Costco.

Red State conservatives drive big, giant trucks with guns in the window. The ever-commuting Blue State liberals lust for a new Toyota hybrid as a cheaper way to get through their long commute.

The Heartland and the South have a nasty history of racism. We liberals to the Far West and Northeast are much too politically correct, liberal, and freedom loving for that.

Southeastern Conference football teams run the ball first, play defense second, and score third. Football teams from the Pac Ten employ the West Coast Offense that originated in finesse-filled San Francisco.

Blue States must deal with soccer moms, while Red States enjoy enduring NASCAR dads. Backyard cooks in the Red States "barbeque." Blue State chefs "grill."

The Blue States are filled with Jews (New York), Catholics (Boston), homosexuals (San Francisco), atheists (Seattle), and tree huggers (Portland, Oregon or Maine). The Heartland and the South are filled with Protestants (insert any city or state), Mormons (Utah), and transsexuals (Miami).

We all get along just fine where we are. I have absolutely no interest in moving to or even visiting either a hick Heartland state or a hillbilly Southern state. And much like your average Red State conservative, people from the Red States who visit the pagan big cities to the North and West—filled with Catholics, Jews, Atheists, and homosexuals—must shake their heads in disgust.

There is an idyllic utopia where Red meets Blue in happiness and sin: Las Vegas.

It is pretty clear to me that Red State and Blue State cultures are very different. But while we are able to live mostly separate lives, we do have to vote for the same president. That is a problem, at least when your block loses the election. Since the 2004 election was a Red State triumph, it was a Blue State disaster. Not because George W. Bush is going to change the lifestyle of the Blue State liberal—he ain't that powerful—but because we have an imbecile as a president. This is a little embarrassing. More importantly, there are times when all of us Blue State liberals worry that our individual rights and freedoms are going to continue to erode because we have a president with Red State values.

On the evening of November 2, 2004, when it was all said and done, I just kind of shook my head and figured that some people (Red State Republicans) get what they deserve. So after the election was over, I came to grips with one thing that made my living in a country that would elect a clown like George W. Bush president. I rationalized it all away by taking a unique, self-centered personal perspective. I live in a Blue State. I have an attractive wife. I have a stable job. I have health insurance. I am about as far away from Iraq as a person can get. Things are just fine for me. Who cares who the president is? I am doing great. There is no doubt that I enjoy watching Southeastern Conference football games on ESPN on Saturday evenings. However, I prefer having access to Blue State dental care.

But, when I hear all of the talk about how "faith" and "morality" entered into the election and I endure members of the Christian Right going on and on about how this is God's country and that the right-wingers are God's people, it makes me cringe.

There is little doubt that religion, a backward religion that contradicts just about everything Jesus said, dominates certain parts of this country. This is to the dismay of millions who acknowledge that Jesus was a liberal.

Red State, Blue State: It's All about Religion

In an effort to see just how much religion, or lack of it, impacts the reality of Red States and Blue States, I looked to find out the religious breakdowns in these two new classifications of our proud states.

I found a detailed research project conducted by The Graduate Center at the City of New York University (NYU) called the American Religious Identification Survey (ARIS).1 The authors, Barry Kosmin and Egon Mayer, analyzed a variety of different factors and how important religion is in our national life. One of the areas that they researched was religious identification by state.

The data confirmed most of what we already assume and know. There are a lot of Protestants, specifically Baptists, in the South. There are more Protestants of varying denominations in the Heartland. There is a high percentage of Catholics and Jews in the Northeast. There is a concentration of Mormons in Utah and other Western states such as Idaho. And, of course, there are the nonbelieving heathens who live out in the Northwest—where I live. None of this was much of a revelation

There is an unquestionable link between religious background and Red State, Blue State status. Data accumulated in this 2001 survey make it apparent that religion impacts how people vote, and, since there are high concentrations of people with certain religions in certain areas, the results are not very surprising.

This high concentration of certain religious affiliations in a state has an election-day consequence. For example, 44% of the residents of Massachusetts claim Catholicism as their religion. Massachusetts always votes liberal. To the contrary, Utah residents claim Mormonism at a 57% rate; this state always votes conservative. While these two states represent an extreme, they are indicative of some trends.

Baptists reigned supreme in southern states such as Mississippi (55%), South Carolina (43%), Tennessee (39%), North Carolina (38%), Alabama (37%), Arkansas (37%), and Louisiana (35%). This trend barely extended to the West with Oklahoma (30%), the only state registering a majority of Baptists. The conclusion is obvious. Southern states, which are predominantly Baptist, all vote Red.

Likewise, states with the combination of Jewish and Catholic voters in the Northeast, such as New York (38% Catholic, 5% Jewish),Massachusetts (44%

Catholic, 2% Jewish), and Vermont (38% Catholic), consistently vote Blue in national elections. Then there is the "No Religion" classification. States such as Washington (25% No Religion) and Oregon (21% No Religion) consistently vote Blue. Other Blue States have blocs of heathens, but they do not have as great a number as the Northwest states. There is no doubt that there are more nonbelievers in Blue States than in Red States. Combining these three groups (Jews, Catholics, and heathens) leads to a Blue state voting bloc.

So there are two primary tendencies in voting that are based on religion. The first is that the higher the percentage of people who classify themselves as Protestant or Mormon, the more likely the state will vote Red. The second is that the higher the percentage of Catholics, Jews, and nonbelievers, the more likely the state will vote Blue. That is the situation. Our nation is divided not only by culture but also by religion.

When people make the assertion that our nation has been hijacked by a bunch of religious extremists—and they believe that fundamentalist Southern Baptists are extremists, they are right. People would also be half right to say that, in general, Protestants cost the Democrats the election.

SHCAK (Self-Hating Catholics against Kerry)

There was one difference between the election of 2000 and the election of 2004. Actually, there were quite a few differences, the most important being that Al Gore actually won the 2000 election. But since that battle is over, it is interesting to note that John Kerry, in spite of four years of Bush failures, actually did worse in the popular vote than Al Gore. One of the reasons was that John Kerry, a Catholic, lost the a segment of the Catholic vote.

The loss of this vote was based solely on religious issues. These religious issues were abortion and same-sex marriage. In key states such as Missouri and Colorado, archbishops went public in their assertion that Kerry should be denied the sacrament of communion because he has views that the Catholic Church does not support.

Likewise, many bishops in the United States used scare tactics against voters, saying that that they would deny communion to Catholic politicians who fail to stand with the church. Bishop Michael J. Sheridan of Colorado Springs, Colorado, went a step further by saying that he would not give communion to Catholic voters. He is believed to be the first to extend the ban on communion to certain Catholic voters who did not vote with Catholic doctrine. Bishop Sheridan wrote, "Anyone who professes the Catholic faith with his lips while at the same time publicly supporting legislation or candidates that defy God's law makes a mockery of that faith and belies his identity as a Catholic."2 Gotta love the self-righteous priest.

I also thought it was great how at the end of this "inspired" letter on how Catholics should vote, Bishop Sheridan referred to himself as the "Most Reverend Michael J. Sheridan." What a nut. So the *revered* Bishop knows exactly how Jesus would vote. Then he gives an order to his flock before they go to the polls, with the additional threat of denying communion to those who do not agree with his views.

This is my first example of how conservative dicks like to take it upon themselves to deny others a right in the name of God and personal politics. It just so happens that in this case it is a group of Catholic priests attempting to take away the rights of other Catholics. It is usually the Red State politicians who engage in this type of behavior that would inevitably lead to a theocratic dictatorship.

In order to expose this type of political and religious grandstanding for the insidious behavior that it is, it is important to go to the source of the sacrament of communion to seek its complete meaning and importance. For this, we should address the text in the Gospels that deals with "The Last Supper": "And he took bread, and when he had given thanks he broke it and gave it to them, saying, 'this is my body which is given for you. Do this in remembrance of me.' And likewise the cup after supper, saying, 'This cup which is poured out for you is the new covenant in my blood'" (Luke 22:19–21). That's it. That is all Jesus said.

Jesus does not give a set of behavioral rules or a requirement for specific political affiliation as a prerequisite for participation in the holy sacrament of communion. Certain scumbags in the Catholic Church created these rules on their own in the effort to deny believers the opportunity to perform religious rites in "remembrance" of their Savior. Conservative religious leaders want to deny followers rites based on personal opinion. It is sickening

In this particular case, Catholics priests were threatening and trying to punish John Kerry and other liberal Catholics for being "different." This behavior is one of the characteristics of a Red State conservative.

It is kind of a shame. I know that, in the city where I work, a group of Catholics bought a full-page advertisement in the local newspaper containing a Catholic voters' guide. Other Catholic churches in the area were quick to say that they were not involved in the advertisement. However, it is troubling that a group of religious leaders were trying to influence the election with the insidious means of divine retribution and guilt. It is clear that this self-hating and immoral behavior by the Catholic Church widened the election results.

The religious Right did a masterful job of garnering the votes of members of all conservative, orthodox religions. So much so that, as mentioned earlier, John Kerry, a Catholic, lost the Catholic vote 52% to 47%. On the other hand,

John Kerry crushed Bush in the religious category of "Other": 74% to 23%. It is too bad for John Kerry and the rest of the country that the "Other" only covers 7% of the electorate.3

Red State, Blue State: the Game

It becomes important, since George W. Bush won the election based on religion, that at some point the religious values of the triumphant political party are put to the test. It is also important, since these religious tendencies impacted our Electoral College vote and indicates a chasm between Red and Blue States, that we look at the health, well being, values, culture, and religion of these two classifications of states. Does Jesus agree with Red State values? Is God actually on the side of the Red State conservative?

It is important to contrast life in the liberal Blue States with life in the conservative Red States. Are the Red States a sanctuary for God's people? Are the Blue States godless municipalities that eat their children and abort their young?

To help answer this question, I developed the game "Red State, Blue State." In this game, I will list different statistics and numbers regarding the quality of life in the average Red State and the quality of life in the average Blue State. I will take an issue, such as infant mortality rates, and then list the tendencies in the liberal heathen states in the North, Midwest, and Far West and compare them with the strongholds of the conservative right in the Heartland and South. It will be fun.

It was, after all, the Red State conservatives that transformed certain political issues into a religious identity and national movement. Do their spoken values in these areas match the realities exhibited in their lives and neighborhoods? We will see.

I do want to give everyone a taste of this interesting game. This one I will make kind of fun. The first category: What percentage of mobile homes makes up the total number of housing units in each state? I am not quite sure what kind of cultural trend this suggests, but it will reinforce some of our stereotypes. Reinforcing stereotypes is actually kind of enjoyable. See, I can be conservative sometimes also.

Here we go.

Percentage of mobile homes as housing units

Rank	State	Percentage of Mobile Homes	Red or Blue
1	South Carolina	20.3	Red
2	New Mexico	18.6	Red
3	West Virginia	16.9	Red
4	Mississippi	16.6	Red
5	North Carolina	16.4	Red
6	Alabama	16.3	Red
7	Wyoming	15.9	Red
8	Arkansas	14.9	Red
9	Montana	14.3	Red
10	Kentucky	14.1	Red

Source: *Structural and Occupancy Characteristics of Housing 2000 Data.*
United States Bureau of the Census.

The next three states in this dubious list are Arizona, Florida, and South Dakota. Delaware was the first Blue State listed in this category. To that end, the thirteen states with the highest number of "trailers" as living units all voted Red in the 2004 election.

Notice that these Red States that have a high percentage of mobile homes are spread all across the country. The existence of trailers as homes is not a Southern phenomenon; they are everywhere in the Red States. Now, the bottom ten look quite a bit different. Not only are the percentages significantly lower, but also all of these states voted Blue in the 2004 presidential election.

Percentage of mobile homes as housing units

Rank	State	Percentage of Mobile Homes	Red or Blue
51	Washington D.C.	0.1	Blue
50	Hawaii	0.1	Blue
49	Connecticut	0.8	Blue
48	Massachusetts	0.9	Blue
47	Rhode Island	1.0	Blue
46	Maryland	1.9	Blue
45	New York	2.7	Blue
44	Illinois	3.2	Blue
43	Wisconsin	4.4	Blue
42	Minnesota	4.5	Blue

Source: *Structural and Occupancy Characteristics of Housing 2000 Data.*
United States Bureau of the Census.

Again, I am no sociologist, so I don't want to make any assumptions as to what all of this means. However, ya'll gotta admit, ya'll know this is true.

Next, since I am a pompous Blue State liberal and I think I know everything, I must be a little condescending towards my Red State brethren. It is time to prove that, here in the Blue States, we are more educated. To prove this, it is appropriate to look at the percentage of residents in each state with at least a bachelor's degree.

Percentage of residents with at least a bachelor's degree

Rank	State	Percentage with Bachelor's Degree	Red or Blue
1	Washington, D.C.	46	Blue
2	Massachusetts	37.6	Blue
3	Maryland	37.2	Blue
4	Colorado	36.0	Red
5	Virginia	34.2	Red
6	New Hampshire	34.0	Blue
7	Connecticut	33.5	Blue
8	New Jersey	33.4	Blue
9	Minnesota	32.7	Blue
10	Vermont	31.2	Blue

Source: *Annual Social and Economic Supplement to the 2003 Current Population Survey.* United States Bureau of the Census.

Blue State dominance held true for states 10 to 20 also. Blue States such as California, New York, Washington, Illinois, Delaware, Rhode Island, and Hawaii are in the next ten. The three Red States in the second ten are Kansas, Utah, and Nebraska.

That means that, out of the nineteen states and District of Colombia that voted Blue in the 2004 election, fifteen of them are in the top twenty of per capita college graduates. For this and other reasons, it is not surprising what the bottom ten is going to look like. The Red States have to be somewhere.

Percentage of residents with at least a bachelor's degree

Rank	State	Percentage with Bachelor's Degree	Red or Blue
50	West Virginia	15.3	Red
49	Arkansas	17.4	Red
48	Mississippi	19.3	Red
47	Wyoming	20.7	Red
46	Nevada	21.2	Red
45	Kentucky	21.3	Red
44	Indiana	22.2	Red
43	Louisiana	22.3	Red
42	South Carolina	22.3	Red
41	Alabama	22.7	Red

Source: *Annual Social and Economic Supplement to the 2003 Current Population Survey.* United States Bureau of the Census.

The ten states with the lowest percentage of college graduates all voted Red in the 2004 election. It is actually a little bit sad. Since I am a liberal, I do have an unfortunate streak of compassion.

Now, wasn't that fun? There is a whole a lot more where that came from. But before I move onto more Red State, Blue State cultural comparisons, I must tend to some pretty important business. Part of this deals with religion. Since it is my premise that Jesus was a liberal and that a form of blasphemous Christianity has a death grip on the Red States, one question must be asked and answered. How in the hell did the message of the most radical liberal in the history of the world become the religion of a bunch of ultra-conservatives?

For this answer, we must look at the Word of God…that means the Bible, in case you didn't know.

PART II

How in the Hell Did the Liberal Jesus Become a Conservative Icon?

3

Contemplating God

A Trinity of Confusion

The 2004 national election brought forth a lot of talk about "God" and "religion." The reason why this is a problem, which can lead to some confusion, is because of Christianity's doctrine that consists of a three-headed deity. In religious circles, this is called the Trinity. The Trinity consists of the Father (God), the Son (Jesus), and the Holy Spirit (?). It is here that all of the confusion starts.

People make vague references to God quite often when looking to justify their half-baked religious ideas. Very seldom do these people invoke the name of Jesus. We will see that these two religious figures are quite a bit different. Liberal Christians everywhere have rolled over and let conservative Republicans claim moral issues and religion as their own. That is why it is imperative that, if conservative Christians insist on making religion an issue, liberals need to make them acknowledge Jesus when they pontificate about ethics and morality. It would be nice to know where all of these Christians get their information on how to be a religious conservative since their Leader was a famous liberal.

At best, the conflict between the teachings of Christ and the Old Testament text is a mixed message. This has caused outright confusion among the followers of Christianity, who try in vain to combine two very different religions and philosophies. The crux of the problem might lie in the way we identify our deities. We are having a difficult time separating one from the other, or, in this case, separating the Father from the Son.

We all know Jesus was as an historical figure, but who exactly is God in relation to the historical figure of Jesus? Is Jesus God? Is God Jesus? Are they different? Did Jesus cancel out the message of God, and, if so, why did God have the wrong message in the first place? Furthermore, how exactly does the Holy Spirit fit in?

To the rational thinker, the answers are all pretty vague. For this reason, we are going to make what was intended to be the Christian assumption: Jesus was the incarnation of God living on Earth. For this reason, we should know that, as Christians, the God of the Old Testament shouldn't be our primary concern. However, it is apparent that fundamentalist Christians invoke the stories and laws of a conservative Old Testament God to justify their hatred, bigotry, and lunacy.

Vague References

Part of the issue is that when people refer to "God," "religion," "faith," and "morality," it is a little bit unclear what they mean. All of these terms are too vague, too general, and too subjective, because they could literally mean anything. The definitions of these terms are all based on personal opinion and bias. There are thousands of value judgments, with literally millions of "moral," "ethical," and "religious" applications.

Using the term "God" needs clarification as well. Is "God" the Old Testament God, the New Testament God, the Muslim God, or one of the many Hindu gods? Who knows? In the United States, it is only assumed that Jesus is somehow involved. This assumption is not only wrong, but it is unfair to Jesus because, out of all of these supposed gods, Jesus was the only one that was a historical figure that walked the Earth and laid down a set of guidelines. Moses, Abraham, and Buddha did not claim to be God in the manner in which Jesus did. These men may have been historical figures. They may have been prophets. They may have been very wise and heroic men. God may have inspired them to do and say great things. But their followers did not believe them to be God walking on Earth. They were men. Jesus claimed to be God.

Likewise, it is erroneous to assume, just because conservatives or any other group call themselves "Christian," that it means they are voting in Jesus's best interest. Using vague religious references keeps these people from being held accountable for their votes, beliefs, and actions.

Liberals need to make conservatives say "Jesus" and make them prove that their conservative agenda is supported by the philosophies and teachings of Jesus. Referring to "God" or "religion" simply isn't good enough.

According to Some, God Likes Cheaters and Morons

George W. Bush and his conservative friends and their continual bragging about their religion, faith, and God are great examples of this type of confusion. Their supposed monopoly on faith allows them to get away with making vague references, which lead to a confusing and biased sense of morality. In 2003, the former executive director of the Christian Coalition and current executive of the GOP in Georgia said he believed that God placed Bush in the White House. Reed said, "He knew George Bush had the ability to lead in this compelling way."1 Who the hell is "He"? Is "He" God? Is "He" Jesus? If "He" is God and "He" is Jesus, why not say, "Jesus knew George Bush had the ability to lead in this compelling way"? Since Reed does not take the time to further explain the meaning of "He," we are left to assume that "He" is the God of the Ralph Reeds of the world. Is Ralph Reed's "God" Jesus? He certainly doesn't say so.

The God of Ralph Reed certainly isn't a God that I am interested in following. So, who gets to claim "God"? The answer to that question has become pretty simple as of late. Ralph Reed and his conservative buddies get to claim God as their own because they talk about Him all the time. I am curious as to when the rest of us "humble" Christians get to claim God? But the Religious Right continually bombards us with the idea that Bush is God's choice, and it is effective. A top aide at the White House once said, "I think President Bush is God's man at this hour."2 This is a very powerful statement.

However, it is so vague that it is impossible to argue with this very disturbing assertion. Conservatives take it as fact, and liberals don't argue with it because we are too afraid to offend someone's religion. It would be tantamount to claiming atheism, which is political suicide.

Again, if all of these guys are all Christians, why not just say, "Bush is Jesus's man at this hour"? That is a little more difficult because Jesus's teachings don't allow too much room for conservative sound bites.

Liberals have found it increasingly difficult to combat right-wing religious propaganda. I, along with millions of liberals, think it is blasphemous and absurd to suggest that "God" or "Jesus" placed Bush, or anyone else for that matter, in the White House. The screwed-up state of Florida placed Bush in the White House! Ralph Nader placed Bush in the White House. To the liberal, God didn't have anything to do with any of these shenanigans.

On the flip side, millions of conservatives believe that Bush is, as a matter of fact, God's choice to lead the United States. Conservatives must think that the fraudulent vote in Florida during the 2000 election was His way of righting the ship. Having the "Supreme" court decide the election was setting a lost country back on course. Bush was going to lose, so "He" helped Florida cheat. "He" persuaded Ralph Nader to stay in the election and capture millions of liberal Votes. Consequently, Bush slips into the presidency with His help. It sounds perfectly logical…to a lunatic.

The end result can only be that the kind of statement involving anyone being "God's chosen one" will only incite strong views from both sides of the fence when, in reality, it is nothing more than a self-serving proclamation that can never be proven with even the slightest amount of accuracy or authority. The Republican assertion that Bush is God's president is ultimately a meaningless piece of vain fantasy.

"Jesus Day" and a State-Sponsored Killing Spree

I must say that I don't really challenge Bush's assertion that he is the tool of a God or the pawn of a religion. I am, however, challenging the notion that his God has anything to do with Jesus—you know, the guy executed by a pack of conservatives for being so "liberal."

It really isn't very surprising that we never really hear Bush say "Jesus" unless he absolutely has to. He only uses the most general terms to bamboozle millions of Red State religious zealots into believing that he has the ear of a divine presence.

Making a direct reference to Jesus as opposed to God is a totally different intellectual and religious experience because Jesus was a man living on Earth. He had a life story supported by history and by our cultural mythology. He had very, very specific ideas and philosophies. Jesus had words. These words can be studied, researched, evaluated, and eventually applied to the life of the individual who chooses to worship Him as God. Believe it or not, it is actually possible to take a modern-day issue and research Gospel text to find out what Jesus said regarding this issue.

If someone does not believe that Jesus was God living on Earth, all of this means nothing to that person. But for those people who have the faith that Jesus was the Savior and a God who laid out a plan for His people, we must seriously consider His words.

Voters have hopped on the Bush bandwagon of referring to a vague term such as "moral issues" to justify a vote. It is a lot more difficult to say, "Jesus influenced my vote and I can prove it with sincerity and documentation from the Gospels." Saying "God" to justify personal opinions and values is much, much easier. I have read hundreds of "Bushisms"—some intelligent, some absurd, some honest, some dishonest, and some childish—but the name "Jesus" rarely comes up in any of his speeches or appearances. He talks about "God" all the time, but never "Jesus." It is not out of the realm of possibility that this is intentional.

One of the only examples I found where Bush actually refers to Jesus was his declaration of "Jesus Day" while he was the governor of Texas. Bush, in his own unique style, states,

> I urge all Texans to answer the call to serve those in need. By volunteering their time, energy, or resources to helping others, adults and

youngsters follow Christ's message of love and service in thought and deed. Therefore, I, George W. Bush, Governor of Texas, do hereby proclaim June 10, 2000, Jesus Day in Texas and urge the appropriate recognition whereof.3

Alas, "Jesus Day" was born. How sweet.

Nobody ever thought to ask what Jesus might think about having His own personal holiday in the state that leads the free world in executions. During his reign of terror (1995–2000) George W. Bush authorized a staggering 152 executions. The government-imposed slaughter began with Clifton Russell, Jr. on January 31, 1995 and ended with Claude Jones on December 7, 2000. Remembering that Jesus emphasized compassion, love, and forgiveness over murder and mayhem, it becomes difficult to support this type of carnage in the name of Jesus.

This type of killing doesn't exactly inspire the need for everyone to "follow Christ's message of love and service in thought and deed." Unfortunately for Mr. Bush, his actions speak louder than his words.

Furthermore, in an interview with *Talk* magazine, Tucker Carlson, *Crossfire's* conservative pundit, said that Bush mimicked a soon-to-be-executed woman's final plea for clemency. Apparently, this man of God mocked the woman by saying "'Please, don't kill me.'"4 Bush was making fun of a terrified woman who was facing her planned execution. This sounds like an arrogant bully, not a follower of Jesus. One of his own, ultraconservative Gary Bauer, lashed out at Bush, "I think it is nothing short of unbelievable that the governor of a major state running for president thought it was acceptable to mock a woman he decided to put to death."5

Now, let's try to imagine Jesus's response to someone who was mourning her impending execution. Would He mock her? No. He would comfort her. Would He ridicule her? No. He would calm her. Would He laugh at her? No. He would treat her with compassion. Furthermore, there is a similar occurrence in the Gospels. Jesus actually has a conversation with a prisoner who is about to die.

We all know that Jesus was crucified alongside two other men, both of them criminals. He told one of them, "Truly, I say to you, today you will be with me in Paradise." (Luke 23:43) This is a little bit different than the response of Dubya, who, if we remember correctly, was placed in the White House by the hand of the most compassionate and loving "God."

Blue State Bible Study Part 1: "Intelligent" Design? I Don't Think So

Simply put, the liberal doctrine of Jesus continues to get lost in the religious shuffle. One of the primary problems has to be that the message of Jesus is ignored because of the sheer length of the Bible. The Bible is a book that is more than two thousand pages long and Jesus appears in fewer than two hundred of them. Furthermore, Jesus's actual words only comprise maybe twenty or thirty total pages of text. All told there are sixty-six books in the Bible. Jesus only directly appears in four of them. It's not a very high percentage. There is little doubt that this adds to the dilution of his message.

Since the Old Testament is the Word of God, perhaps we can come to some conclusion as to where conservatives get their wacky ideas about being "Christians." Perhaps they are confusing the Word of God with the words of Jesus, at times two very conflicting messages.

From what I understand, and I am no theologian, the Old Testament has three primary functions: Jewish history, Jewish law, and prophecy of a messiah. Moses was the author of the first five books, and the rest of the Old Testament was written by a variety of different authors and/or prophets who were all "divinely inspired," another vague reference to God.

To the ultraconservative, Red State Christian, every word was not only sent directly from God, but every word is to be taken as absolute historical fact. A literal interpretation of biblical text is the backbone of conservative doctrine. This, of course, presents some problems not only for the followers of Jesus, but also for the proponents of common sense.

Problems with the Old Testament start almost immediately with what Evangelical Christians like to call "Intelligent Design." If people want to believe that it is historical fact that Adam and Eve were the first human beings, that a snake tempted them with a forbidden fruit from the Tree of Knowledge, and that they ate this forbidden fruit, which caused the creation of sin—that is their business. It is strange, but it is their business. But how in the hell does anyone explain the first family tree without getting real creepy?

We all know the story. Adam and Eve had two sons, Cain and Abel. Cain killed Abel. As punishment for this act, God sends Cain and his wife to the land of Nod.

First problem: Where did Cain's wife come from? Adam and Eve are the only people created by God and they had two sons. The only logical explanation is that Adam and Eve, the world's first two people had an unnamed and unmentioned daughter, which makes Cain's wife his sister. Yuk! Alas...that is against God's law: "Cursed be he who lies with his sister, whether the daughter of his father or the daughter of his mother."(Deuteronomy 27:22) In this case, it was the daughter of both mother and father. The first people can't be allowed to break God's law! That would lead to anarchy!

Since God would not place his first two subjects in a position of breaking a commandment, it must be that there was no daughter. So after the death of Abel, there was only father, mother, and one remaining son (a third son Seth came along later). If there was no daughter, then Eve left Adam for her only remaining son—who killed her other son—to settle in Nod where they populated the Earth. This would mean that, when Cain and Eve had children, their children would then need to copulate, which means that Cain's son would be forced to copulate with his sister and niece. Does any of this make sense? Maybe that's why we have all of these problems.

So, if "Intelligent Design" is historical fact as the conservative would believe, all of us human beings are the product of an incestuous relationship between Cain and Eve, which is something that we should not be promoting in public schools. Furthermore, brother-mother incest is condemned with the utmost ferocity in Leviticus20:11: "The man who lies with his father's wife has uncovered his father's nakedness; both of them shall be put to death, their blood is upon them." This, of course, means that, according to Old Testament law, their angry Creator killed Cain and Eve because of an incestuous relationship.

If God enforced his own law, this troubled family tree would have ended with Adam alone commiserating the loss of one of his sons, who was killed by his brother. He would also be left longing for his wife, who left him for his other son, that same son who killed his dead son. My guess is that poor old Adam would be extremely pissed off at an omniscient God who had a very bad plan about how to populate the Earth.

If I were God, I would have made twenty or thirty families in the beginning. It would have been a nice little neighborhood. I would have made sure that there was no inbreeding in that family tree. This would have been "Intelligent Design."

Anyway, most intelligent people (liberals and scientists) wave away these kinds of problems presented by a literal interpretation of the Bible with a metaphorical reading of these lessons. Seeing metaphor and acknowledging science is, of course, the "intelligent" way. Evangelical conservatives have yet to rise to that order of higher-level thinking.

Blue State Bible Study Part 2: "Spilling Semen," Horse Issues," and the Strange Ways of God

I did a little more research and started looking for some more oddball punishments sent down by this angry conservative God. I can't say that I was completely surprised at what I found, but it was a little amusing and kind of disturbing. God is kind of weird.

I was more than a little alarmed when I discovered that God did not approve of my chosen method of birth control. Ya see, I don't like condoms all that much. My wife doesn't like them too much either, so I "pull and pray." It has worked so far, as I remain childless. I'm not sure what the medical term for this is, so let's just say that I withdrawal." My wife is also on birth control, so we have our bases covered. We are Blue State, professional liberals, so we won't be having kids until right before it is almost too late.

I just didn't know that my lifelong method of avoiding unwanted pregnancy was punishable by death! According to Old Testament scripture, poor Onan found it out the hard way. "But Onan knew that the offspring would not be his; so when he went in to his brother's wife he spilled the semen on the ground, lest he should give offspring to his brother. And what he did was displeasing in the sight of the Lord, and He slew him also." (Genesis 38:9–10) It is unclear what Onan's sin was, screwing his brother's wife or "spilling" on the ground. Either way, God slew the poor guy.

Ever since Janet Jackson decided to expose her fake tit during the Super Bowl halftime show, the moral police have been on our collective ass. Conservatives are big on blasting the evils of Howard Stern, HBO, and other purveyors of smut. Yet, in my research, I discovered that the Old Testament has some very odd porn stories of its own.

There is one biblical tale in particular that belongs on the pages of *Penthouse Forum*. Since it is in the Bible, it is highly unlikely that it would be classified as pornography, but it is more than a little indecent. The author of this story describes a woman's reminiscing about her slutty behavior in detail that would make Larry Flynt proud: "Yet she increased her harlotry, remembering the days of her youth, when she played the harlot in the land of Egypt and doted upon her paramours there, whose members were like those of asses, and whose issue was like that of horses." (Ezekiel 23:19–20) So this gal, who liked to mess around in her youth, starts messing around again because she longed for her ex-lovers who were hung like donkeys and had the "issues" of horses. There is no word about why this is included in "The Good Book." It only gets more disturbing.

A few years back while watching public television, I heard mythology guru Joseph Campbell say that the Old Testament God was an angry God. "A lot of laws, no mercy" was what he said, if memory serves me correctly. Most punishment meted out by God was death, destruction, and slaughter. Other times, God showed some creativity in His effort not only to exact revenge on his disobedient subjects, but also to do so in a most embarrassing fashion.

It seems that God likes to be worshipped and gets real pissed off when He is not worshipped in the correct manner. In this case, this particular form of disrespect results in a very degrading threat and possible future punishment. The Lord says,

> If you will not listen, if you will not lay it to heart to give glory to my name, says the Lord of hosts, then I will send the curse upon you and I will curse your blessings; indeed I have already cursed them, because you do not lay it to heart. Behold, I will rebuke your offspring, and spread dung upon your faces, the dung of your offerings, and I will put you out of my presence. (Malachi 2:2–3)

That's right, the old "shit on the face" punishment. Evidently, because God does not get the praise He so richly deserves in the manner in which He wants it from His followers, He will not only take all of their possessions, but He will spread poop on their faces before He sends them away. It sounds like it would be a good idea if God's people just got down on their knees and sang His praises.

Perhaps part of the reason conservatives hate everyone who does not share their "sacred" beliefs comes from more bad interpretation of the Bible. Sometimes, God's word teaches an inherent divine right that occasionally rears its ugly head in ancient biblical texts. In the Old Testament, God has an unfortunate history of destroying not only members of his own group who disobey or do not praise Him enough, but He also has a propensity to enjoy the massacre of all of His enemies. He even orders the murders of breast-feeding infants. That just isn't very nice.

As the story goes, Samuel, a messenger of God, tells Saul that, in order to ascend to the throne of Israel, he must destroy the enemy. The order goes, "Now go and smite Am'alek, and utterly destroy all that they have; do not spare them, but kill both man and woman, infant and suckling, ox and sheep, camel and ass." (1 Samuel 15:3) Saul moves along and commences to perform God's order of killing all men, women, children, and suckling babies. The problem is good ol' Saul didn't exactly perform God's commands to perfection. He only killed all of the people—and suckling infants—but he kept the animals as the spoils of a hard fought slaughter of men, women, and babies. God had a punishment for Saul's disobedience. Saul was sent away and did not become the king of Israel. Saul killed the babies but kept the cattle. Now that is an abomination!

The Father and the Son

All of this craziness leads most intelligent, liberal thinkers to conclude that there are stories in the Bible that are probably not meant to be taken literally. Find the metaphor, find the lesson, and maybe some of this stuff can be of use in a human life. This realization, that all things in the Bible cannot be taken literally, shocks the hell out of the Red State fundamentalists who, when confronted with stories like these, are left unable to adequately explain either God's plan or His tendency towards bizarre violence.

Christian fundamentalists can quote Old Testament scripture all they want. But, if they are Christians, I am sure they have no problem agreeing with the notion that Jesus does represent a new way of thinking and a new kind of leadership. The differences are not even subtle. They are immense. Here is one example.

The Old Testament says, "Anyone who injures another person must be dealt with according to the injury inflicted—fracture for fracture, eye for eye, tooth for tooth. Whatever anyone does to hurt another person must be paid back in kind." (Leviticus 24:19) This was the original "eye for an eye, tooth for a tooth" law. Conversely, in the Gospels, Jesus states, "You have heard that it was said, 'Eye for eye, and tooth for tooth. But I tell you, do not resist an evil person. If someone strikes you on the right cheek, turn to him the other also." (Matthew 5:38–39)

Could any two laws of how to deal with a personal injury be any different? The concern of the Old Testament was punishment and revenge. The concern of Jesus in the Gospels wasn't getting temporal revenge, but securing personal and eternal salvation.

Two totally different ideas and solutions to the same ethical dilemma are found in the same religious book that attempts to merge two very different Gods. It is no wonder that everyone is confused.

A Religious Oxymoron: Conservative Christians and Liberal Jews

Jesus did indeed usher in a new way, and, for that reason and for our purposes of reclaiming Jesus as a radical liberal thinker, it becomes necessary that we separate Jesus's love, forgiveness, and understanding from the angry God of the Old Testament, who was hell-bent on killing everyone in sight. Jesus, the radical liberal, stands in direct opposition to his ultraconservative Father. So, whom do we believe—the Father or the Son? Like it or not, Christians are supposed to believe the Son.

Jewish people don't acknowledge Jesus as the Son, so they believe the Father. That is their religion. However, in what is a shocking revelation, evangelicals in Red States tend to be a whole hell of a lot more conservative than Jewish people living in Blue States.

Obviously, there are many instances in the Old Testament where God shows His love and mercy. That said, it is important to remember that liberals have never been the ones to declare a religious war against the Jews. Liberal Christians love Jewish people. It is always the conservative "Christians" who launch anti-Semitic attacks in the name of Christ.

There is no doubt that Jewish people in America are an intelligent, thoughtful group of people who care about their God and their fellow Americans. Exposing some of the odd behavior of the Old Testament God is not meant to criticize the Jewish faith.

However, in trying to find the root of the anger, hatred, and discrimination that has been at the heart of conservative politics, there needs to be some kind of starting point. The anger in the Old Testament is a valid place to start. It does appear that the angry conservative God of the Old Testament sidetracks the goofy religious Right. This is a predicament that does not befall most thoughtful Jewish Americans.

Jewish people in the United States vote overwhelmingly liberal. Going back to CNN polling data, 74% of the Jewish population who voted in the 2004 presidential election voted for John Kerry; 59% of Protestants and 52% of Catholics voted for Bush. The problem for liberals is that only 3% of the population of the United States is Jewish. I, for one, wish there were more Jews in the United States.

So, the Jews are the ones who are supposed to have the angry, conservative God, yet they vote liberal. And the Christians, the ones with the loving, liberal God, vote conservative. What the hell is going on? There must be some other reason.

I know the reason and I know who is to blame.

4

Blaming Paul

The Early Years

Before I move on and state the differences between the religious philoso-phies of Paul and Jesus, it is important to note that prior to their roles as founders of the Christian faith, Paul and Jesus had what appear to be opposing lifestyles.

The Bible is vague about the early life of Jesus. There is only one incident recorded in the Gospels about His childhood and that is when, at the young age of twelve, went out on His own and was found instructing Jewish scholars in a temple.

> And when he was twelve years old, they went up as usual for the fes-tival. When the festival was ended and they started to return, the boy Jesus stayed behind in Jerusalem, but his parents did not know it. Assuming that he was in the group of travelers, they went a day's journey. Then they started to look for him among their relatives and friends. When they did not find him, they returned to Jerusalem to search for him. After three days they found him in the temple, sitting among the teachers, listening to them and asking them questions. And all who heard him were amazed at his understanding and his answers. When his parents saw him they were astonished; and his mother said to him, 'Child, why have you treated us like this? Look, your father and I have been searching for you in great anxiety.' He said to them, 'Why were you searching for me? Did you not know that I must be in my Father's house?' But they did not understand what he said to them. Then he went down with them and came to Nazareth, and was obedient to them. His mother treasured all these things in her heart. And Jesus increased in wisdom and in years, and in divine and human favor. (*Luke 2:42-52*)

In this instance, Jesus alarms his parents because they do not know that He went to the temple. When He is found, He recognizes their concern and becomes further obedient to His parents. This is uncommon wisdom for a twelve year old.

Throughout the New Testament, Jesus is consistently portrayed as a respectful child, a humble carpenter, a compassionate teacher, an intelligent Jewish scholar, not to mention a radical social liberal. Paul's pre-Christian days were a little bit different.

In the days before Paul's miraculous conversion, Mr. "of Tarsus" was known as Saul and he was presented as being neither humble nor intelligent. This was due to his self-proclaimed status as a persecutor of a small group of people called "Christians". I am not totally sure of the complete duties performed by a persecutor of people. Maybe he teased them. Perhaps he threw rocks at them. Who knows, it is even possible that he had them arrested or killed. Since none of this is made very clear, Paul should be given the benefit of the doubt. It may be true that Paul may have never actually jailed or killed a Christian. However, it is unmistakable that at the very least, he stood in negative, oppressive, and potentially violent judgment of one segment of a human population based totally on their religious convictions. Paul continued to do this well after his conversion.

This is not the "Christian" way. However, we will soon discover that it is the "Pauline" way. Based on different parts of Paul's teaching, it is obvious that Paul never really exorcized his judgmental demons.

After reading all of Paul's Epistles, it is apparent that his overly critical and exclusive ways continued well after he became the voice of Christianity. After his revelation and self-anointing as the primary spokesperson of Jesus, Paul no longer stood in harsh judgment of Christians. Nevertheless, he targeted anyone different from himself for his own special form of divine judgment and threats of earthly and eternal punishment. It is here that Paul laid the groundwork for his philosophy of violent discrimination of other groups of people. This message has permanently slandered Jesus and His liberating message.

The differences between the two primary messengers of the Christian faith are evident from the beginning. Prior to his life as a messiah, Jesus developed a philosophy of inclusion and selfless love and practiced this in His adult life and communicated this to his followers. To the contrary, even after he became a Christian, Paul continued to be exclusive. Because his hatred for those who were different remained, Paul not only blasphemed his Lord and Savior Jesus Christ, but he became the inspiration for the oppression even murder of millions. It is because of Paul's dangerous and message that many crimes against humanity have been enacted in Jesus's name.

If you think that I am crazy, just keep reading.

A Red State Hallucination on the Road to Damascus

As the story goes, Saul of Tarsus was a rabid Christian hater and intense prosecutor and persecutor of the early followers of Christianity. He had it in for them. Then one day, he decided to go to Damascus. Jesus has been paying for that trip ever since.

> But Saul, still breathing threats and murder against the disciples of the Lord, went to the high priest and asked him for letters to the synagogues at Damascus, so that if he found any belonging to the Way, men or women, he might bring them bound to Jerusalem. Now as he journeyed he approached Damascus, and suddenly a light from heaven flashed about him. And he fell to the ground and heard a voice saying to him, "Saul, Saul, why do you persecute me?" And he said, "Who are you, Lord?" And he said, "I am Jesus, whom you are persecuting; but rise and enter the city, and you will be told what you are to do." The men who were traveling with him stood speechless, hearing the voice but seeing no one. Saul arose from the ground; and when his eyes were opened, he could see nothing; so they led him by the hand and brought him into Damascus. (Acts 9:1–8)

Why is it that the extremists are always the ones to have prophetic hallucinations and subsequent transformations? Paul definitely set the stage for the other kooks who live a life of sin: get "inspired" and then make everyone else suffer. It sounds kind of like our current president, doesn't it?

Conservatives tell us that we are supposed to take the Bible literally. Since some of the stories in the Bible are a bit absurd when taken literally and since I am a liberal, it could be possible that Paul's transformation was just an example of the ravings of a complete and total lunatic. That's what I believe anyway. As a consequence of his transformation, Paul dedicated the rest of his life to spreading the message, his message, to the masses.

Paul's writings were permanently placed in the Bible in the fourth century. That would be four hundred years after the death of Christ. These writings consist of thirteen epistles. The Epistles are Romans, First Corinthians, Second Corinthians, Galatians, Ephesians, Philippians, Colossians, First Thessalonians, Second Thessalonians, First Timothy, Second Timothy, Titus, and Philemon.

An epistle is essentially a letter that is meant for reading by more than one person—kind of like a sermon, my least favorite part of church, but in writing. The letters are sent, one guy reads them, and then he reads them to the group.

The group gets happy and spreads the message. In this case, the group spreads the message of Paul. It had to be the message of Paul that was being sent because most of these people did not have easy access to the Gospels. This is how the Pauline message was distributed. It is unfortunate that Paul wasn't sending around the Gospels instead of his dumb letters. Paul could have just copied the Gospels and told the followers of Christ, "Please read this. I am only a man. Read the Word of God. What I say is not important." Paul was a little too self-involved for that.

"Everybody vs. Paul"

Before people start going crazy and declaring me insane because I am accusing Paul of subverting the message of Christ, it is important to note that I am neither the first nor the last to believe that Paul completely undercut the message of Jesus. I was surfing around the Internet one day and I arrived at a pretty interesting Web site called "liberalslikechrist.org" where I found an entire section devoted to Paul bashing. I liked it so much I bookmarked it for future reference. When I bookmarked the page, the bookmark in my "favorites" folder read "Paul vs. Everybody." This is a bit of an exaggeration, since not everyone is against Paul. Red State conservatives love him.

Before we get to the good stuff of proving how the writings of Paul are vastly different and even undermine the words of Christ in some very key areas, I think it is important to hear what a few brainiacs have to say about our good friend Paul.

> Where possible Paul avoids quoting the teaching of Jesus, in fact even mentioning it. If we had to rely on Paul, we should not know that Jesus taught in parables, had delivered the Sermon on the Mount, and had taught His disciples the 'Our Father.' Even where they are especially relevant, Paul passes over the words of the Lord. (Nobel Prize winner, Albert Schweitzer)1

On Paul's filibustering and ultimately ignoring of the words of Jesus:

> Paul hardly ever allows the real Jesus of Nazareth to get a word in. (Carl Jung)2

On the difference between the teachings of Jesus and the teachings of Paul:

> My long-time view about Christianity is that it represents an amalgam of two seemingly immiscible parts—the religion of Jesus and

the religion of Paul. Thomas Jefferson attempted to excise the Pauline parts of the New Testament. There wasn't much left when he was done, but it was an inspiring document.
(Carl Sagan)3

Sagan brings up an interesting point when he brings up Thomas Jefferson's distaste for America's favorite apostle. Our preeminent founding father was so disgusted by Paul's ignoring of the Christian message that he tried to put together another version of the Bible, leaving out the drivel eschewed by Paul of Tarsus, the lifelong Jesus hater.

Paul was the first corrupter of the doctrines of Jesus.
(Thomas Jefferson)4

It is pretty amazing that a man every Red State conservative in the United States holds up as the spokesperson for freedom wanted the teachings of Paul eliminated from the Bible. The truth is that Thomas Jefferson really wasn't a big fan of the conservative way of thinking at all. In his day, the no-fun, "everyone is a sinner" (except me, because I am "saved") conservative movement was led by the Calvinists. Jefferson was unrelenting and accurate in his attack of their ultra-ultraconservative doctrine.

The doctrines of Jesus are simple, and tend all to the happiness of man.
1. That there is one only God, and He is all perfect.
2. That there is a future state of rewards and punishments.
3. That to love God with all thy heart and thy neighbor as thyself is the sum of religion.
These are the great points on which he endeavored to reform the religion of the Jews. But compare with these the demoralizing dogmas of Calvin.
1. That there are three Gods.
2. That good works, or the love of our neighbor, are nothing.
3. That faith is everything, and the more incomprehensible the proposition, the more merit in its faith.
4. That reason in religion is of unlawful use.
5. That God, from the beginning, elected certain individuals to be saved and certain others to be damned; and that no crimes of the former can damn them; no virtues of the latter can save them.
—To Dr. Benjamin Waterhouse, June 26, 1825

The Calvinist doctrine sounds pretty familiar, doesn't it? It sounds a lot like modern-day fundamentalism, which has its roots in the Red States of America. Calvin and today's fundamentalists conserve the old way. Jefferson, by simplifying the message of Jesus, seeks to liberate not only the messages, but also the would-be Christian.

The "Faith" of Paul

The two important elements of Jefferson's list of demoralizing dogma are at the center of the conflict between Paul and Jesus. It's the never-ending battle between works and faith as a means to justification and salvation. Jesus, the proponent of "works," battles Paul, the defender of something mysterious called "faith."

Faith is usually defined as something along the lines of a belief or a trust in God or a belief in something for which there is no verifiable proof. Faith is unseen. People have faith in God even though this faith cannot be proven by empirical data. Faith is a good thing. I know that my faith in the existence of God is personal and that I would have a hard time trying to prove His existence in a scientific way.

Works, on the other hand, are visible actions that can be proven by the existence of witnesses. Jesus emphasized works, while Paul emphasized faith. Paul is obsessed with faith. He believes that a man's faith justifies him in the eyes of the Lord. He repeatedly states that, if a man has faith that Jesus was the Son of God, died on the cross for all of our sins, then he is free. He is saved. He is justified. It's a pretty easy way to salvation, I must say.

It is simple, because in Paul's faith-based doctrine, Jesus does all of the work. Jesus lives the life of purity. Jesus spreads a controversial message intended to liberate mankind. Jesus is punished. Jesus is strung up on the cross. Jesus is crucified until death. In Paul's world, the Christian doesn't have to do anything! This type of Christian says a few words, believes a few things, and "poof," like magic, he or she is "saved." A substantive change in life or personality doesn't have to happen at all.

This leads to the George W. Bush type of Christian, who declares the need for a "Jesus Day" but teases a dying woman, or, worse yet, while declaring a strong Christian faith, refuses to go to war himself but is more than happy to send others off to a foreign country for suspect reasons.

One of my main problems with American Christianity is that modern-day Christians allow the changing of Jesus' message to fit their lives rather than changing their lives to fit Jesus' message. All of this is possible because of Paul's doctrine of justification by faith, where Jesus does the work and we reap the benefits.

Now we never really know who achieves salvation, so, while they are on Earth, people are able to get away with a distortion of a very important tenet of the Christian message. Unfortunately for Jesus, Paul does not include a behavioral component to the requirement of salvation. Salvation by faith alone is some pretty selfish shit, not to mention a very dangerous doctrine.

The scary thing is that, in our culture, we hear about "faith" and the lack of emphasis of works on the road to salvation quite often. It is one of those ideas that unfortunately does have some biblical documentation. But this documentation is not from Jesus.

People like the evangelicals, looking for an easy way to salvation, run with it. Paul gives them their defense: "For we hold that a man is justified by faith apart from works of law." (Romans 3:28) This, I guess, is fine. God is great. God is good. God is powerful, and it is His decision, so salvation is dependent on Him. However, it does get dangerous, especially when Paul not only talks about faith as the only way, but also disparages those who do good works: "And to one who does not work but trusts him who justifies the ungodly, his faith is reckoned as righteousness." (Romans 4:5) This gives fundamentalists an excuse to replace faith with works.

The result is a lot of words about personal salvation from Christians, without the love and compassion modeled by Jesus. According to this faith-based doctrine, people can do whatever they want, and, as long as they "believe," they have earned personal salvation. Likewise, people who dedicate their lives to the service of others can be denied, because they lack something called "faith." The whole conservative doctrine of Christianity is based on the very selfish and simplistic use of another extraordinarily vague religious idea.

Paul actually disparages those who do good works by saying: "For by grace you have been saved through faith; and this is not your own doing, it is the gift of God—not because of works, lest any man should boast." (Ephesians 2:8–9) I guess Paul is trying to hammer home the point that all things are possible with Jesus—the idea that an individual can be a selfish jerk—like George Bush, John Ashcroft, Donald Rumsfeld, and Dick Cheney—and still be allowed into the Kingdom of God and given eternal life is because of the shortsighted message of Paul. All you gotta do is talk about your faith, and, brother, you are saved.

Furthermore, in this passage Paul indicates that people who are doing good, compassionate works, like giving alms to the poor, clothing the needy, teaching the uneducated, and healing the sick—things that Jesus did throughout his life—are only doing these things only so they can "boast" about their good works. Paul has a very negative view of the compassionate, intelligent human being. But then again, he is a conservative and that is the conservative way. So, if salvation by faith is the chosen doctrine, everybody with a big mouth gets "saved." Everyone who likes to talk about God goes to Heaven. People who are born with silver spoons in their mouths, discriminate against other religions, deny constitutional rights to those who don't share their views, cut programs to aid the poor, and invade other countries for no reason will enter the Pearly Gates because they are justified by their "faith."

That's great, if that's the doctrine. However, Jesus of Nazareth, the one the religion is named after, says something completely different.

The "Works" of Christ

Jesus doesn't even waste any time making His point about "works" as a manifestation of the Christian life. In the fifth chapter of Matthew, Jesus gives His first public speech in "The Sermon on the Mount," which is just about the most liberal public lesson ever put to paper. The first words out of His mouth are the Beatitudes, with each containing a very specific behavioral component that leads to a spiritual blessing.

> Blessed are the poor in spirit, for theirs is the kingdom of heaven.
> Blessed are those who mourn, for they shall be comforted.
> Blessed are the meek, for they shall inherit the earth.
> Blessed are those who hunger and thirst for righteousness, for they shall be satisfied.
> Blessed are the merciful, for they shall obtain mercy.
> Blessed are the pure in heart, for they shall see God.
> Blessed are the peacemakers, for they shall be called sons of God.
> Blessed are those who are persecuted for righteousness' sake, for theirs is the kingdom of heaven.
> Blessed are you when men revile you and persecute you and utter all kinds of evil against you falsely on my account.
> Rejoice and be glad, for your reward is great in heaven, for so men persecuted the prophets who were before you.
> (Matthew 5:3–12)

I find it interesting that, in each one of these commands, Jesus indicates that His presence in a follower's life is supposed to lead to a visible behavioral outcome.

Christians are to be "meek." Christians are to "mourn." Christians are to be "merciful." Christians should expect to be "persecuted." All of these commands are works that are the by-product of spiritual change. As opposed to "faith," all of these "works" can be seen. Jesus mentions nothing about "faith" or other misleading terms and ideas that do not have a visible outcome. Furthermore, if each one of these commands is practiced, there will be a permanent spiritual reward for the disciple.

George W. Bush and his Red State friends don't hold up too well against the Beatitudes. They are not "meek," for they brag about their religion and morality. They are not "peacemakers," because they invade other countries in the name of a nonviolent God. As multimillionaire politicians and religious showoffs, they are definitely not "persecuted". But, then again, they don't have to be like the Christian Jesus describes in the Beatitudes. The modern-day evangelical is not a Christian. He or she is a "Pauline" who is justified by his or her "faith," which, according to Paul, is much more important than "works." This faith without works might please Paul, but Jesus repeatedly warns us against the absence of works.

Jesus is remarkably consistent about works being a manifestation of spiritual change. People must show their devotion through their works, which are a by-product of spiritual change. The internal change has a very definite external effect. "Let your light so shine before men, that they may see your good works and give glory to your Father who is in heaven." (Matthew 5:16) Jesus never wavers in this point, and He has the strength, courage, and wisdom to practice what He preaches.

He gives to the needy. He prays with the poor. He practices compassion. He works miracles to relieve the suffering of downtrodden people. His entire life and message are based on the accumulation of works that support His words, doctrine, and life philosophy.

The life of Christ was not based on the accumulation of meaningless words without action. His life was all about helping people, being compassionate, and promoting forgiveness and selfless love.

Jesus did find it necessary to warn us against Paul's false doctrine: "For by your words you will be justified, and by your words you will be condemned." (Matthew 12:37) According to Jesus, Christians don't talk about their "faith." Christians live the lives of good works.

In Defense of Jesus: the Message of James

Not that Jesus needs anyone to take His side, but his very own brother took up the cause of Christ in this doctrinal battle. It is safe to say that Jesus shared some kind of personal relationship with his brother James. By the same token, Jesus never even met Paul. Even though Jesus and James had different fathers, their mother inextricably links the two. Mary raised Jesus from birth to death and was one of only two followers who were at the cross at the time of his death. This was undoubtedly a profound experience for the mother, which was undoubtedly relayed to her other son, so profound that, at least to some degree, James spread the message of his brother. One element of this message was the book of James.

It is no surprise that Paul did not have any direct contact with Jesus during his life, that is, except for that damned trip to Damascus where Paul had his famous hallucination and decided to embark on his mission to destroy the Christian message. The truth is that he never really met Jesus. A lot of these Red State revelations can be chalked up to vain fantasy and an overblown sense of self-importance.

At any rate, the mood and the words of James are diametrically opposed to the teachings of Paul. In regards to the apparent conflict between faith and works as the primary means to the end of salvation, James sides with his brother. It is interesting that James's words are almost the exact opposite of the words of Paul. Paul says, "For we hold that a man is justified by faith apart from works of law." (Romans 3:28) In almost the exact same phrasing, James says the direct opposite, "You see that a man is justified by works and not by faith alone." (James 2:24)

It is actually pretty amazing that these two opposed sayings about the same topic are allowed in the same book. But, this happens all the time in the Bible. It is almost as if James read the words of Paul and wrote a letter himself condemning this primary tenet of Pauline morality and thought. James knew that Paul was wrong!

In his wisdom, James agrees with his brother. In this particular doctrinal battle between the apostle Paul and Jesus's brother James, Jesus emphatically breaks the tie. It is clear that Paul missed the point and, in so doing, set down a dangerous tenet of faith that is not supported in the Gospels. Works in the religious life are important because Jesus says so.

The Christian is justified by his or her works, which are a byproduct of faith. Faith, by itself, is nothing. It means nothing, because, if people have faith in their God but have a wrong or misguided moral or ethical code of conduct, the good works never appear, and some pretty insidious stuff happens in the name of an innocent and misinterpreted God.

Justification for this is the Red State conservative Christian movement that turned a liberal message into conservative nonsense. Paul must share a great deal of the blame. If we continue to examine Paul's teachings, we find that he is even more conservative than most people could ever imagine.

Paul "Justifies" Slavery

The United States of America prides itself on being the one true bastion of freedom and democracy in the history of the world. While it is true that we have done a lot better than most countries in this area, we do have our faults, both past and present.

If there is one major embarrassment in the history of the United States of America, it must be the existence of racism in our supposedly free society. This racism exists more in some parts of the country (Red States) than it does in other parts (Blue States). The embarrassment of this attitude was embodied in our Southern states (all Red States) in the form of hundreds of years of slavery and segregation.

How can a free society that worships a God that exudes freedom and compassion have laws that not only enforce but protect the abominable act of owning slaves? Furthermore, how can the slave owners use God as a defender of this abominable institution?

For that answer, we must look no further than Paul, who provided biblical ammunition for the practice upheld in the South for over a hundred years, the owning of slaves.

We all know the sordid details. Slavery and segregation were conservative institutions that were defended by Red State interests. It was only through the selfless work of liberals that slavery was finally abolished. Remember, of course, that conservatives conserve the old way of things, while it is the liberal's job to liberate, so slavery did not go quietly, The United States had a war over it. It was only after this war that the conservatives in the South were forced to give up on slavery.

Considering Paul's status as an icon to the conservative religious Right, it is not very surprising that he not only condoned slavery but also believed that slaves should honor their masters with the utmost degree of reverence. This undoubtedly secured Paul's place as the Red State conservative's favorite biblical figure. Here is a sampling of Paul's attitude toward the slave and master relationship.

> Let all who are under the yoke of slavery regard their masters as worthy of all honor, so that the name of God and the teaching may not be defamed. Those who have believing masters must not be disrespectful on the ground that they are brethren; rather they must serve all the better since those who benefit by their service are believers and beloved. Teach and urge these duties. (1 Timothy 6: 1–2)

Not only does Paul tell the slaves to honor their masters, but he also makes a specific plea to be extra respectful to slave masters who are Christians. It never really got through to Paul that a Christian probably shouldn't own other people. Paul held Christian slave owners in such high regard that he instructs the slaves to believe the Christian slave master more than the pagan slaveholder.

The result is that Christian slave owners had biblical authority to expect the utmost devotion from their slaves due to their status as believers in Christ. That is pretty disgusting. Is it any wonder that slavery in the Red States was allowed to flourish by Christian slave owners and politicians? They had biblical authority.

But Paul doesn't stop there. Paul goes one step further by threatening the slaves with damnation if they disobey their masters: "Slaves, be obedient to those who are your earthly masters, with fear and trembling, in singleness of heart, as to Christ; not in the way of eye-service, as men-pleasers, but as servants of Christ, doing the will of God from the heart, rendering service with a good will as to the Lord and not to men." (Ephesians 5:5–7) According to Paul, it is the will of Christ for slaves to obey their Christian masters. It is one of Paul's bizarre acts of "faith."

Not only must slaves be obedient, but they must also obey with "fear and trembling" in the same way that they are humbled and terrified of Christ. Paul, of course, gives the obligatory order to slaves that their hard work ultimately pleases God and is His will. That sure is nice of him. The work of the slave doesn't just please the master; it pleases Jesus as well. So, according to Paul, the benevolent, loving God of all mankind (Jesus) condones slavery. It is ridiculous. The liberals who inspired the abolition of slavery and subsequent Civil Rights Act of 1964 put Paul and the Red States of the South to shame.

The Good Samaritan

There was not one time in the Gospels that Jesus ever indicated that slavery was in any way an ethical or moral endeavor sanctioned by God. He certainly felt the opposite. The parable of "The Good Samaritan" tells Jesus's side of the story the best.

> And behold, a lawyer stood up to put him to the test, saying, "Teacher, what shall I do to inherit eternal life?" He said to him, "What is written in the law? How do you read?" And he answered, "You shall love the Lord your God with all your heart, and with all your soul, and with all your strength, and with all your mind; and your neighbor as yourself." And he said to him, "You have answered

right; do this, and you will live." But he, desiring to justify himself, said to Jesus, "And who is my neighbor?" Jesus replied, "A man was going down from Jerusalem to Jericho, and he fell among robbers, who stripped him and beat him, and departed, leaving him half dead. Now by chance a priest was going down that road; and when he saw him he passed by on the other side. So likewise a Levite, when he came to the place and saw him, passed by on the other side. But a Samaritan, as he journeyed, came to where he was; and when he saw him, he had compassion, and went to him and bound up his wounds, pouring on oil and wine; then he set him on his own beast and brought him to an inn, and took care of him. And the next day he took out two denarii and gave them to the innkeeper, saying, 'Take care of him; and whatever more you spend, I will repay you when I come back.' Which of these three, do you think, proved neighbor to the man who fell among the robbers?" He said, "The one who showed mercy on him." And Jesus said to him, "Go and do likewise." (Luke 10:25–37)

Keeping in mind that the Samaritans were not friends of the Levites, it is interesting that Jesus's directive to "love your neighbor as yourself" extends to all people, even people from different cultures and ethnic backgrounds. According to our Red State fundamentalists, Christians are only supposed to love people who are just like them. Everyone else is going to Hell in a hand basket.

Going back to the idea of faith as the only means of salvation, it is also interesting that, in this parable, Jesus included the occurrence of a priest ignoring the man who was a victim of thieves. The religious man, full of piety and "faith," ignored him. The Samaritan, even though he was a godless heathen, practiced Christian compassion and generosity. The Samaritan earned salvation. The priest had no idea that, when he ignored a man in need, he was neglecting his duties as a child of God.

The priest does not recognize that a man from another background was his neighbor. In the same way, Paul had no idea that slaves were his neighbors. Paul was an idiot.

It becomes apparent that Paul completely missed the point of "loving your neighbor as yourself" and that he secured his place—not as the world's greatest proponent of Christianity—but as one of the most flagrant blasphemers of the Christian message. But people wouldn't know that because they look to the Epistles for the easy answers, while ignoring the difficult answers located in the Gospels. Jesus provides the difficult answers, Paul the easy ones. It is much easier to own and justify slavery in an age that condones slavery than it is to take a stand against it.

So, it was from Paul that slave owners received their biblical justification for slavery. Is it any wonder that every single state that at one time condoned slavery in the United States voted Red in the 2004 election? It isn't surprising to me. What is surprising and even ironic is that this part of the country is called "The Bible Belt." Paul's legacy lives on. What a shame.

Paul "Justifies" Misogyny

Since Paul was an outspoken advocate of slavery and slave owner's rights, it isn't too surprising that he was also a bit of a misogynist. It's hard to believe, but Paul didn't think equal rights should be extended to women.

The church has struggled with the issue of how much women should be involved in religious proceedings for years. Historically, most Christian denominations have been on the side of Paul. It is only until recently that some denominations have ordained women ministers. The Catholic Church continues to be way behind the times. But, if Paul had anything to do with it, women wouldn't be involved at all. "Let a woman learn in silence with all submissiveness. I permit no woman to teach or to have authority over men; she is to keep silent. For Adam was formed first, then Eve; and Adam was not deceived, but the woman was deceived and became a transgressor." (1 Timothy 2: 11-14) It is almost funny that a man could be so uptight and so wrong and yet still be considered a source of information about religion. In two sentences that are supposed to be accepted as infallible because of their inclusion in the Bible, Paul tells women to be silent and listen to men. Additionally, he then goes back to Old Testament conservative doctrine and blames women for the fall of mankind. Paul's discrimination is almost too good to be true. But it doesn't stop there.

According to Paul, women shouldn't just be silent in church, but they need to consult their husbands for their religious information and education. "The women should keep silence in the churches. For they are not permitted to speak, but should be subordinate, as even the law says. If there is anything they desire to know, let them ask their husbands at home. For it is shameful for a woman to speak in church." (1 Corinthians 14:34–35) Paul never mentions the law that does not allow women to speak in church. Wherever this law comes from, it certainly does not come from Jesus.

Paul would be hysterical if he weren't so dangerous. Paul, the infallible spokesperson for Jesus, lays down the law should anyone question his Christian philosophy and his qualifications as the one and only prophet when he says, "What! Did the word of God originate with you, or are you the only ones it has reached? If any one thinks that he is a prophet, or spiritual, he should acknowledge that what I am writing to you is a command of the Lord." (1 Corinthians 14:36–37)

There you have it. Paul's word is the infallible word of God. Paul should have just cut the crap and announced that he was God. This precious piece of self-absorption comes right after announcing that women need to close their mouths in church and obey their husbands. Paul really had a bug up his butt regarding women. Not only does Paul think women should shut up and do what their husbands say, but he also says that there shall be no challenging of his authority. It is he who is the one true prophet. This is some pretty scary and pretty blasphemous stuff.

But alas, Paul's anti-woman doctrine is even too much for the churches in the Red States of America. If I am not mistaken, I do believe that in a Red State a woman can speak in church. The United States accuses and convicts Middle Eastern countries of oppressing women, but shouldn't we be continuing our Pauline doctrine of putting women in their place? If we were truly following biblical teachings, we would be doing the same thing as the members of the Taliban. We condemn them, but it is they who, according to Paul, are following the teachings of God. It seems we get to pick and choose which biblical policies we want to obey.

This, of course, leads us right back to Jesus and how this whole notion of justification by faith apart from works is a very dangerous message. Jesus knew it. It is too bad Paul couldn't get it through his thick, conservative skull. It is a Red State nightmare that slavery is now illegal and women have been granted the right to vote. If it weren't for those liberals, things would have been fine. The Red State South would have been a Pauline paradise: a lot of blacks doing Red State work and a lot of women seen and not heard.

A Gospel Hero

Before moving along, it is important to note that, in the Gospels, women tended to be pretty heroic figures. Jesus befriended a female prostitute and defended her to His death. Mary Magdalene was probably Jesus's most loyal friend. Mary was not one of the people who denied Jesus.

It is interesting that all of Jesus's male disciples either disappeared after Jesus was arrested or denied Him altogether. It was two women who had the bravery and strength to place themselves at the foot of Jesus's cross upon His death. Paul probably did not know this since he gives us no evidence that he ever actually read the Gospels. I wonder what Jesus would have said to Paul had He known that Paul was telling women to shut their mouths in church. The thing is, I doubt if Paul even read the Gospels. This was another of his ultraconservative characteristics. There is no doubt whatsoever that Paul shares a some of the responsibility for the bastardization of the Christian message. While it may not be all Paul's fault, he certainly gave Christians Biblical justification for a lot of irresponsible and atrocious behavior. Thank God liberals got it straight and saw that slavery should be outlawed and that there is nothing wrong with women enjoying a full relationship with their Savior

The continued misinterpretation of the liberal Christian message took a serious hit when Paul started writing his misinformed and ill-applied letters. There has not been any person in the history of mankind who has undermined the liberal message of Christ more than Paul. Listen to a conservative Bible study or a Red State religious service and it is undeniable that the pastor or whoever is leading the service is relying heavily on Paul for a great deal of his or her information. When Christ is quoted, it is to justify the teachings of Paul, not vice versa. A strong case can be made that the modern American church is not Christian, but Pauline.

Jesus Never Had a Chance

Let's face it. Paul was a self-serving, arrogant, piece of shit. He never directly quotes the Gospels, indicating that there is no evidence that he ever read the words of Christ. Yet, because of his hallucination on the road to Damascus, he anoints himself the spokesperson for the Christian religion. He tells people that they shouldn't do anything they want and that they will be "saved" because of their faith. He tells slaves to honor their masters. He is obsessed with other people's sex lives. He tells women to honor their husbands, shut up, and do what they're told. It all sounds very Red State of him.

For some crazy reason, Paul isn't thrown off the pages of the Bible. Thomas Jefferson had the right idea in trying to eliminate Paul from the New Testament. It is too bad that he couldn't pull it off. In Paul's early days he used to persecute Christians. After he had his "revelation, "he decided to execute his lifelong effort to kill Jesus's message permanently. Way to go, Paul! Mission accomplished! A conservative zealot undermined the liberal message of Christ before other followers could spread a liberal message. The Christian Right has found its icon, and it ain't Jesus.

In the end, almost 2,000 pages of angry, Old Testament conservatism and a load of Pauline selfishness and bigotry surround the four chapters of the liberal Christian doctrine espoused by Jesus that is contained in the Gospels.

Jesus never had a chance.

5

Wolves

Honor among Men

Even though I am claiming myself as a heathen, I understand that, by criticizing the modern-day blaspheming of Jesus, I am opening myself to becoming just like "them." In my defense, there is one difference. I am not trying to prove that I am a better Christian than the Red State evangelical with salvation as my personal domain. I am trying to prove beyond a shadow of a doubt that the conservative Christian, whether from a Red State or Blue State, is a hypocrite who lacks biblical knowledge and spreads a very self-serving message.

Conservatives have been judging liberals with their snide remarks for years. It is only recently that they have had the balls to castigate liberals in the name of a liberal God. Quite frankly, it is time to expose them as hypocrites who do not have any knowledge of the Gospels or any interest in Jesus. To that end, Jesus does warn us against people who will twist His message to serve their own selfish needs.

One of the best ways to expose this type of hypocrisy is to make the initial determination that just about any religious person who loves the spotlight may have missed the point. Some people show a disturbing need to be loved by their fellow man. Some people have a need to be famous and feel important. All false prophets and all hypocrites achieve some sort of public trust by deceiving the masses with lies and half-truths.

At this point, it seems pretty clear that the messages of Jesus and Paul are quite a bit different. Before moving any further, it is appropriate to take a moment and uncover one more significant difference between the liberal message of Jesus and the conservative doctrine of Paul. It seems that Paul thinks that honor in the sight of men is very important, while Jesus thinks that people who enjoy the praise of men are self-centered jerks. Jesus prefers that people do God's will and avoid the pitfalls that come with fame and fortune. It is the man who seeks approval among men that makes the greatest and most dangerous hypocrite.

It is apparent how certain public figures, especially the religious ones, can get confused since Paul continually takes the opposite position of Jesus on most issues. Paul believes that success among men is success that is heralded and condoned by God, which, of course, has led to the ubiquity of religious leaders lining their coffers and declaring that monetary gifts are given to them from God because of their devotion. Paul says, "For we aim at what is honorable not only in the Lord's sight but also in the sight of men." (2 Corinthians 8:21) Jesus says the opposite, "But he said to them, 'You are those who justify yourselves before men, but God knows your hearts; for what is exalted among men is an abomination in the sight of God.'" (Luke 16:15) I wonder how all of our Christian politicians and evangelists deal with this one?

It is obvious that, as the differences between Paul and Jesus continue to grow, more and more people find it much easier and more convenient to align themselves with the conservative Paul rather than the liberal Jesus. Without question, the boastful religious leaders and, unfortunately, some of the politicians of our day are following Paul's lead in seeking honor among men. Jesus sees that what is exalted among men is not the primary interest of God. When our political leaders seek approval because of their supposed relationship with God, they are missing the point. Their vanity, brought on by their popularity and millions of dollars in campaign funds, must be considered an affront to Jesus, who wants His followers to see these scoundrels for what they are and get away from them as fast as possible.

These people who are in power become consumed with their personal greatness and declare that they are on a mission from God to save people. Paul is their unabashed leader, "I try to please men in everything I do, not seeking my own advantage, but that of many, that they may be saved." (1 Corinthians 10) The modern-day braggart evangelists are actually convinced that, in spite of breaking the laws of Christ, they are on a mission from God. Pride is an ugly thing.

Jesus warns them, but they do not listen, "Woe to you, when all men speak well of you, for so their fathers did to the false prophets." (Luke 6:26) Jesus not only tells us that we should not desire men to speak well of us, but He also notes that this notion of people declaring they are agents of God because they are popular has all happened before, so it will happen again. People love to be enamored with and follow the false prophets who seek to undermine His message and our lives. The masses follow these people to their own demise.

The Third Commandment

It would be nice if people were more careful regarding what they say about "God" and "religion." For all of us imperfect individuals, when eternity is at stake, getting something wrong or inadvertently blaspheming an all-powerful God can threaten personal salvation. The public figures that pontificate about "their God" and "their religion" can blur the lines between being a unique witness for Christ and a "false prophet" or a "hypocrite." The false prophet can lead millions astray. The hypocrite is just self-serving, self-righteous, and very annoying.

This is one of the reasons for the Third Commandment in the Old Testament. While everyone know some of the commandments, "Thou shall not kill," "Thou shall not commit adultery," "Thou shall not bear false witness," the Third Commandment is largely ignored. This commandment is the one in which God metes out a very specific and eternal punishment. God holds the breaking of this commandment as an unforgivable sin.

Nine of the commandments give simple instruction on what *not* to do— this is the Old Testament way. However, there is not a specific punishment associated with any of these commandments. The only commandment that gets special attention is commandment number three.

The Third Commandment is not the commandment against murder or against worshipping false idols. It is the one that many take to be the most innocuous of all of God's laws. The unforgivable commandment from the Lord is this: "You shall not take the name of the Lord your God in vain; for the Lord will not hold him guiltless who takes his name in vain." (Exodus 20:8) Pretty simple. Don't take the Lord's name in vain, or, as most people think, don't swear.

It is hard for a rational person to think that taking the Lord's name in vain—saying the name "God" or the name "Jesus" as part of a profane statement—is the ultimate sin. We all do it. We say "Jesus Christ" when we are angry. We say "Goddammit" when we are frustrated. We even combine other vulgar words with these lofty names. I do it all the time. For some reason, my favorite expression when I am really pissed off is "Jesus F'ing Christ." I understand that this is not very nice, but how can this be worse than murder? Furthermore, while making this kind of statement is certainly disrespectful and wrong, how can it be singled out as being the one in which the breaking of it holds people guiltless and beyond forgiveness? Is it worse to slit someone's throat or to say, "Jesus Christ, I lost my goddamn motherfucking car keys"?

Certainly, murder is worse, but that commandment is not singled out for any special retribution or punishment. That commandment only says, "Thou shall not kill." This is not really surprising, considering that the Old Testament God is pretty bloodthirsty. But is it worse than swearing? Everybody does that, and everybody does it a lot.

Consequently, there has to be a deeper meaning concerning the Third Commandment. This commandment must not deal with profane statements as its focal concern. There must be something more insidious and crucial regarding God and the sanctity of this law. It is for this reason that we must believe that, in this commandment, God is trying to protect himself and His followers from "false prophets" and "hypocrites" who blaspheme His name. We all know them, the people who talk about God and they are wrong. They are pontificating self-righteous windbags like Paul of Tarsus, Jerry Falwell, or George W. Bush. They are the people who spend countless hours attributing their personal beliefs and opinions to divine inspiration. They are the people who use God's name to promote their own ideology, hatred, and discrimination. By consistently invoking the name of God, some people actually believe that God inspired their kooky ideas. And when they are wrong, and they are wrong often, these "false prophets" lead millions down the wrong path. Now, that sounds like an unforgivable sin.

It is obvious why this is the one with the "special punishment," for it is the one commandment that can eternally disparage God and lead lost souls down a permanent path of personal and spiritual self-destruction.

Some people might think that the First Commandment, "You shall have no other gods before me," is more important than the third. I don't think so. It certainly is the one that is more familiar. It is also less open to misinterpretation. While the First Commandment links with the Second Commandment that states that God's people should not worship false idols, both have different consequences than the third.

God doesn't declare that the first two are beyond guilt and are ultimately unforgivable because the damage done by worshipping a false idol is easily reversed. Change religions, declare the past worship of a false god part of a troubled or disillusioned past, and move ahead. This is what Paul of Tarsus did, and we are taught that his conversion was divine. Paul changed his ways. This is kind of like the deathbed conversion that I have planned for myself.

If someone decides to worship another god, it is at his or her own peril and at his or her own personal risk. According to God, it is wrong, but, on the list of eternal sins, it isn't as bad as taking the Lord's name in vain because people worshipping the false idol are not blaspheming God. To a certain degree, they are leaving Him alone and not necessarily causing a problem for all eternity. The "false prophet" is leading people down the wrong path in the name of God. This can impact a lot of people over a lot of years. It has impacted numerous nations and cultures, including our own.

For this reason, it is very dangerous for public figures to pontificate about their relationship with God or their knowledge of His plans. Public figures, especially preachers and politicians, wield great power and influence over large numbers of people. Because they are in power, these people become so sure of their message, they begin to believe that God is speaking through them as some kind of reward for being a dutiful servant. However, if they are wrong, and they are wrong often, these charlatans and wolves can lead millions away from God's message. That is why the breaking of the Third Commandment leads to eternal damnation. This gives me some hope that someday these conservative, evangelical jackasses will have to pay for their idiocy and arrogance.

Identifying False Prophets

Throughout the Gospels, Jesus makes very specific commands to his followers to be on the lookout for false prophets. One of his most famous declarations on this issue was, "Beware of false prophets, who come to you in sheep's clothing but inwardly are ravenous wolves. You will know them by their fruits. (Matthew 7:16–17) This has to be considered one of Jesus's most famous sayings because even nonreligious people are able to understand the meaning of the "wolf in sheep's clothing." It is a brilliant metaphor that conveys the sinister side of the person who approaches with a smile only to stab in the back. Jesus does give us some instructions on how to identify these people. We will know them by the "fruits" of their labor. This is just another lesson from Jesus as to the importance of works in the religious life.

If people preach about the Gospels and about love and compassion, they are doing God's work, and it will show. By the same token, if people preach about their strong faith, their rigid beliefs, and their devotion to Christianity, but their works do not reflect the true meaning of Christ's teachings, then they need to be declared the false prophet or "the wolves in sheep's clothing" that they are.

Everyone knows that there is a huge difference between the likes of Mother Theresa and Martin Luther King when they are compared to Jerry Falwell and Pat Robertson. Both pairs are religious and both pairs claim Christianity, but the fruits of one pair are a lot different than the fruits of the other. And just to rub it in a little bit, Martin Luther King Jr. and Mother Teresa were liberals, while Falwell and Robertson are Red State conservatives.

It is exceedingly important to make sure that a person's beliefs are in tune with the person they are following. Christians are compelled to follow Christ and His words. Jesus has a doctrine. He has a philosophy, and it is part of written and historical record. Christians should be following the doctrine of Jesus, not the doctrine of some religious bozo that has fallen in love with himself and his crackpot ideas.

The Attack on Hypocrites

It is also interesting that a careful review of Jesus' words shows that He pays special attention to "hypocrites." Jesus shows disdain towards those people who consistently brag about their faith and religious leanings. As a religious leader, Jesus had a very unique and special call to His followers to be very humble in prayer and devotion. It is the boastful ones that irk Jesus. "And when you pray, you must not be like the hypocrites; for they love to stand and pray in the synagogues and at the street corners, that they may be seen by men. Truly, I say to you, they have received their reward." (Matthew 6:5) Apparently, some people like to be religious show-offs. I think we all can name a few of those without any prompting. We are instructed by Jesus to question their sincerity.

The people of the United States are continually bombarded with religious and secular public figures who boast about their relationship with God and about how they know the way to personal salvation and everlasting life. The most disturbing of these images are seen on television in the form of televangelists. These people give their message in the most public haunts of men. They ask for money. They build gaudy stages and churches that are more like amusement parks than houses of worship. These preachers violate almost every direct commandment of Jesus in their public displays of their faith. If you need any proof, just check out The Sermon on The Mount in The Gospel of Matthew.

However, I am sure that Paul is quite pleased, especially considering that, at one point while showing a continued propensity to violate a teaching of Jesus, Paul says, "but take thought for what is noble in the sight of all men." (Romans 12:17) Way to go Paul.

To most of us liberals who live in the Blue States, the existence of televangelists and other religious show-offs who populate our nation is somewhat harmless and even a little amusing. If people in the Deep South and Southwest want to follow false prophets and give their money to a group of charlatans and scoundrels, that is their business. In spite of Red State efforts, the United States is a free country. But now we have our politicians declaring themselves messengers of God, and the idea that there is a misguided man of God as president of the United States is more than a little disturbing.

However, it is our own fault, since we are supposed to be a Christian nation and our leader Jesus warns us against this phenomenon, "For false Christs and false prophets will arise and show great signs and wonders, so as to lead astray, if possible, even the elect." (Matthew 24:24) That's right. Jesus tells us that even our elected officials will use His name to lead us astray.

At this point, it is really important to give Jesus the credit He deserves. He was a very revolutionary thinker who wanted His followers to have the intelligence and strength to be able to tell the difference between the true followers of a faith and those who seek to deceive us. Jesus even has a special warning for us to be afraid of the "elect." Bravo! Two thousand years ago, Jesus predicted and warned us that those who we choose to govern us will use His name to further their power and influence all in the effort to lead us astray.

The Chosen Ones

Leaders from all over the world and from all historical periods have consistently declared that, since they are in power, God is on their side. There is a persistent view among conservative Christians that God was involved in the 2000 and 2004 President Bush victories.

The idea that God appoints leaders is nothing new. In the Old Testament, God has a very accomplished history in this area. From Abraham and Moses to King David and King Solomon, God's chosen people exhibit faith and belief in the Almighty, and they are rewarded for it with positions of power. This wasn't Jesus's message, but it was the message of God. There is little doubt that the message in the cases of these four chosen people of the Old Testament was that God was in their corner and it was He who put them in their lofty positions. Since this message was sent with such veracity, it is not surprising that leaders throughout the history of the world have declared that divine intervention placed them in power. This leads to a variety of problems when it comes to the world leadership of fallible human beings. They come to the conclusion that they have been "elected" or placed in power because God is on their side. Some of the worst political and governmental leaders of our time have all claimed God's presence in their lives. Here is a sampling:

> "Who says I am not under the special protection of God?"
> (Adolf Hitler)1

> "I place my trust in God and not in some illegal political tribunal. God has already told me that this period in history is a part of the inevitable human process. My sacrifice will be recognized in many years. That is my hope and my faith."
> (Slobodan Milosevich)2

> "It is the duty of Muslims to prepare as much force as possible to terrorize the enemies of God."
> (Osama Bin Laden)3

God is on our side, and Satan is on the side of the United States."
(Saddam Hussein)4

I've heard the call. I believe God wants me to run for president.
(George W. Bush)5

It is pretty obvious that there is a significant problem here. All of these men claim God is on their side, yet they are notorious in some circles for their crimes against humanity. They had their enemies, and—whether these enemies were Jews, Americans, Croats, or Iraqis—they set out to destroy them in the name of their God.

Some Americans will freak out at the idea of placing George W. Bush in the same category as Hitler, Milosevic, Bin Laden, and Hussein, but there are good, suffering people in the world that regard George W. Bush as just as big a criminal as any other dictator in human history. Both George W. Bush and his namesake authorized the invasion of the same country based on some pretty suspect principles. Are law-abiding Iraqi civilians who now hate America any different from the Americans who hate Al Qaeda after the World Trade Center bombings? It's difficult to say.

There just isn't any way to know what world leaders have God on their side. Being a leader of a national government is a pretty messy business, which is why Jesus instructed His followers to place their priorities elsewhere. "Do not lay up for yourselves treasures on earth, where moth and rust consume and where thieves break in and steal, but lay up for yourselves treasures in heaven, where neither moth nor rust consumes and where thieves do not break in and steal. For where your treasure is, there will your heart be also." (Matthew 6:19–21) In His instructions, Christ is pretty consistent about the difference between earthly dominance and spiritual sanctity. The followers of Christ should not let their lust for power in the world damage their souls. This is something that every political leader does. People can't have it both ways. Earthly governmental dominance was never a Christian ideal.

Paul Does It Again

Another biblical contradiction to the teachings of Christ comes once again from the big mouth of top-notch evangelical Paul of Tarsus. Paul says some very frightening things about how Christians need to obey and respect their elected officials.

It is quite amazing that Paul actually tells the followers of Christ to obey their leaders because God has placed these people in power. "Let every person be subject to the governing authorities. For there is no authority except from God, and those that exist have been instituted by God." (Romans 13:1) Now this is pretty strange, considering that Jesus was crucified by the governmental leaders of His day. It was these same leaders who were in the habit of persecuting not only Christians, but also anyone who was different than the members of the conservative and oppressive Roman state.

Not only does Paul tell us to follow these leaders blindly because they have been "instituted by God," he tells us that we will be punished if we don't. "Therefore he who resists the authorities resists what God has appointed, and those who resist will incur judgment." (Romans 13:2) Not only are we ordered to follow our leaders, but we are also told not to question them and that, if we disobey our leaders whether they are good or bad, Hell will be our destination. I hate Paul more and more all the time.

Paul continues with this line of insanity with his bizarre assertion that all of God's governmental leaders are somehow infallible. "For rulers are not a terror to good conduct, but to bad. Would you have no fear of him who is in authority? Then do what is good, and you will receive his approval." (Romans 13:3) Tell this to the Jews in Europe, the Iraqi civilians in Iraq, the wretched in Cuba, or the millions who suffered or were murdered under Stalin.

Paul's instructions in this area may be the most irresponsible advice in human history. Obey your rulers because they are always good! Talk about leading the flock to the slaughterhouse!

But Paul continues and actually gives the evil dictator the right and authority to convict, punish, and kill those who do not follow his orders. "For he is God's servant for your good. But if you do wrong, be afraid, for he does not bear the sword in vain; he is the servant of God to execute his wrath on the wrongdoer." (Romans 13:4) Great! Government leaders are the servants of God. So they have the right to execute their enemies.

Finally, Paul adds the concept of divine punishment to the equation. The punishment is now twofold. If you don't follow your leader, your leader is justified in killing you. Furthermore, after your death, God is going to get you as well. "Therefore one must be subject, not only to avoid God's wrath but also for the sake of conscience." (Romans 13:5) Pretty weird. This is way different than what Jesus told us about not trusting the elect. But Paul contradicts Jesus all the time. It is pretty clear where all the Red and Blue State evangelical Christians get the idea that God placed "His man" in the White House. Once again, Paul trumped the message of Jesus.

So, according to some people, George W. Bush was elected because of his religion. He and Karl Rove have forced it down the nation's throat for years in an effort to garner a victory by hoodwinking Red State conservatives. This divine idea started even before George W. Bush ran for the presidency in 2000. Even his contemplation of the idea of being president was divinely inspired. "I can't explain it, but I sense my country is going to need me. Something is going to happen...I know it won't be easy on my family, or me but God wants me to do it. God speaks through me."6 Talk about a God complex. George W. Bush had a "burning bush" hallucination.

I need George W. Bush as my president about as much as I need prostate cancer. The whole idea that we need George W. Bush is preposterous to more than 50 million Americans. But hey, we got him. I guess God hates us. We do need to hold the Red States responsible for this predicament. It was this group of states that spawned the modern-day fundamentalist, evangelical movement that has tried to place God in government. It is they who consistently promote the idea that George W. Bush is God's president.

Praising Bush

I hate guys like Charles Colson. We all know them, the lifelong criminal and arrogant scumbags who get caught doing dirty deeds and then have religious transformations. They use their miraculous change of heart as a way to force-feed their dumb religion to millions. Does any of this sound familiar? They think they are the modern-day prophets because they have been "saved".

Anyway, Colson is one of the people who believe that God performed one of His magic tricks in an effort to plant the chosen one in the White House. Colson indicates that God may have helped George W. Bush cheat in the 2000 election. "This was Providence. Anybody looking at the 2000 election would have to say it was...a miraculous deliverance, and I think people felt it again this year." Colson continues," By allowing Bush to stay in office, God is giving us a chance to repent and to restore some moral sanity to American life."7 Interesting that a spoiled kid of a Texas millionaire is going to restore "moral sanity" to our lost nation. As disturbing and insane as that is, there is more:

> Millions were relieved at the election results and gave God their praise! Yesterday America cried out and He heard from heaven and answered our prayers. PRAISE GOD!!
> (E-mail from Jim Rogers of Mission America)8

Others chose not to praise the godliness of Bush, but to attack the hedonism of John Kerry.

The Bible says godly leadership is a sign of God's blessings and a lack of godly leadership is a sign of God's judgment. I don't see Kerry as a godly leader.
(Richard Lamb, Southern Baptist Leader)9

Apparently, George W. Bush needs our prayers. He ain't getting one from me.

Recently I have felt the Lord speak to me (remember, I'm a conservative Presbyterian, I rarely use those words) that our President needs someone fasting for his every day in the office for his holiness.10

In a very disturbing pro-Bush ass kiss fest at the Republican National Convention, George Pataki gets down on his knees and heaps Dubya's an abundance of praise. He even links him to God.

He is one of those men God and fate somehow lead to the fore in times of challenge.
(George Pataki)11

Pataki can't stop himself as he continues to service George W. Bush while exploiting the attacks on September 11 for Republican political gain.

I thank God we had a president who understood that America was attacked, not for what we had done wrong, but for what we did right.
(George Pataki)12

A flock of Red State psychos want us to fast—not in honor of God, but in honor of George W. Bush.

God is raising up multitudes of Christians (regardless of political affiliation) to fast and pray for the holiness of President George W. Bush and our nation. Join us in God's grassroots movement.
(Bob Sjogren, Fast for George W. Bush)13

Rudy Giuliani declares God's love for George Bush.

And I say it again tonight: Thank God, George Bush is our president."
(Rudy Giuliani)14

Finally, the father of George W. Bush, not God but his other father, believes that God somehow directed his loss in the 1992 presidential election so that his son could be president later.

> If I'd won that election in 1992, my oldest son would not be president of the United States of America. I think the Lord works in mysterious ways. 15

Like father, like son. What an overblown, arrogant piece of shit. Bush Sr. lost the election in 1992 because the country hated him and Bill Clinton was a better candidate. Even losing is divine to moronic, self-centered Red State Republicans. Their stupidity and hubris know no limit.

The people of the United States have been bombarded with this kind of crap for years, and it gained momentum in the recent election. It is too bad that the Blue State liberals and those in the rest of the country have to suffer because so many evangelical morons fell for this line of religious crap. It was they who delivered the presidency to a religious kook, not God. George W. Bush is just another in the long line of history's world leaders who mistook their good fortune and luck for divine intervention.

Quoting Hitler

Being a card-carrying liberal, I'm no fan of Adolf Hitler, but, when it comes to knowing evil and manipulating the public for personal and evil gains, he does have some wisdom. It is here that Hitler's words actually provide some insight into what is happening in the United States.

First of all, considering the constant bombarding of the American people with the idea that George W. Bush is God's president, Mr. Hitler actually believed that it is possible to make the masses believe that the big lie is a bigger truth.

> The great masses of the people will more easily fall victims to a big lie than to a small one.16

I wonder if Karl Rove knows this?

Hitler would have made a great campaign manager, as he continues to espouse the benefits of the great, oft repeated lie:

> Make the lie big, make it simple, keep saying it, and eventually they will believe it.17

Millions of conservatives bought "The Big Lie" of Bush being God's chosen one. Millions of freethinking liberals called "bullshit" when that crap came down the pike.

Additionally, Hitler hits the nail on the head when he says,

Great liars are also great magicians.18

The rise of George W. Bush into the presidency in the name of God has been nothing short of magical.

Finally, Hitler communicates the belief that, in every society, there are people who will follow the lie with grins on their faces. These people will never ask questions. They will never challenge authority. They will never truly stand up for their rights when confronted with a leader who is so eager to take advantage of the weak. They are the followers of Paul. They are Red State conservatives. Hitler says,

How fortunate for leaders that men do not think.19

Napoleon Bonaparte, another notorious "leader of men," echoed this sentiment.

Religion is excellent stuff for keeping common people quiet.20

Ya hear that Red States?

Thank Your Local Liberal

There is one saving grace for us. We are in America, and, thankfully; we are *not* living under a religious dictatorship. We're on the way, but there are too many liberals to ever let this happen. It is about time that the Red Staters thanked the liberal Americans for all of our hard work and dedication in the effort to keep the United States from becoming a religious dictatorship. There is no doubt in my mind that if it weren't for the Blue State liberals that occupy half the electorate of our country, we would be under the leadership of an out-and-out religious dictatorship.

Evangelicals, fundamentalists, conservatives, Republicans, right-wing fanatics, whatever you want to call them, would be under the dominance of a dictator if it weren't for the work, intelligence, and bravery of the American liberal. Because of the blindness and stupidity of the Red State conservative and of conservatives everywhere, it will always be the work of the Blue State liberals to keep the United States of America something that resembles a democracy. It is becoming a pretty difficult job.

This, my friends, is a fact. Instead of criticizing us, conservatives should be thanking us. We keep democracy alive. Those Red State freedom-haters try to kill it. It has always been and will always be this way. The liberals preserve democracy and defend the rights of the individual.

Striving for democracy and promoting individual freedom all started with that radical liberal named Jesus, who warned us against "false prophets," "hypocrites," and the "elect." It is pretty amazing that religious politicians and their blind followers who say they are all about Jesus are able to completely miss or selfishly ignore these pretty simple and thoughtful instructions. Politicians and religious leaders ignore these instructions to their benefit. The followers of these wolves in sheep's clothing completely miss these warnings to their own demise.

Perhaps I will see them in Hell.

PART III

Conservative Issues and the Message of the Liberal Christ

6

The Sanctity of Life

Roe v. Wade Makes Sense

Throughout the years, one of the favorite conservative Christian issues has been a moral preoccupation with the right for a woman to terminate her pregnancy.

Conservatives, because they have anointed themselves as the ones who protect the sanctity of human life, are convinced that they have taken the high road on this controversy. They have turned this into a hotly debated religious issue. In their minds, God does not want innocent babies killed. Consequently, abortion is wrong because abortion is murder.

Pro-choice advocates argue that the issue is not so much about abortion and whether it is right or wrong, but that it is an issue concerning what a woman does with her body. Any intrusion from the government is a violation of a woman's right to control what belongs to her. Essentially, the Roe v. Wade decision gave women a constitutional right to do what they wanted with what belongs to them. In the Roe v. Wade opinion, the Supreme Court stated, "The Constitutional right to personal privacy, the roots of which are found in the 5th, 9th, and 14th Amendments, is broad enough to encompass a woman's decision whether or not to terminate her pregnancy."1

The Court did determine that the state has no "compelling interest" to protect an unborn fetus when an abortion is performed in the first trimester.

However, the Court did conclude that, since a woman's health is at risk during a second trimester abortion, the state does have some interest in protecting the methods of abortion. Likewise, because the fetus can support itself outside the womb, the state may have the right to proscribe a third trimester abortion, except in the case of a life-threatening situation involving the mother.

As everyone knows, Roe v. Wade made abortion legal in the United States. It would be hard to argue for abortion. There are not many people, conservative or liberal, who think that abortion is a good idea. Most people, while believing that women have the right to control their own bodies, also believe that abortion is a bad form of birth control.

I'm a pretty pragmatic guy, and I actually think the *Roe v. Wade* decision contains a great deal of common sense. If the fetus cannot survive on its own, it is hard to call it a life. In fact, most people refer to a fetus as an "it," not as a "he" or a "she." Likewise, as the development of the fetus progresses, so does the chance that the fetus can't survive. As a result, the Supreme Court put some restrictions on abortions, especially concerning those in the third trimester. This makes sense. This is one of the more divisive issues in the United States, and there is really no reason to argue about any of it. Neither the pro-choice activists nor the pro-life advocates are going to change their minds any time soon.

The point here is not to talk about what I think or to make the arguments about whether or not abortion is right or wrong or if women should have control of their bodies. Conservatives have made this one of their favorite religious issues. Consequently, it is important to consult scripture and see what the Bible and its primary authors, a conservative God, a liberal Jesus, and a conservative Paul, say about an issue that has only become important during the latter half of the twentieth century.

George W. Bush seems to agree with the sentiment of the conservative when he says, "I worry about a culture that devalues life and believe as your president I have an important obligation to foster and encourage a respect for life in America and throughout the world."2 That is a charming statement from a warmonger, isn't it? Consequently, it is important to evaluate whether or not the fruits of his labor are consistent with his words.

At least Bush isn't as bad as his conservative buddy Jerry Falwell, who blames Roe v. Wade for the September 11 attacks on the World Trade Center, "The abortionists have got to bear some burden for this because God will not be mocked. And when we destroy 40 million little innocent babies, we make God mad."3 Interesting to note that Falwell says that abortionists "make God mad." It would be hard to imagine Jesus, the Prince of Peace, sending three planes into the World Trade Center buildings, killing thousands of people due to some people's stance on a political issue. This is one of those vague references that people need to be wary of. Attacking two buildings and killing thousands of innocents may be the behavior of God, but it is not the behavior of Jesus. This is an important qualification and shows Falwell's lack of knowledge of and his ability to manipulate scripture based on personal opinions. His statements and also exposes his faith...the faith of a psychopath.

Biblical Mass Murder and the Sanctity of Life

We all know that the conservative God of the Old Testament was an angry God that had a propensity towards violence. For this reason, it is no surprise that the members of the pro-life movement probably should not look towards this particular God if they are to find biblical justification to prove their point that human life is somehow sacred. The violence in the Old Testament is not going to help their cause. In fact, it is going to do just the opposite.

Since God was more than willing to hand down the death penalty for things that in modern-day society we do not even consider crimes, the fact that He not only instigates murder and violence but promotes it is consistent with His behavior and His personality.

It all starts with Noah's ark. This tale is one of the most well-known stories in the Bible. In it, humans have run amok and God wants to start all over. God, in His infinite wisdom and infinite power, decides to punish the entire world population with death by drowning. As we all know, God floods the Earth, killing everyone, except for Noah, his family, and two of each of the animals that populated the world. They all march "two by two" onto the ark. Ducks, giraffes, elephants, snakes—you name it—they all are saved. This is an instance in which God saves animals but kills humans. What a guy. It all makes for a great children's story. However, this mass death doesn't sound very fair or very nice, especially to the child population of the world. In this case, God did not protect the innocents. All of which begs the question, namely, how many pregnant mothers were killed? How many fetuses were destroyed? How many innocent babies drowned in a worldwide flood? Is this the action of a God who thinks that all life is sacred?

This story blames man's disobedience for God's violence, but it is violence nonetheless. It is also violence that kills both the guilty and the innocent. God made no distinction beyond Noah and the animals. He killed them all. Is life really sacred to a God who so wantonly kills all of His subjects? God's violence against mankind does not stop there. After murdering the world's population, God shifts His focus to the enemies of His people. On numerous occasions, God tells His followers to destroy cities and kill all members of races that are not from His chosen group. The result is bloodbath after bloodbath, killing both the old and the young. Joshua, for instance, is commissioned by God to destroy at least six different cities. This killing spree is described in fewer than two pages of The Holy Bible.

The city of Ai was the first attacked and it fell quickly.

And all who fell that day, both men and women, were twelve thousand, all the people of Ai. For Joshua did not draw back his hand, with which he stretched out the javelin, until he had utterly destroyed all the inhabitants of Ai. Only the cattle and the spoil of that city Israel took as their booty, according to the word of the LORD which he commanded Joshua. So Joshua burned Ai, and made it forever a heap of ruins, as it is to this day. (Joshua 8:24–29)

Makkedah was next.

And Joshua took Makke'dah on that day, and smote it and its king with the edge of the sword; he utterly destroyed every person in it, he left none remaining; and he did to the king of Makke'dah as he had done to the king of Jericho. (Joshua 10:28)

The God-inspired killing continues at Libnah.

Then Joshua passed on from Makke'dah, and all Israel with him, to Libnah, and fought against Libnah; and the LORD gave it also and its king into the hand of Israel; and he smote it with the edge of the sword, and every person in it; he left none remaining in it. (Joshua 10:29)

Joshua then moved his reign of terror to Lachish.

Horam king of Gezer came up to help Lachish; and Joshua smote him and his people, until he left none remaining. And Joshua passed on with all Israel from Lachish to Eglon; and they laid siege to it, and assaulted it; and they took it on that day, and smote it with the edge of the sword; and every person in it he utterly destroyed that day, as he had done to Lachish and Elgon. (Joshua 10:33–34)

Finally, it comes to an end after all of the residents of Hebron and Debir are smote.

Then Joshua went up with all Israel from Eglon to Hebron; and they assaulted it, and took it, and smote it with the edge of the sword, and its king and its towns, and every person in it; he left none remaining, as he had done to Eglon, and utterly destroyed it with every person in it. Then Joshua, with all Israel, turned back to Debir and assaulted

it, and he took it with its king and all its towns; and they smote them
with the edge of the sword, and utterly destroyed every person in it.
(Joshua 10:37–38)

That's a lot a' killin' by one guy on a mission from God. But, as they say,
"With God, all things are possible." It is especially violent when it is understood that the Bible makes it perfectly clear that, in each of these cities, everyone was killed. Man, woman, child, infant, and fetus, all were butchered with
the utmost cruelty. It sure doesn't seem like this God values human life. People
will try to justify this wanton destruction of human life by saying that biblical
times were different and violent—that it was a time of war and "God's people"
were fighting for survival. The Israelites had been oppressed in the past and
needed to fight back or else they would be oppressed in the future. It was a violent time that needed a violent God.

This still doesn't explain the killing of women and children. It seems particularly vicious and cowardly. Nonetheless, God instigated and ordered multiple
killing sprees.

Well-Known Stories of Biblical Infanticide

It is surprising that God also unleashes His wrath on children. Yes, God kills
children. It is in the Bible.

There is another well-known biblical story about Abraham and his son
Isaac. The tale is supposed to be some kind of a metaphor or lesson about how
strong a person's faith and trust in God is supposed to be. As the story goes,
God ordered Abraham to travel to the top of a mountain and kill his son. The
order to Abraham was to sacrifice his son in order to show his devotion.
"When they came to the place of which God had told him, Abraham built an
altar there, and laid the wood in order, and bound Isaac his son, and laid him
on the altar, upon the wood. Then Abraham put forth his hand, and took the
knife to slay his son." (Genesis 22:9–10)

That is a lot of trauma. Just imagine the scene. A father ties up his son, lays
him on a rock, takes out a knife, and puts it to the poor boy's throat, ready to
kill. The son has to be going crazy. The father must be grief stricken and out of
his mind. God watches it all with glee because He is getting His devotion. But
God finally comes to the rescue and substitutes a lamb for Isaac. Consequently,
Abraham does not kill his son and is duly rewarded for his faith.

It is important to remember that Abraham did make the move to kill Isaac.
It was God who saved the boy, not Abraham. Abraham would have killed his
son.

By myself I have sworn, says the Lord, because you have done this, and have not withheld your son, your only son, I will indeed bless you, and I will multiply your descendants as the stars of heaven and as the sand which is on the seashore. And your descendants shall possess the gate of their enemies, and by your descendants shall all the nations of the earth bless themselves, because you have obeyed my voice. (Genesis 22:16–18)

In the end, everything turns out perfect. God gets His "sacrifice." Abraham becomes a leader of his people and is rewarded with the promise that his people will rule the world.

Some stories of child killing from God don't have such happy endings. The most famous of these stories involves God's order to execute the firstborn of every Egyptian family. This just isn't very nice, even if the Egyptians are the enemy. "At midnight the Lord smote all the first-born in the land of Egypt, from the first-born of Pharaoh who sat on his throne to the first-born of the captive who was in the dungeon, and all the first-born of the cattle." (Exodus 12:29) There is not a lot to explain here. God killed thousands of innocent children whose only crime was that they were Egyptian. This behavior sounds pretty conservative to me.

"Mr. Poopy Pants": a Not So Well-Known Story of Biblical Infanticide

There is another example of God-inspired child killing in the Bible. This particular tale is kind of amusing, yet it is left out of most children's Sunday school classes. In this one, God actually kills obnoxious and rude children. Who hasn't wanted to do that at one point in their lives? In the Old Testament, our unrealistic fantasy becomes God-sanctioned reality.

As the bizarre story goes, one of God's favorites, Eli'sha, is taking a stroll through the forest when he encounters some very rude boys. The result is a serial killer's fantasy. Forty-two children are slaughtered in a matter of minutes.

He went up from there to Bethel; and while he was going up on the way, some small boys came out of the city and jeered at him, saying, 'Go up, you baldhead! Go up, you baldhead!' And he turned around, and when he saw them, he cursed them in the name of the Lord. And two she-bears came out of the woods and tore forty-two of the boys.

From there he went on to Mount Carmel, and thence he returned to Sama'ria. (2 Kings 2: 23–25)

That's right. Some obnoxious kids called one of God's favorites "baldhead," so old "baldhead" prays to God and the children are torn to pieces by some very hungry bears. Now that's justice!

After this insult, Eli'sha continues his journey without incident, that is, until he runs into a few Samarian schoolgirls who notice a stench emanating from Eli'sha. One of the insolent little girls calls him "Mr. Poopy-Pants." These girls are sent into a magical trance. In a sleep-like state they march in unison to the edge of a mountainous cliff. One after the other they proceed to jump to their deaths until there is a grisly pile of corpses at the bottom of a ravine. It is a total massacre.

Just kidding.

That was a sick attempt at humor. No schoolgirls were killed in this incident. But we are left to assume that Eli'sha had God's protection from further insults from petulant children. Some of people aren't so lucky.

We are told growing up that all of these stories have a lesson. I am sure there is some kind of a lesson here; I just can't figure out what it is. I do know that, as a teacher, I have had quite a few interactions with some pretty insolent kids. I have had students call me a faggot, a motherfucker, just about everything in the book. The greatest punishment any of them received was maybe some sentences or a two-day suspension from school. Instead of sending these brats to the principal, I should have said a prayer requesting their brutal murder. My prayers probably would be unanswered since I am not a devoted servant like Eli'sha was.

But these stories of child killing do not really address the issue surrounding the fetus. These are children who were killed, and they obviously did something wrong. They were born to Egyptians, lived in a pagan city, or called a prophet "baldhead." Maybe they got what they deserved. Who knows? I am one of the pagans that believe most of this stuff is fantasy or mythology at best, so I am hopeful that, even in ancient times, violent soldiers went easy on the child population of conquered cities and let them live. I also doubt that God had a she bear kill a group of children because they teased an old man. But maybe, because I am a liberal, I give God more credit than He deserves. I seriously doubt that a God, if He were good, would order the execution of anyone.

If multiple cities were razed by God's soldiers, it stands to reason that, if all women were killed, one of them must have been pregnant and maybe even was in the third trimester when the baby could have lived on its own. It is logical to believe that not only did God order the execution of potentially millions of children, but that a fetus was murdered along the way as well. This behavior from God does undermine the religious arguments of the conservative that the fetus is somehow important and should be valued and saved. Still, does God say anything about the murder of a fetus? If so, He must surely be against it, right?

Wrong.

A Shekel for Your Fetus

In a shocker, God does address the murder of an unborn baby. It is a story that destroys the conservative idea that God values the rights of an unborn fetus. He clearly does not.

As the story goes, God is doling out some more of His rules and regulations and applicable punishments. In this case, He is describing what should be done when men beat a woman who is with child and the result of this beating is a miscarriage. God says,

> When men strive together, and hurt a woman with child, so that there is a miscarriage, and yet no harm follows, the one who hurt her shall be fined, according as the woman's husband shall lay upon him; and he shall pay as the judges determine. If any harm follows, then you shall give life for life, eye for eye, tooth for tooth, hand for hand, foot for foot, burn for burn, wound for wound, stripe for stripe. (Exodus 21:22–25)

Sorry, Mr. Falwell. Apparently the death of a fetus does not "make God mad."

According to scripture and God's law, when a fetus is killed because a woman is beaten by a group of men, God only issues a fine as recompense for the destroyed fetus. Incidentally, while Roe v. Wade makes a distinction between a first and third term abortion, in this instance, God does not. A dead fetus is a dead fetus and it is only worthy of a fine.

This law from God is a bit amazing. A group of men beat a woman, there is a miscarriage, and as long as "no harm follows," the men who beat the woman and destroy the fetus only deserve a fine. There isn't even jail time or the bearing of iniquity, only a fine! God kills everyone in sight, yet, when a fetus is destroyed, it is only worth a couple of shekels. Unbelievable.

This does hurt the argument from the evangelical Christian that abortion is murder. And before religious goofballs everywhere go crazy and note that this was the Old Testament and not Jesus, they should remember that they quote the Old Testament to persecute gays and justify their hatred for just about everything and everyone. Evangelicals talk about God all the time to promote their hatred and judgment of others. It is only reasonable and fair that pro-life advocates should likewise be able to quote Old Testament theology to justify their point regarding the fetus.

This issuing of a fine as punishment to the death of an unborn baby is of interest in modern American law and politics. Recently, in a decision hailed by just about every American, George W. Bush signed a law that was inspired by the recent murders of Lacy Peterson and her unborn baby. The law reads, "Anytime an expectant mother is a victim of violence, two lives are in the balance, each deserving protection and each deserving justice. If the crime is murder and the unborn child's life ends, justice demands a full accounting under the law."4 Not to make light of this, but this is against God's law as outlined in the Bible.

I thought George W. Bush was "God's Man" in the White House? This law is a blatant violation of an instruction from God. The murderer of the mother gets punished in kind. The murder of a fetus only results in a fine.

Now that we know that God doesn't give a crap about children or babies or infants or fetuses, it is time to move on to the more liberal and compassionate voice in the Bible. It is time to see what Christ says about the most compelling and controversial religious issue of our day.

When an Embryo Kicks

Being a liberal and understanding that Jesus was the preeminent liberal philosopher, it would be difficult for me to imagine Jesus being for abortion. Likewise, it would be hard for me to imagine Jesus telling women that the government had the authority to tell them what to do with their bodies and how to handle their pregnancies. Consequently, it is difficult to imagine where Jesus would stand on this issue.

However, it is unfortunate that, just as in the case of homosexuality, Jesus never mentions abortion, a woman's right to choose to get an abortion, or anything about a fetus. We are left with no direct quotes to evaluate Jesus's stance on this controversial issue.

As I browsed through different pro-life literature looking for references to Jesus and the pro-life movement, the closest I could come to finding anything in the New Testament regarding unborn babies had nothing to do with first trimester issues surrounding whether or not a fetus is a human life. The one Gospel passage that pro-choice advocates cite deals with a baby jumping in a womb.

And when Elizabeth heard the greeting of Mary, the babe leaped in
her womb; and Elizabeth was filled with the Holy Spirit and she
exclaimed with a loud cry, "Blessed are you among women, and
blessed is the fruit of your womb! And why is this granted me, that
the mother of my Lord should come to me? For behold, when the
voice of your greeting came to my ears, the babe in my womb leaped
for joy." (Luke 1:41–44)

So a baby jumps in a womb. Big deal. This happens all the time. We call it
kicking. Since most of these "jumps" or "kicks" do not happen in the first
trimester, it has no relation to the argument regarding a fetus. The Supreme
Court said as much in *Roe v. Wade*.

Most pro-choice Christians seldom advocate second—or third-term abortions unless the mother's life is at stake. This biblical reference only states that
the baby leaped in the womb. It never qualifies whether the baby was a fetus. If
it was a fetus, could it have "leaped for joy"? It is highly unlikely. If the baby was
still in the fetus stage, why didn't Elizabeth say, "the fetus leaped for joy"? This
is the one Gospel citation most frequently used by Pro-Life literature.
Ultimately, it means nothing for either side of the argument.

Likewise, when trying to find a Christian argument to justify a woman's
right to choose, there are also no substantive references from Jesus to support
that position. Neither does Paul.

Chinese Abortions

Since Paul was for slavery and against women's rights, it is hard to imagine
that he would be for a woman's right to manage her own body. Paul hardly
cares about anybody that is not just like him. In his world, it is the man who
controls a woman's body.

I imagine, and this is just my opinion, that Paul would hate abortion for his
people, but not give a rat's ass about abortions from other people (pagans). I
only think this because Pauline philosopher Pat Robertson, who hates the idea
of abortion in America, thinks that, in China, abortion is just fine. Mr.
Robertson said, "They've got 1.2 billion people, and they don't know what to
do. If every family over there was allowed to have three or four children, the
population would become completely unsustainable. So, I think that right now
they're doing what they have to do. I don't agree with forced abortion, but I
don't think the United States needs to interfere with what they're doing inter-
nally in this regard."5

Once again, the big-mouthed evangelical wants it both ways. In this case,
Chinese abortion is practical. In other cases, it is murder condemned by God.

Robertson's stance simply does not make sense because it only values the life of some fetuses, not all of them.

The pro-life movement uses a couple of Paul's quotes to try to prove its points, but again these are so vague that it is illogical to think that, in any of these instances, Paul is making a distinction between a fetus in its first or third trimester. So, when Paul says that babies are born with the proverbial "clean slate," he does not make the qualification of when a fetus becomes a baby or if a fetus is human life, "Though they were not yet born and had done nothing either good or bad, in order that God's purpose of election might continue, not because of works but because of his call." (Romans 9:11) Paul is only saying that, when babies are born, they have a calling to serve God. This is hardly an argument that supports the right to life of a first trimester fetus.

The simple truth is that all of this is a total waste of time, because at no point in the New Testament do Jesus, Paul, or anyone else address the issue of the fetus or of a woman's choice to terminate her pregnancy. The New Testament guidance on this issue simply does not exist.

However, there is ample information in the New Testament on how we are to treat those infants and children who are living. It is here that the religious Right's arguments about the sanctity of a child's life fall apart. The culture that they espouse and love simply does not take care of its most vulnerable members.

School Days

It is well known that children are the most vulnerable members of our society. They are young, so they can't work to support themselves. They are naïve, so they need guidance. They are small in stature, so they need protection. In my job as a teacher at a public school, children surround me on a daily basis. What I have seen over the last fifteen years has been nothing short of amazing. I grew up in the typical American nuclear family of the 1970s and 1980s. I lived with both of my parents and my siblings in a middle-class neighborhood. There was always food on the table, clothes on our backs, and stability in the home. This is not the life of the average child growing up in America. I would say that, out of the 10,000 or more students I have taught, less than half grew up in a house with both birth parents.

I have taught children who lived with only their mother, only their father, different forms of stepparents, their grandparents, their aunts, their uncles, their brothers, their sisters, their cousins, and more than a few who lived with foster families.

Additionally, I have taught children who were physically, emotionally, or sexually abused by family members; children whose parents were active gang members; children whose parents were convicted murderers; children whose parents were addicted to alcohol, crack, or crystal meth; and children who had one parent living under a restraining order from the other parent.

As far as my students are concerned, I have taught children who had babies before they were fifteen years old, children who became pregnant by adults, children who joined street gangs before they became teenagers, children who were thieves, children eventually convicted of murder, and children capable of violence and behavior that is completely shocking. All of these occurrences were at two different schools that, while they are diverse, were still surrounded by middle-class neighborhoods. Even with my experiences, it is hard for me to imagine what teachers see on a daily basis who work in large urban centers such as New York, Chicago, or Los Angeles or rural impoverished communities.

There is no doubt about it—as a society, we do not take care of our children. After seeing all of the unfortunate things children have to go through on a daily basis, it is a little difficult for me to get worked up about a fetus. There are far too many living children with problems that, in a democracy, are quite frankly a national disgrace. Not everyone gets to be the children of George W. and Laura Bush.

If I Was King

My students are pretty familiar with my attitudes regarding having children and different methods of birth control. Every year, I teach the novel *Animal Farm* to my ninth grade students. And every year, as Napoleon takes over the farm and becomes a dictator, I tell my students what I would do if I were the dictator of the United States.

Let's call this a teaching point. I tell all of my students that, if I were the dictator, I would have my best and brightest scientists work to develop a birth control pill that would last for thirteen years. All members of the society would have to take the pill when they were twelve years old. It would last until they were twenty-five. Here's the reason behind this: no teenagers or uneducated, unemployed people would be having kids. In my mind, this would go a long way in the effort to wipe out poverty.

It is funny, because the children with educated parents, or a background that is not somehow impoverished, chime in with comments like, "Sounds good to me. I don't want to have kids until I am finished with college" or "I'm not having kids." Other students, who have grown up in poverty or a seriously dysfunctional family, say things like, "I wanna have kids before I'm twenty" or "That's weak" or "Why would you want to do that?"

The reason why I want to do this is a little heartless and not very fair, but there are too many of the wrong people having children. If a teenage girl who is poor has a baby, she and the baby are going to be poor forever. At some point, the cycle of poverty needs to be broken. Having kids without education or the skills for a decent paying job destroys the future of the parent and the child. The cycle of poverty continues to turn and is difficult to break.

Unwanted children far too often live a life of desperation, unhappiness, and violence. It is justifiable that, if we are not going to take care of these children, they should not be born. Believe it or not, Jesus does, at least in part, support me on this one.

Living in Infamy

Judas was an unfortunate soul that has become one of the most notorious figures in human history because of his betrayal of Christ. He has even suffered the indignity of having an awful heavy metal band named after him (Judas Priest). Pitiful.

His historical shame has been unbearable, and Jesus knew this when He said in regards to Judas's life and times on Earth, "The Son of man goes as it is written of him, but woe to that man by whom the Son of man is betrayed! It would have been better for that man if he had not been born." (Matthew 26:24) There it is: Jesus says that a human being, destined to be miserable, should never have been born.

I agree with Jesus. The unwanted child that is going to grow up unloved by a parent is destined to live a horrible life because society will refuse to take care of him or her when everything goes awry. Far too many of these children become the murderers, thieves, and criminals that conservatives want to put away for life under laws like "three strikes, you're out." Others become the serial killers and psychopaths that, in conservative Red States, ultimately arrive on death row, or in some cases the evangelical pulpit. Conservatives lust for punishment and declare the ungodly state of our country, yet they want more and more children to be born under difficult circumstances, and they refuse to take care of them. Red Staters cut social programs that benefit children, try to put child criminals in jail where they learn to be worse criminals, yet somehow they try and convince us that the life of a child is sacred. It is absurd. The people destined to be the miserable scourges of our society should never be born.

Now, if we were more committed to helping these children live a meaningful, nonviolent life, all of that changes. But, at this point, nothing is going to change. So why bother? Some children should never be born because our society does not show a compelling interest to take care of them. I am for population control. I am also *for* abortion. That's right. I actually think abortion is a great thing, not because I enjoy killing fetuses, but because—if we aren't going to take care of children who are not wanted and who will not be taken care of by their parents or by our society—to paraphrase Jesus, it is best that they were never born. I have on numerous occasions told my students, friends, and family that we should build a monument, not a statue, but a monument to honor the first person who performed a safe and legal abortion. A culture that doesn't take care of its disadvantaged kids shouldn't be having disadvantaged kids.

The Miracles of Jesus: Acts of Compassion or Arrogant Displays of Power

Obviously, since Jesus was a kind, compassionate, liberal soul, He would want us to take care of our children. There is one incident that is outlined in three of the Gospels in which some parents were excited about the prospect of meeting Jesus and having Him bless their children. As the story goes, they had a hard time getting to Jesus. Interestingly enough, the people that were causing this problem were His disciples. "Then children were brought to him that he might lay his hands on them and pray. The disciples rebuked the people; but Jesus said, 'Let the children come to me, and do not hinder them; for to such belongs the kingdom of heaven.'" (Matthew 19:13–14) So Jesus likes kids. Who doesn't?

The same story is repeated in Mark. "And they were bringing children to him, that he might touch them; and the disciples rebuked them. But when Jesus saw it he was indignant, and said to them, 'Let the children come to me, do not hinder them; for to such belongs the kingdom of God. Truly, I say to you, whoever does not receive the kingdom of God like a child shall not enter it.' And he took them in his arms and blessed them, laying his hands upon them." (Mark 10:13–16)

This isn't a whole lot of information in regards to developing a solid conclusion about taking care of children first and adults second. But there are some other instances in which Jesus not only wants to bless children, but also pleads with His followers to take care of any person who is in need and vulnerable.

Since children are in need more than adults, children should be taken care of first. To that end, Jesus tells a mother to feed her children first and her dog second. That's right. This lady needed to be told that her daughter came before her dog.

> But immediately a woman, whose little daughter was possessed by an unclean spirit, heard of him, and came and fell down at his feet. Now

the woman was a Greek, a Syrophoeni'cian by birth. And she begged
him to cast the demon out of her daughter. And he said to her, 'Let
the children first be fed, for it is not right to take the children's bread
and throw it to the dogs.' But she answered him, 'Yes, Lord; yet even
the dogs under the table eat the children's crumbs.' And he said to
her, 'For this saying you may go your way; the demon has left your
daughter.' And she went home, and found the child lying in bed, and
the demon gone. (Mark 7:25–31)

It is too bad that this particular reference deals with feeding children before
dogs. It seems way too obvious, but maybe in biblical times they needed the
dogs for work or protection or something. At any rate, when she agreed to feed
the children first, her daughter was healed. See? Jesus loves the little children.
In these Gospel references to children, it is obvious that Jesus insisted on blessing children and delivered a miracle to a mother who promised to make her
child a priority. Jesus is sending a message that children are important, if not
the most important members of a society. This is a good message, a message
that is much different from the child-killing God of the Old Testament.

In terms of specific references to children having a priority in a society,
there are only these three references, and, to a certain degree, that is enough.
Jesus has a long-standing interest and well-documented message that defends
the rights of the poor and disinherited. He teaches that taking care of those
who are less fortunate is a means to personal salvation. This is a message that is
completely ignored by conservative evangelicals.

The Gospels are filled with acts of compassion and miracles performed by
Jesus. Conservative doctrine wants to suggest that Jesus's miracles are performed as some kind of display of His super powers. This makes Jesus some
kind of a magician or superhero who wants to display His powers for attention
and "oohs" and "aahs," not as manifestations of a divine presence on Earth.
Liberal doctrine is more concerned with promoting Jesus and His miracles as
acts of compassion. Conservative doctrine emphasizes miracles as an arrogant
display of power. The conservatives are wrong again.

This is evident in the different stories in which Jesus is able to feed thousands of people with only some loaves of bread and a few fish. When I was a
child, a misguided Sunday school teacher relayed this to me as some kind of
magic act. A closer reading shows the feeding of the masses was a somber act of
compassion. Jesus was feeding people because they were hungry, not because
he wanted attention and glory. This is much different than the Old Testament
God, who convinced a man to murder his son as a display of devotion. Before
Jesus distributed his gift to 5,000 hungry people, he found out that John the

Baptist had been beheaded. This is the famous scene in which John's head was served on a platter, courtesy of King Herod. Jesus then goes away to pray, and His disciples are sending people away to get their own food before Jesus steps in and stops them.

> Jesus said, 'They need not go away; you give them something to eat.' They said to him, 'we have only five loaves here and two fish. And he said, 'Bring them here to me.' Then he ordered the crowds to sit down on the grass; and taking the five loaves and the two fish he looked up to heaven, and blessed, and broke and gave the loaves to the disciples, and the disciples gave them to the crowds. (Matthew 14:17–19)

This miracle was an act of compassion and kindness from a man who was mourning the death of a friend.

The Gospels are more direct in noting the compassion of Jesus the other time He gives food to thousands of hungry people. In this instance, Jesus is healing the sick, out of His compassion for their pain, before He feeds the masses.

> And great crowds came to him, bringing with them the lame, the maimed, the blind, the dumb, and many others, and they put them at his feet, and he healed them, so that the throng wondered, when they saw the dumb speaking, the maimed whole, the lame walking, and the blind seeing; and they glorified the God of Israel. Then Jesus called his disciples to him and said, 'I have compassion on the crowd, because they have been with me now three days, and have nothing to eat; and I am unwilling to send them away hungry, lest they faint on the way.' (Matthew 15:30–32)

It is important to note that Jesus is not giving a group of greedy people money and riches, the oft-heard conservative prayer request. He is healing people with serious and painful afflictions and feeding people who sacrificed their comfort to show Jesus their affection.

As the Gospels continue, Jesus's message of taking care of those in need becomes much more aggressive, much more radical, and much more liberal.

Jesus: the Radical Liberal

In a scene that must offend conservatives and even the proponents of capitalism to a grand degree, Jesus doesn't just tell His followers to give to the poor and the needy but instructs His followers to give to those people who ask for anything. That's right. If people ask, they receive. More than that, His followers are supposed to give these people more than they ask for, "and if any one would sue you and take your coat, let him have your cloak as well; and if any one forces you to go one mile, go with him two miles. Give to him who begs from you, and do not refuse him who would borrow from you." (Matthew 5:40–42) This has to be some of the most liberal economic ideology in the history of mankind. This is an economic message even more radical than communism.

Conservatives conveniently ignore all of this. This is confirmed by looking at the modern-day conservative politician's attitude towards welfare recipients. In light of the comments made by Jesus, the insinuations of the 1990s—about welfare recipients in poor communities being lazy, welfare mothers milking the system to avoid work, people taking advantage of food stamps—seem downright unchristian in nature. According to Jesus, if people need something and they are in a position to give, Christians are supposed to give. They are not supposed to make wild, prejudicial accusations.

Christians don't seek to humiliate them. Christians just give, and they are supposed to give until their neighbors are satisfied. While this might blister the Red State conservatives with rage, these acts of kindness and compassion are supposed to satisfy our souls. This is wildly liberal doctrine. These kinds of statements from Jesus, ignored in the evangelical movement, prove that Martin Luther King Jr. was right. Jesus was not just a liberal. He was a radical liberal.

Jesus also adds an element of salvation to our generosity to the poor and unhappy. Evangelicals like to talk about their personal salvation and how they are "saved," but seldom do we hear about these people being charitable to those who are different from them. It is more likely the case that they tend to be more judgmental of others than compassionate.

Children are the most vulnerable members of our society. Jesus is forceful in His notion that, in order to receive salvation, the Christian must exhibit compassionate and extraordinary selfless behavior to those who are less fortunate. "But when you give a feast, invite the poor, the maimed, the lame, the blind, and you will be blessed, because they cannot repay you. You will be repaid at the resurrection of the just." (Luke 14:13–14) This doctrine, different from the conservative evangelical who emphasizes words over action, is undervalued in the modern-day church, both by liberals and conservatives. There were times in the Gospels when Jesus was put to the test regarding not only Jewish religious doctrine, but on the appropriate steps to living the religious life. It is apparent that Jesus was not concerned with individual sin, but with the compassionate life of His followers, and this was a critical element of His doctrine. It is here that Jesus gives a profound lesson on the greatest commandment.

> And one of the scribes came up and heard them disputing with one another, and seeing that he answered them well, asked him, "Which commandment is the first of all?" Jesus answered, "The first is, 'Hear, O Israel: The Lord our God, the Lord is one; and you shall love the Lord your God with all your heart, and with all your soul, and with all your mind, and with all your strength.' The second is this, 'You shall love your neighbor as yourself.' There is no other commandment greater than these." (Mark 12:28–31)

Jesus does not make the qualification here as to who is a person's neighbor. It should be obvious, from this and other comments from Him, that all people are our neighbors, regardless of race, economic status, or creed. Additionally, if we are to be considered followers of Christ, we are to pay special attention to those who are less fortunate: more liberal doctrine from a radical liberal.

In another one of His more profound and compassionate lessons, Jesus personalizes all of this. He identifies himself with the struggles of the poor, the pains of the hungry, the victims of loneliness, the despair of the prisoner, and the desperation of the homeless and all others who are victims of life's inevitable pratfalls and disappointments. Jesus commands His followers that not to help these people is an affront to Him as God living on Earth and that He feels their pain.

> For I was hungry and you gave me food, I was thirsty and you gave me drink, I was a stranger and you welcomed me, I was naked and you clothed me, I was sick and you visited me, I was in prison and you came to me. Then the righteous will answer him, 'Lord, when did we see thee hungry and feed thee, or thirsty and give thee drink? And when did we see thee a stranger and welcome thee, or naked and clothe thee? And when did we see thee sick or in prison and visit thee?' And the King will answer them, 'Truly, I say to you, as you did it to one of the least of these my brethren, you did it to me.' Then he will say to those at his left hand, 'Depart from me, you cursed, into the eternal fire prepared for the devil and his angels; for I was hungry and you gave me no food, I was thirsty and you gave me no drink, I was a stranger and you did not welcome me, naked and you did not clothe me, sick and in prison and you did not visit me.' Then they also will answer, 'Lord, when did we see thee hungry or thirsty or a

stranger or naked or sick or in prison, and did not minister to thee?'
Then he will answer them, 'Truly, I say to you, as you did it not to one
of the least of these, you did it not to me. (Matthew 25:35–45)

This is probably one of the most poignant and liberal of any of Jesus's messages, that is, if you have a heart!

People are supposed to take care of one another. If people are down,
Christians pick them up and help them get back on their feet. This is a far cry
from the blame game that conservatives play in the United States, where some
heartless assholes tend to believe that poor people are poor because they are
lazy and unloved by God.

The Sanctity of Vegetables and Stem Cells

There was nothing more disturbing than the nation's preoccupation with
the Terri Schiavo case. It is not my intention to review the specifics of this
problem but to point out the national furor and Red State lunacy this circum-
stance caused. As we all know by now, Terri Schiavo was declared by court-
appointed neutral doctors to be in a persistent vegetative state beginning in
1990. Essentially, Ms. Schiavo was a "vegetable" for almost fifteen years. Her
husband wanted to "pull the plug" by disconnecting a feeding tube that was
keeping her alive. On the other hand, her hyper-religious parents wanted her
to "live" in the hopes that some day, after fifteen years as a vegetable, she would
recover. Crazy but true.

The entire argument about whether or not to pull the plug on this woman
was not only troubling but divided the nation in a variety of ways.

People across the United States were not so much concerned about whether
or not Terri Schiavo should be allowed to die. The primary issue that concerned most Americans was whether or not an invasive government should be
involved in a private, family matter. As we all know, Red State evangelicals are
obsessed with the private lives of others and this case was no different.
However according to many, they found themselves on the wrong side of this
"moral" issue.

According to an ABC news poll, Americans supported the removal of Terri
Schiavo's feeding tube by a 63% to 23 % margin. Likewise, 70 percent of
Americans believed that it was "inappropriate for Congress to get involved" in
the effort to keep or remove the feeding tube. Furthermore, by a margin of
67% to 19% people polled thought politicians were becoming involved in this
case for "political advantage."6

The thing that I don't understand is why these "Christians" were so
adamant about defending Terri Schiavo's right to be stuck on a feeding tube

indefinitely. Forgive me if I am wrong, but the whole evangelical reason for being a Christian is to get to Heaven and spend eternity with Jesus. This group has created an entire religion that revolves around the selfish pursuit of the forgiveness of their sins and the gift of eternal life. These religious handouts are a freebie based on their "faith." The end result for this lazy faithfulness is being able to spend an eternity in a perfect place upon death. What did Terri Schiavo do to have this date delayed by fifteen years! Talk about punishment. It is nothing short of unbelievable that Schiavo's religious parents would not let her go and be with her God in her Heaven.

I know I wouldn't want to spend my remaining years in a hospital bed with no brain function, having others wiping my drool and changing my diapers, and a life full of bed sores and being treated like a circus freak. Consider this my living will, and a message to my wife and family. Let me die! I also know what my older non-evangelical sister would want. She told me that she would haunt me from the grave if I kept her alive under such miserable circumstances.

It appears that we are not alone in the viewpoint. According to the same ABC news poll mentioned earlier, "Half of Americans say that as a direct result of hearing about this case, they've spoken with friends or family members about what they'd want done if they were in a similar condition. Nearly eight in 10 would not want to be kept alive." However, Terri Schiavo's parents, Bill Frist, Tom Delay, Jeb and George W. Bush, and even the loudmouthed Jesse Jackson were convinced that they knew better and their arguments were all somehow based on their religious views. These people wanted to keep this poor woman away from spending an eternity in Heaven with her God for a further indefinite amount of time. Unbelievable! All of this was done in the name of promoting a "culture of life."

In spite of the vast support of all sane Americans on this issue, our liberal leaders dropped the ball because they are so afraid of the Religious Right. The response of the liberal politicians on Capitol Hill was embarrassing. It was silence. All told, 47 Democrats voted in favor of congressional intervention in Terri Schiavo's life and death, 53 voted against intervention, and 102 didn't even show up to vote. This Red State hot potato was too controversial for the Democrats. The complete results in the House of Representatives was that 253 voted for congressional intervention and 58 voted against. This is disturbing in light of a poll that suggested that 70 percent of Americans thought it was "inappropriate" for Congress to get involved. Liberal politicians had the whole goddamn country on their side and they botched it and left it to the judicial system to let this woman die with dignity.

The insanity of George Bush and the Religious right defending the non-living at the expense of the living does not stop with Terri Schiavo. As everyone knows, Dubya is also against the funding of stem cell research. Their gripe is of course that scientists using stem cells to research the causes and ultimate cure for an array of diseases and infirmities does not respect human life. Now, I am no scientist, but I wasn't aware that a stem cell packed away in a freezer sitting harmlessly in a Petri dish is now considered human life. But it is and the kooky evangelicals need to protect these cells.

Hell, even Nancy Reagan, the wife of conservative hero Ronald Reagan is calling for Bush to back off on his federal ban on stem cell research. She says, "I don't see how we can turn our backs on this. We have lost so much time. I just can't bear to lose any more."7 She isn't the only conservative to question Dubya's allegiance to the extreme religious right. Orrin Hatch, ultra-conservative U.S. Senator from Utah and Mormon bishop says, "I do not believe that life begins in a Petri dish and, like many others, hope that these excess embryos can benefit mankind."8

However, Bush refuses to listen. He recently declared that there was no way he would ever change his mind as he vowed another veto on a recent bill allowing some research of some additional stem cells. "I made my position very clear on embryonic stem cells...I made it very clear to the Congress that the use of federal money, taxpayers' money, to promote science which destroys life in order to save life is—I'm against that."9

According to the Religious Right, clinging to life no matter how miserable it is and denying a better life for millions by refusing to research cells that will never become human beings is "fostering a culture of life".

It seems the Red State religious nuts have it all wrong. Terri Schiavo should have been allowed to pass into Heaven years ago. Likewise, I am with millions of Americans who believe that a cell that will never become a human life should be researched to benefit the sick.

As it turns out, these two scenarios are not the only things that Red State conservatives have all wrong. The poor Red States, which are all about fostering a culture of life, have a hard time taking care of the living, which leads us to our next few editions of *Red State, Blue State*.

Red State, Blue State: Growing Up in America

So how does all of this fit into the modern-day conflict between conservative and liberal political policy and the battle between the conservatives in the Red States, who say they are God's people and love the unborn fetus, and those of the Blue States, who are godless, child-killing pagans?

To answer this, we must play a little more *Red State, Blue State*, and see which states treat life as if it is sacred. We are not going to be hypocrites and measure our recognition of the value of life by how many people go to abortion rallies. We have shown that Old and New Testament attitudes and judgments regarding abortion are vague at best. With that in mind, it is important that we investigate how we treat our living children under certain "quality of life" issues.

This edition of *Red State, Blue State* will compare the states by looking at different trends that concern the raising and productivity of all of God's little children. In so doing, we will be able to find out which of these groups does a better job of taking care of its children or, as George W. Bush says, "foster and encourage a respect for life in America."

The first game of *Red State, Blue State* deals with simple abortion rates. In this category, the demonic Blue States do not perform very well. I think it is great, since I am for abortion, but some liberals might not be too proud of this. There was no data for Alaska, California, New Hampshire, and Wyoming.

Highest rates of abortion occurrence by state

Rank	State	Abortion Rate	Red or Blue
47	Washington, D.C.	37	Blue
46	New York	30	Blue
45	Delaware	28	Blue
44	Florida	26	Red
43	Nevada	23	Red
	Rhode Island	23	Blue
41	Kansas	21	Red
40	Washington	20	Blue
	Oregon	20	Blue
39	New Jersey	19	Blue
	Connecticut	19	Blue

Source: National Vital Statistics 2002 data, National Center for Health Statistics, Centers for Disease Control and Prevention

There you have it. Eight out of the bottom eleven states with the highest rates of abortion are heathen Blue States. This is a bummer for all of those crazy Catholics who hate John Kerry. They should probably follow their convictions and move to Idaho or Kentucky, like that will ever happen; they enjoy their freedom way too much.

Lowest rates of abortion occurrence by state

Rank	State	Abortion Rate	Red or Blue
1	Idaho	3	Red
2	Kentucky	4	Red
3	Colorado	5	Red
4	Mississippi	6	Red
5	Missouri	6	Red
	South Dakota	6	Red
	West Virginia	6	Red
8	Utah	7	Red
9	South Carolina	8	Red

Source: National Vital Statistics 2002 data, National Center for Health Statistics, Centers for Disease Control and Prevention

Well, my fellow Blue State heathens, it looks like they got us in that one. We need to somehow regroup. I know, let's forget about the first trimester fetus and look at some quality of life issues. Maybe this will show how well we liberals in the Blue States take care of our living children.

Conservatives pontificate about how concerned they are about the fetus. But are they concerned about the healthy fetus? One of the ways we determine whether or not a pregnant woman is healthy and has a healthy pregnancy is through infant mortality rates. It is not too surprising that Red States have the highest infant mortality rates in the United States, while Blue States have the lowest.

Highest rates of infant mortality by state

Rank	State	Deaths per live birth	Red or Blue
50	Mississippi	10.2	Red
49	Louisiana	9.7	Red
48	Tennessee	9.2	Red
47	South Carolina	8.8	Red
46	Arkansas	8.8	Red
45	Delaware	8.7	Blue
44	Georgia	8.6	Red
43	Alabama	8.6	Red
42	Michigan	8.4	Blue
41	Maryland	8.4	Blue

Source: National Center for Health Statistics 2002–2003 data, Centers for Disease Control and Prevention

Before any conservative gets too happy about the presence of three Blue States on this list, the next eight states having the highest rates of infant mortality are all Red (West Virginia, North Carolina, Missouri, Ohio, Wyoming, Oklahoma, Indiana, Florida, and Virginia). Out of the eighteen states that have the highest rates of dead babies, fifteen voted with their morality on their sleeves when they voted Red in the 2004 election.

Unquestionably, it is the Red States, especially those in "the Bible Belt," which have the highest rates of infant mortality. To the contrary, Blue States dominate the list of states with the lowest infant mortality rates.

Lowest rates of infant mortality by state

Rank	State	Deaths per live birth	Red or Blue
1	Vermont	4.3	Blue
2	New Hampshire	4.4	Blue
3	Maine	4.6	Blue
4	Massachusetts	4.9	Blue
5	California	5.0	Blue
6	Minnesota	5.0	Blue
7	Utah	5.3	Red
8	Washington	5.4	Blue
9	Iowa	5.4	Red
10	Connecticut	5.6	Blue

Source: National Center for Health Statistics 2002–2003 data, Centers for Disease Control and Prevention

Eight out of the ten states with the lowest infant mortality rates in the country are Blue States. It could have been nine out of ten, but for some reason Iowa decided to vote Red, linking them forever with Red State immorality. Shame on them.

Teenage pregnancy can be a bit of a problem. If responsible women had their druthers, they would prefer to have a child when they have a job, a stable relationship, an education, and plans for a successful future. These positive circumstances typically do not befall a girl who becomes pregnant at a young age. And as we shall see, this unfortunate event that leads to a life of poverty for both the mother and the child happens far more often in Red States than in Blue States.

Highest rates of teenage pregnancy (age 15-19) by state

Rank	State	Rate	Red or Blue
1	Mississippi	64.7	Red
2	Texas	64.4	Red
3	New Mexico	62.4	Red
4	Arizona	61.2	Red
5	Arkansas	59.9	Red
6	Louisiana	58.1	Red
7	Oklahoma	58	Red
8	Georgia	57.7	Red
9	Alabama	54.5	Red
10	Tennessee	54.3	Red

Source: "National Vital Statistics Report" *Center for Disease Control,* 2002

The next five states are Nevada, South Carolina, North Carolina, Kentucky, Colorado, Delaware, West Virginia, Indiana, Florida, Missouri, and Kansas. They are all Red. Out of the twenty one states with the highest rates of teen mothers, twenty voted Red in the 2004 election. Delaware was the only Blue State in the top twenty of teenage pregnancy.

Once again, the occurrence of so many Red States at the top of this list will tell us what the bottom ten of teenage pregnancy rates will look like.

Lowest rates of teenage pregnancy (age 15-19) by state

Rank	State	Rate	Red or Blue
50	New Hampshire	20	Blue
49	Massachusetts	23.5	Blue
48	Vermont	24.2	Blue
47	Maine	25.4	Blue
46	Connecticut	25.8	Blue
45	New Jersey	26.8	Blue
44	North Dakota	27.2	Red
43	Minnesota	27.5	Blue
42	New York	29.5	Blue
41	Pennsylvania	31.6	Blue

Source: "National Vital Statistics Report" *Center for Disease Control,* 2002.

Beyond this ten, the next six states (Wisconsin, Iowa, Washington, Michigan, Maryland, and Rhode Island) are Blue as well. Unbelievably, fifteen of the sixteen states with the lowest rates of teenage pregnancies are liberal leaning Blue States.

Teenage pregnancy does have a result and that is poverty and in many cases a lack of education that begins an eternal cycle of poverty. Unlike the residents of Red States who are consumed with their divine right to protect the fetus, we heathens in the Blue States actually take care of our pregnant women and their unborn.

Sometimes, after children are born, they grow up in families that struggle with economic difficulties. Poverty creates a variety of issues that hinder growth and hope for a better life. An inevitable lack of nutrition, high rates of illiteracy, poor education, and living in unsafe neighborhoods plague children who grow up poor. This is another area where we can judge how well different communities value human life.

There is an imbalance between the Blue States and the Red States when we look at percentages of children growing up plagued by poverty. The results are only surprising if you are under the assumption that Red States make children a priority.

Highest percentage of children growing up in poverty by state

Rank	State	Percentage of children	Red or Blue
50	New Mexico	26.9	Red
49	Arkansas	26.8	Red
48	West Virginia	26.7	Red
47	Louisiana	25.5	Red
46	Texas	24.0	Red
45	North Carolina	23.1	Red
44	Mississippi	23.1	Red
43	Alabama	22.3	Red
42	Montana	20.2	Red
41	Oregon	20.1	Blue

Source: Current Population Survey, March 2004, United States Bureau of the Census

Once again, we see that Red States dominate a list that should cause them moral shame. It is hard to believe that four states in the freest country in world history have more than a quarter of their children growing up in poverty. All of these are "moral" Red States. With Bush in office another four years, we should expect that number to grow.

Lowest percentage of children growing up in poverty by state

Rank	State	Percentage of children	Red or Blue
1	New Hampshire	7.2	Blue
2	Minnesota	9.7	Blue
3	Connecticut	10.1	Blue
4	Maryland	10.6	Blue
5	Vermont	10.9	Blue
6	Delaware	11.0	Blue
7	Nebraska	11.0	Red
8	Alaska	11.2	Red
9	New Jersey	11.2	Blue
10	Colorado	11.2	Red

Source: Current Population Survey, March 2004, United States Bureau of the Census

Blue States once again abound, seven states of the top ten states being among the states with the lowest rates of child poverty.

It is also important to the development of children and families that they have access to some kind of health insurance. Once again, the performance of the moral Red States is beyond dismal.

Highest percentage of residents without health insurance by state

Rank	State	Percentage without Insurance	Red or Blue
50	Texas	24.6	Red
49	New Mexico	22.1	Red
48	Louisiana	20.6	Red
47	Oklahoma	20.4	Red
46	Montana	19.4	Red
44	Nevada	18.9	Red
44	Alaska	18.9	Red
43	Idaho	18.6	Red

42	California	18.4	Blue
41	Florida	18.2	Red

Source: Current Population Survey, March 2004, United States Bureau of the Census

It is interesting to note that the home state of George W. Bush leads the nation, with almost a quarter of its population without health insurance. Hopefully, this won't influence national policy. Additionally, Mississippi, Arkansas, North Carolina, Oregon, Colorado, Arizona, West Virginia, Georgia, and Wyoming appear in the next nine. Out of the bottom nineteen states with the highest percentages of residents who do not have health insurance, eighteen voted Red in the 2004 election. Now that is a lesson in how to not take care of children.

This is becoming boring. The "immoral" Blue States once again did well, giving us the top nine and ten out of the top eleven.

Lowest percentage of residents without health insurance by state

Rank	State	Percentage without Insurance	Red or Blue
1	Minnesota	8.7	Blue
2	Vermont	9.5	Blue
3	Hawaii	10.1	Blue
4	Rhode Island	10.2	Blue
5	New Hampshire	10.3	Blue
6	Connecticut	10.4	Blue
7	Maine	10.4	Blue
8	Massachusetts	10.7	Blue
9	Michigan	10.9	Blue
	North Dakota	10.9	Red
	Wisconsin	10.9	Blue

Source: Current Population Survey, March 2004, United States Bureau of the Census

It's too bad that North Dakota and Wisconsin had to tie. It was almost ten out of ten in the Blue State column. This still undoubtedly proves the point that Red States don't make the health of their children a very high priority.

More Lies Told by Even More Idiots

It could very well be that, in the eyes of the Lord, abortion is in fact murder. The Bible does not say so, but, by most accounts, abortion is a horrible form of birth control. But how do residents in the Red States who are all about "Jesus" justify not taking care of their children? Abortion is not the only issue that deals with the dignity and quality of a child's life. Likewise, religious conservatives latch on to some very bizarre issues (Schiavo and stem cells among others) in their Red State efforts to convince us that they care about human life. All the while, their beloved Red States are the worse places for children to grow up. With high rates of infant mortality, high rates of uninsured children, and high rates of children living in poverty, it sure doesn't seem like they value the living. It appears they only value the non-living, the barely living, or in some cases the already dead.

Red State Christians love to pontificate about how much they love God, but they do not take adequate care of those people who are in need: a direct violation of an order of Jesus and a prerequisite for salvation. This lack of action and honesty not only leads to a myriad of social problems, but it makes their Christian stand on abortion and other issues regarding protecting children meaningless, short-sighted, and, once again, hypocritical.

The continued blabbering of the religious Right and the conservative residents of the Red States from both the Heartland and the South regarding the inherent value of human life is nothing more than a big pack of lies told by a bigger pack of hypocritical idiots.

7

The Defense of Marriage

Dixiecrats

Red State conservatives have been force-feeding us their wacky sense of morality for years. The notion that we have only recently been taken over by a theocratic form of government is silly. Blasphemous religious zealots have been influencing our government for quite some time.

Even if Bill Clinton was in office for eight years, the nation was still compelled to weather a conservative moral crusade brought on by Newt Gingrich and others in the 1990s. These clowns started us down the road of capitulating to conservative religious leaders who are magically able to convince hordes of people to vote against their own economic self-interest in the name of something almost indescribable called "morality."

There is little doubt that conservative doctrine takes hold more in the South than in other areas of the country. This is no accident. Not since John Kennedy in the sixties have we had a liberal, Democratic president who did not hail from the South. Jimmy Carter was from Georgia, Bill Clinton was from Arkansas, and even Al Gore, who won the popular vote in the 2000 presidential election, was from Tennessee. If Gore had won a single Southern state, he would have won the electoral vote as well and become president.

To a certain degree, because of where John Kerry is from, he never had a chance. The South will never vote for a Northern Democrat. This is why he chose John Edwards as his running mate. He was hoping that having a Southern Democrat on the ballot would have delivered him the one Southern state he was going to need to win the election. Big mistake. If he would have chosen someone from a swing state like OHIO, he may have had a better chance of winning OHIO. But that is another story.

Gettin' Hitched

One of the issues that was said to be a divisive one in the 2004 election was the controversy surrounding same-sex marriage. George W. Bush went on record saying that he wanted to amend our beloved U.S. Constitution because he did not think that two men or two women marrying each other was good for the sacred union of marriage. A religious crusade began. Thanks of course to George W. Bush and Karl Rove, this issue became the centerpiece of the ethical component of the 2004 election, simply because it was a new issue. Not very many heterosexuals cared about same–sex marriage until recently.

It is hard to figure out why there are so many people concerned about what happens in other people's bedrooms and personal lives. This is another trait of the Red State conservatives that Blue State liberals struggle to understand. If two guys or two gals want to get married, it only affects those two people and maybe a few other immediate family members. The national furor is a mystery to me. Alas, I am in the minority. It appears that the majority of the United States wants some kind of law preventing two law-abiding, homosexual American citizens from get married. Some people are in favor of "civil unions" as a way for gay couples to surrender their freedom.

Marriage is some kind of a religious rite of passage for two people in love, while the "civil union" is a legal contract. When I got married, we needed two documents: one was a marriage license from the State of Washington, and the other was a Certificate of Marriage given to me by a Lutheran pastor that I didn't know. The certificate from the pastor seemed meaningless to me. The certificate from the state was a legally binding document putting me in eternal bondage to my wife and vice versa. The legal contract from the state meant more than the document supporting the religious ritual. But then again I am a heathen.

The Defense of Marriage Begins

Believe it or not, this ridiculous battle to defend marriage started back in 1996 when Bill Clinton was president. As it turns out, ten members of the House of Representatives decided to propose a law called the Defense of Marriage Act (DOMA). The senators who proposed this legislation were Bob Barr from Georgia (Red State), Steve Largent from Oklahoma (Red State), Jim Sensenbrenner from Wisconsin (Blue State), Sue Myrick from North Carolina (Red State), Ed Bryant from Tennessee (Red State), and a trio from Missouri (Red State), Bill Emerson, Harold Volkmer, and Ike Shelton. I will get to the hypocrisy of the Red States attempting to defend marriage a little later, but, out of the ten representatives authoring this legislation, nine hailed from conservative states and one from a liberal-leaning state. Mr. Sensenbrenner from Wisconsin is a Republican. Go figure.

The Defense of Marriage Act did two things. First, it declared that individual states do not have to recognize same-sex marriages that were performed in other states. This protects the Red States from the immorality of the Blue States. Second, it gave a legal definition to the terms "spouse" and "marriage." These legal definitions had the direct intent of making marriage only legal between a man and a woman.

The House of Representatives overwhelmingly supported this idea. The Senate followed, with another overwhelming vote of 84 in favor and only 15 against. The Defense of Marriage Act became law when noted philanderer Bill Clinton put pen to paper. Bill Clinton signing an act defending marriage is more than a little bit ironic. A married man gets an adulterous blow job from a young intern, leaves a semen stain on her frumpish blue dress, and has the audacity to sign a law that defends the sanctity of marriage. Call me crazy, but this is the height of hypocrisy. So what if he signed the legislation before he was caught with his pants down or, as this case may have been, before he was caught with his pants unzipped. The accusations of "cigar play" made Clinton's betrayal of his "sacred" marriage even more disturbing.

But who cares? He was a good president. He just wasn't loyal to his wife. That is her problem.

At any rate, at least one philanderer signed the Defense of Marriage Act. I'm pretty sure Mr. Clinton wasn't the only one. Considering the behavior of some of our elected officials, it is hard to understand why we have to take a right away from other people to defend an institution that not very many people in government or in the United States respect.

In Support of Homosexuals

The United States Census Bureau estimates that around 50% of all marriages will ultimately end in divorce. Marriage was struggling before homosexuals wanted the right to perform and live under this "sacred institution." There is still no rational explanation as to why so many people think marriage is under an assault by homosexuals.

There is a good case to be made that the divorce rate might go down if homosexuals were allowed to get married. There are no statistics to support this assumption, only my personal experience as a heterosexual married man who, in my own way, has observed some pretty positive homosexual behavior. This behavior did not take place in the bedroom, but in the workplace. I am not obsessed with the bedroom behavior of other people; this is different than some people we know.

My wife works in retail in the downtown-shopping core of Seattle, Washington. In retail jobs, gay guys are everywhere, and, to borrow a phrase from Homer Simpson, gay people work like "Japanese beavers;" that is, they work all the time. You ever heard of a poor gay person? The ones who have come out of the closet certainly aren't poor. They move to populated urban centers, get jobs, and are able to support their own unique sense of fashion that I could never afford. Gay men work to afford fancy clothes, perfume, and life in a big city! Furthermore, how is a metrosexual going to buy cologne if there isn't a gay guy around to sell it to him?

How's that for reinforcing stereotypes?

That is why I repeatedly tell my wife, "I love gay people." They contribute to the economy. They pull their own weight. They pay their taxes. They work. Let them get married. Who gives a shit? Most homosexuals work and have money, so they may even stay married! So they enjoy receiving anal sex, who doesn't?

A Blue State Takes a Stand

Same-sex marriage became an election issue in part because the idiotic Defense of Marriage Act of 1996 set off a chain reaction in which honest taxpayers had to fight for their rights. Unfortunately, they were being stopped at every turn by people with nothing better to do than work to deny people what should be and is a legal right for all law-abiding adult Americans: the right to sacrifice their freedom and get married. People have the right to live in self-inflicted bondage.

In 2001, a group of gay Americans living in Massachusetts decided they wanted to get married, so they applied for marriage certificates. They were denied. Ultimately, they took the Department of Health of the State of Massachusetts—the ones in charge of issuing marriage licenses to court. The plaintiffs in the Massachusetts lawsuit were found to be hardworking, ethical citizens. Some were even good parents! Their occupations included "business executives, lawyers, an investment banker, educators, therapists, and a computer engineer."1 They worked, they paid taxes, and they were denied the legal right to get married. It doesn't make sense. The Massachusetts Supreme Court ruled in favor of the plaintiffs. The court reasoned in part that the denial of the right to marry

> barred access to the protections, benefits, and obligations of civil marriage, a person who enters into an intimate, exclusive union with another of the same sex is arbitrarily deprived of membership in one of our community's most rewarding and cherished institutions. That exclusion is incompatible with the constitutional principles of respect for individual autonomy and equality under law. (*Goodridge v.Massachusetts Department of Public Health*)

Conservatives are great at talking about freedom and liberty under God. However, they have shown throughout history that they have some problems extending this freedom to people who share different backgrounds and interests. It's not very Christian or American of them. The Massachusetts decision corrected the conservative and oppressive Defense of Marriage Act that was overwhelmingly approved by Congress. It took a neutral court of law to determine that the DOMA, authored and supported by paid lawmakers, was illegal.

That's right. A vast majority of our elected "lawmakers" and one president signed into effect a law that was found to be illegal. This doesn't inspire too much confidence.

Furthermore, it was ruled that the "civil union" that everyone wants—for other people—does not afford the same legal rights as a marriage. They declared that the proposed law supporting civil unions was insufficient.

> For no rational reason the marriage laws of the Commonwealth discriminate against a defined class; no amount of tinkering with language will eradicate that stain. The bill would have the effect of maintaining and fostering a stigma of exclusion that the Constitution prohibits. It would deny to same-sex "spouses" only a status that is specially recognized in society and has significant social and other advantages. The Massachusetts Constitution, as was explained in the Goodridge opinion, does not permit such invidious discrimination, no matter how well intentioned. (Opinions of the Justices to the Senate 440 Mass. 1201, 802 NE2d 565 Feb. 3, 2004).

Now I am no lawyer, but this shit makes sense in a society that is based on and seeks to protect individual freedoms. This well-written and fair decision took all the power away from the Defense of Marriage Act and the representatives who proposed it.

The battle lines were once again drawn. A Supreme Court in the United States of America declared it unconstitutional for the federal government to deny two law-abiding citizens the right to enter into a contract of marriage. It was in response to this decision that "God's man in the White House" decided to embark on his personal crusade to defend marriage. Something had to be done, so the patron saint of all backward conservative issues stepped in. President Bush proposed to amend the U.S. Constitution to take away a right from American citizens. I thought it was a bad day for America.

A lot of other people disagree. People are right when they say that this is an ethical or even a religious issue. It is an ethical issue because some people are trying to write into law an amendment that would take away a legal right from law-abiding, tax-paying citizens because they are different. This is not good in a free society. I believe it is called discrimination.

The Speck in Your Eye Is Hurting Me

So George W. Bush gets on his high horse and defends marriage against a bunch of pagan homosexuals and their liberal friends. On October 28, Bush made his inspired revelation to the country by saying, "I believe marriage is between a man and a woman, and I think we ought to codify that one way or another. And we've got lawyers looking at the best way to do that."2

Bush even got a little biblical on our asses by paraphrasing a liberal teaching of Jesus, his favorite philosopher, about being judgmental when He said, "I caution those who may try to take the speck out of the neighbor's eye when they've got a log in their own."3 Talk about using scripture to his personal advantage! This is a violation of the Third Commandment—we all know where that leads.

George W. Bush cautions us about judging, as he tries to take away a right from a citizen! Additionally, by saying that we need to take the log out of our own eye before we pick at the speck in someone else's, Mr. Bush cleverly made a value judgment that homosexuality is a sin. Now the battle lines are really drawn. George W. Bush has brought religion into the argument.

We all know that homosexuality is a sin. It is an abomination. It is sodomy. It is a disgrace. Furthermore, we all know that God believes homosexuals are perverted scum that will not be allowed entrance into the Pearly Gates upon death. Our conservative politicians and religious leaders from the South and other Red States tell us this every day. More than that, homosexuals are trying to destroy our culture and our churches. Just ask Pat Robertson, who said, "Homosexuals want to come into churches and disrupt church services and throw blood all around and try to give people AIDS and spit in the face of min-isters."4 This happens all the time, and it needs to be stopped. We can't give equal rights to people who are trying to give churchgoers AIDS! This is out-landish. It isn't very surprising that Robertson never references exactly how he knows that gay people want to give other people AIDS by splattering contami-nated blood in churches. Maybe he is speaking in parables.

God hates gays, so we have to hate them also. God wants these promiscuous heathens punished, and He is doing so as we speak. They cannot be supported in their battle against the gay man's curse. We need to follow the lead of our Christian brother, Jerry Falwell, when he says, "AIDS is the wrath of a just God against homosexuals. To oppose it would be like an Israelite jumping in the Red Sea to save one of Pharaoh's charioteers."5 This is a war between good and evil. It is a war between God and Lucifer. The homos must be stopped.

There Is a Plethysmograph on Mike Hocke

Before moving along, it is important to address the issue of gay bashing and latent homosexuality. I have always felt that those people who are vehement in their consistent and violent animosity towards homosexuals are doing so because they have something to hide.

To this end, whenever I hear people referring to gay people in derogatory ways, I refer him or her to a study I read about a few years ago. This study, which revealed the true desires of the frustrated and angry homophobe, sounds perfectly logical to me. It turns out that it is possible that violent reaction to homosexuals indicates repressed homosexual urges.

Some guys at the University of Georgia did a little experiment. They took sixty-four male subjects, some of who were aggressive in their anti-gay feelings, and placed calipers on their penises. These calipers are called plethysmographs. Then they showed them porn. Gay porn. Eighty percent of the men who expressed feelings of animosity towards homosexuals experienced some growth as measured by the penis calipers.[6] That's right; homophobes were aroused by gay porn. Gotta love it. These newfound homosexuals denied that they had been aroused by gay porn. Unfortunately for them, penis calipers don't lie. Someone needs to get Jerry Falwell, Pat Robertson, and Karl Rove drunk and hook them up to a plethysmograph and show them *Donny Does Dallas*. It would be interesting to find out what these sexually oppressed freaks are really into.

I am sure that people are going to think that I am nuts for believing this study to be true. Since I have already shown that I have a disturbing and conservative propensity to stereotype others, I must admit that I do believe that at least 80 percent of homophobes are latent homosexuals. In a stroke of luck, and with only a limited amount of research, I was able to find three different occurrences of a right wing politicians, and religious kooks who have been forced out of the closet. One of these unfortunate occurrences happened in my beloved Blue State of Washington.

But first, there is a religious nut from Pennsylvania who was recently convicted of criminal "solicitation to commit involuntary deviate sexual intercourse." The honorable Reverend Stephen A. White started a club at Temple University called the "Soldiers for Christ". As president and CEO of this club the good reverend used his bully pulpit and, "Preached against homosexuality and atheists, using a bullhorn to rile at students and faculty about 'fornicators,' 'whores' and 'sodomites.'"[7] Unfortunately, the Soldiers of Christ at Temple University lost their leader after he was convicted of crimes associated with his request of a 14 year old boy to perform certain sexual acts on him.

Bummer.

There is another tale of a crackpot named Neal Horsley. While Mr. Horsley is not a household name, he does have his very own page on the Southern Law Poverty website. He is violently against abortion doctors and of course homosexuals. According to the SPLC website, Otis O'Neal Horsley is, the implacable enemy of homosexuals who promises regularly to 'arrest faggots, a man who proposes to use nuclear weapons in a bid for Southern secession, the Scripture-quoting theocrat who wants to force his version of Bible law on American society. This is the Horsley that rails on about "desecration," "pagans," "lust" and "perverted tolerance." And then there is the Neal Horsley who boasts to a young acolyte about having sex with men and with mules, the aging Vietnam War protester who says that "smoking dope, fucking and boozing, that's who I am naturally."8

Sounds like Mr. Horsley is the life of the party. A perverted party. He even admits that all of this is true. an interview with liberal pundit Alan Colmes, included this disturbing revelation about Horsley and the state of Georgia.

> Horsley: "Hey, Alan, if you want to accuse me of having sex when I was a fool, I did everything that crossed my mind that looked like I…"

> Colmes: "You had sex with animals?"

> Horsley: "Absolutely. I was a fool. When you grow up on a farm in Georgia, your first girlfriend is a mule."9

Pretty amazing stuff.

Finally, conservatives are even up to these kinds of shenanigans in my very Blue state of Washington. It just so happens that Spokane's Mayor, Jim White, was exposed not only as a homosexual, but he has also been accused of molesting young boys.

Since, every dog deserves his day in court, and the molestation part of this tale has yet to be proven, and even conservatives deserve the benefit of the doubt, I will not condemn Mr. White for this particular crime. On a side note, while apparently God hates man on man anal sex, we are going to discover very shortly that he is silent on man-on-boy fondling. Troubling.

Anyhoo, this Blue State Republican politician was "outed" by Spokane's very own local newspaper in one of those hard-hitting journalistic exposes that we all love. As truth would have it, West was flirting with young men on gay.com and may have been offering some of his conquests special governmental perks. Nothing wrong with scouring the internet for sex, it is what the it is for. Furthermore, finding same-sex dates and relationships is one of the benevolent services of gay.com.

However, this hypocrite was a lifelong hater of everything homosexual and he used his political power to deny equal rights to homosexuals and offer the state of Washington his wisdom on all sexual issues.

> "In more than 20 years in the Legislature, West had initiated legislation to outlaw sexual contact between consenting teenagers; supported a bill that would have barred gays and lesbians from working for schools, day care centers and some state agencies; voted to define marriage as a union between a man and a woman; and, as Senate majority leader, allowed a bill that would ban discrimination against gays and lesbians to die in committee without a hearing."10

This sure doesn't sound like the behavior of a freedom-loving homosexual. It sounds more like the behavior of a self-hating, uptight, Red State homophobe.

Just imagine what the plethysmograph would have done if Jimbo was one of the university of Georgia subjects. The penis caliper might have exploded under the stress of this guys bulging schlong when gay porn was playing. This is all unfortunate for Jim White and his Republican family and friends. Mr. White had a perfect plan to disguise his homosexuality. Beating up on homosexuals and denying them their rights as citizens should have kept him safe from being outed. But this political horndog couldn't stay off gay.com.

That's alright Jim, neither can I.

Now that his political career is over he will be able to feel the discrimination that other homosexuals receive at the hands of Red State republicans and other religious zealots. Perhaps now that he is officially out of the closet he will lighten up and see the error and hypocrisy of his evil, freedom-hating, Red State ways.

These events have been great for me. I need help supporting my stereotype that the majority of homophobes are latent homosexuals.

Thanks guys!

Sent from Above: a Long List of Sexual Abominations

According to the Red State religious leaders of our day, God hates homosexuals. At least that is what we are told. Goddammit! It looks like they are right. Homosexuality is an abomination. It is even punishable by death. The Lord says, in regards to a man lying with another man, "You shall not lie with a male as with a woman; it is an abomination." (Leviticus 18:13) Shit! The first time I try to prove these conservative assholes wrong, I find that they are right. But, alas, I continued reading this section of the Bible, and I discovered that Chapter 18 of Leviticus lists about a dozen or so "sex crimes" that are an abomination as well. Furthermore, in Chapter 20 of Leviticus, God not only lists the crimes one more time, He also doles out the punishment.

Leviticus 20 must be God's special section on sex crimes. It is essentially a long list of rules and regulations regarding certain types of inappropriate sex, with almost all of them being punishable by death. Only a few of these activities are punished by something other than extermination. The bloodthirsty God of the Old Testament appears to be up to His old tricks: "a lotta laws, no mercy."

The first on this list of sex crimes is an offense that millions of Americans, including conservative Christian do-gooders like Jimmy Swaggart, Jim Bakker, Newt Gingrich, Neil Bush, and Rudy Giuliani, amongst others, commit on practically a daily basis. It is a national scourge that should be reducing our population at an alarming rate. But for some reason, God has convinced lawmakers in the United States to relax on His divine punishment. I thought we were God's country?

> If a man commits adultery with the wife of his neighbor, both the adulterer and the adulteress shall be put to death. (Leviticus 20:10)

That's right. Commit adultery and die. It says it so right in the Bible. A nice way to control population and leave a lot of kids orphans, but not a real good idea as a constitutional amendment; it would disrupt the American way of life. And George W. Bush would have to execute at least one family member.

God gives another stern command against another insidious crime. The man who sleeps with his father's wife brings death to both the man and woman. It does not say whether the father's wife is the son's mother (see diatribe against Adam's family tree in Chapter 2).

> The man who lies with his father's wife has uncovered his father's nakedness; both of them shall be put to death, their blood is upon them. (Leviticus 20:11)

So if the son sleeps with the father's wife, he uncovers his father's nakedness? It sounds pretty gay to me.

A man may not have sex with his son's wife either. This crime is punished by more death.

> If a man lies with his daughter-in-law, both of them shall be put to death; they have committed incest, their blood is upon them. (Leviticus 20:12)

For some reason, it is incest for a father to sleep with his son's wife. In the United States, I don't even think that, if a guy humped his son's pretty young wife, he would be arrested for it. It is certainly inappropriate but not illegal. There we go again, breaking more of God's laws and not demanding His punishment.

Here's the one we have been waiting for: the great command against homosexuality. But it is just another crime that results in death for both participants: top and bottom.

> If a man lies with a male as with a woman, both of them have committed an abomination; they shall be put to death, their blood is upon them. (Leviticus 20:13)

For some reason, God does not have a law against being a lesbian. God's cool! What guy doesn't like a little lesbian action?

God gets a little down and dirty with the next one by forbidding a man the joy of a mother-daughter threesome. This makes rock stars and professional basketball players sad.

> If a man takes a wife and her mother also, it is wickedness; they shall be burned with fire, both he and they, that there may be no wickedness among you. (Leviticus 20:14)

This crime is only punished with a burning at the stake. There is still hope for the man desiring a more traditional threesome with two women who are not mother and daughter. God doesn't say anything about sisters or twins. Hallelujah!

This next one is kind of obvious. No bestiality. Both the man and beast shall be killed. It is again important to note here that the United States is not following God's laws. I believe that bestiality is illegal in the United States. I wouldn't know. I don't live in Georgia. However, we do not execute the perpetrators of this crime. A fine, perhaps some jail time, and a whole lot of embarrassment punishes the unfortunate farm boy.

> If a man lies with a beast, he shall be put to death; and you shall kill the beast. (Leviticus 20:15)

Interesting that God takes such a strong stand against bestiality. Us city boys would never think of doing anything like this. God's people lived in an agrarian society, so the youngsters must have developed some bad habits. Poor sheep.

Next up, same thing, different gender: Bestiality from a woman is condemned with the sternest of language. God orders death.

> If a woman approaches any beast and lies with it, you shall kill the woman and the beast; they shall be put to death, their blood is upon them. (Leviticus 20:16)

It is interesting that, for the woman committing the sin of bestiality, God orders death to the woman three times in one sentence.

God isn't a big fan of brother-sister incest either. However, the most merciful God does not order death. He only sends them away. Apparently, they all settled in Nod…or Kentucky.

> If a man takes his sister, a daughter of his father or a daughter of his mother, and sees her nakedness, and she sees his nakedness, it is a shameful thing, and they shall be cut off in the sight of the children of their people; he has uncovered his sister's nakedness, he shall bear his iniquity. (Leviticus 20:17)

This might support the notion that we are all descendents of Cain and his unnamed sister. Brother and sister have sex. Brother and sister are sent away…sounds vaguely familiar.

I have to agree with the idea behind God's order on the next one: no sex during a woman's menstrual cycle. While I agree with the sentiment, it is the only one of God's "sex crimes" that I ever have committed.

> If a man lies with a woman having her sickness, and uncovers her nakedness, he has made naked her fountain, and she has uncovered the fountain of her blood; both of them shall be cut off from among their people. (Leviticus 20:18)

The punishment for this, banishment, still seems a little harsh. But at least my crime isn't punishable by death. Also, I'd like to see Dubya try to enforce this one with a constitutional amendment.

A man can't have sex with either of his aunts either. There's no punishment of death here, just bearing of iniquity, whatever that means.

> You shall not uncover the nakedness of your mother's sister or of your father's sister, for that is to make naked one's near kin; they shall bear their iniquity. (Leviticus 20:19)

This is yet another sex crime that is allowed in the United States in spite of being forbidden by scripture.

For some reason, God attempts to protect the sanctity of the nephew-uncle relationship. There's no punishment by death here either, but neither the nephew nor his aunt will be allowed to have children.

> If a man lies with his uncle's wife, he has uncovered his uncle's nakedness; they shall bear their sin, they shall die childless. (Leviticus 20:20)

What is with all of the man-on-man uncovering each other's nakedness? Also, the punishment for this crime isn't very harsh. No kids for the two of them. It is possible that Aunt Sue had children before she seduced her little nephew. This is probably a blessing. She doesn't need any more kids, especially when her nephew would be the father and she would be their aunt.

Finally, another childless group of people result in a relationship between a man and his brother's wife. Some of us would think that not having kids is hardly a punishment. No harm, no foul.

> If a man takes his brother's wife, it is impurity; he has uncovered his brother's nakedness, they shall be childless. (Leviticus 20:21)

This one contains another reference to men uncovering each other's nakedness. All of this man-on-man nakedness is getting pretty repetitive.

Interestingly enough, after this diatribe against various forms of sex, I noticed that God does not have a punishment against a man having sex with his daughter. He can't have sex with his son's wife, but is it possible that having sex with his child is not a sin? At least it isn't in Leviticus Chapter 20. On a fairly innocuous note, while God forbids anal sex between two men, he does not forbid anal sex between a woman and man. There is no order in Leviticus that "If a man lies with a woman as with a man, both of them have committed an abomination; they shall be put to death, their blood is upon them." It seems like God, with all of His rules, would have had some kind of law against this type of "unnatural sex." But He doesn't.

Also, while there are laws against a man having a sex with a woman during her period, there is no law forbidding a man or woman having sex with a minor. God could have at least given His subjects some kind of a guideline in this area. In the United States, we have enough common sense to put some age restrictions on a grown man or woman having a sexual relationship with a child. Is it possible that in the Old Testament God condoned a sexual free-for-all in regards to adult-child relationships?

In different parts of the Old Testament, God does order His male subjects to seek virgins for wives. Is it for this reason that He does not make a condemnation of "statutory" rape? God doesn't even make a condemnation against "ordinary" rape. This is all pretty scary.

God's list is either incomplete, or He condones certain types of sexual activities that in the modern world are heinous crimes. Is it possible for an omniscient God to formulate an incomplete list of sex crimes?

If the conservative Christians were controlling the United States and God's laws were imposed on all of us under a strict, literal, and conservative interpretation of the Bible, millions and millions of Americans would be on death row.

Not only would homosexuals be put to death, but adulterers and perpetrators of certain types of incest and bestiality would be wiped from the face of the Earth as well. It is also possible that rapists, pedophiles, and dirty fathers would be walking the streets unpunished because their sexual deviancy is not a crime.

All of this sounds like the religion of the conservative Islamic terrorists that are the enemies of our country. Furthermore, all of these sex laws and disturbing omissions might fly in Alabama, Texas, or…Iraq, but it certainly would not work in the Blue States in the Northeast, Midwest, and West Coast of America. We like our freedom. We like our mother-daughter threesomes. We like sex during a woman's period. We want to punish rapists. And yes, some Blue Staters even engage in homosexual acts.

All of this is just a little food for thought for those who seek to judge the sexual behaviors of others in the name of God. It seems that the vague laws of the Old Testament God that conservative Christians love to quote, especially the one about homosexuality being an abomination, are rendered meaningless in our culture because we absolutely refuse to condemn any of God's other sex crimes.

Conservatives can't have it both ways. They can't pick one scripture to condemn an entire group of people they don't like and ignore other scripture that condemns their adulterous friends like Jimmy Swaggart, Jim Bakker, Newt

Gingrich, Rudy Giuliani, and a litany of other conservative Christians known and unknown. All of these Red State heroes would be dead if God's elected officials were following His plan.

Paul vs. Everybody

The conservatives go to their patron saint Paul for some homophobic rants as well. It isn't going to be surprising to anyone that a man who condones slavery and is against women's rights would once again come down on the side of the conservatives who believe that equal rights should not be extended to homosexuals.

Paul was not a slave, so he thought slavery was fine and dandy. Paul was not a woman, so he thought women should shut their mouths and do what they are told. Likewise, Paul is not gay, so we assume, and he gives conservatives everywhere ammunition in their hatred of gay people.

Paul is much like the God of the Old Testament in that he believes all sexual activity is inherently evil. He doesn't even waste any time. In Romans, the first of the Epistles, Paul barely gets through with his greetings and declaration that he knows the word of God before he starts to blast away at all types of fornicators, including homosexuals.

> For this reason God gave them up to dishonorable passions. Their women exchanged natural relations for unnatural, and the men likewise gave up natural relations with women and were consumed with passion for one another, men committing shameless acts with men and receiving in their own persons the due penalty for their error. (Romans 1:26–27)

See? Paul is no fun. He does something even God couldn't do. It is Paul who finally condemns lesbians. I hate this guy more and more all the time. He is undoubtedly at the forefront of those who believe that all sex is a sin. Paul seems consumed with addressing the Genitals, not the Gentiles. Ha! Ha! Pauline humor.

This is just one more area in which Paul is an extremist. It does seem like it is always the extremists who live the boring life, have a revelation, and become extreme in their hatred for just about everything. Paul is also vain enough that he wants to declare that the Kingdom of God is only for people who think and act just like him.

Paul gives frequent examples of his views on God's justice. He is the role model for the naïve religious leader who is trying to scare the masses into a conversion. Most don't convert because most are not afraid of "Hell."

He does try his best to convert the multitudes of sinners. "Do you not know that the unrighteous will not inherit the kingdom of God? Do not be deceived; neither the immoral, nor idolaters, nor adulterers, nor sexual perverts, nor thieves, nor the greedy, nor drunkards, nor revilers, nor robbers will inherit the kingdom of God." (1 Corinthians 6:9–10) Not only is Paul after the perverts and homosexuals, he is also after anyone who is immoral, an idolater, an adulterer…again, a thief, a drunk, a tax collector, or a robber. Who is left?

Some have suggested that Paul's diatribes against sex, his hatred of women, and his hatred of homosexuality could indicate a form of latent homosexuality. This is possible, but I just think he was just crazy.

It seems that any time Paul discusses any type of sexual contact, he is pleading for people to be just like him. Sound familiar? "I wish that all were as I myself am. But each has his own special gift from God, one of one kind and one of another. To the unmarried and the widows I say that it is well for them to remain single as I do. But if they cannot exercise self-control, they should marry. For it is better to marry than to be aflame with passion." (1 Corinthians 7:7–10) Paul is begging for people to live his life.

I actually like the King James translation of 1 Corinthians 7:10 much better. "Better to marry than to burn" does a better job of capturing the modern-day conservative, Pauline attitude towards sex and Hell. Just think of all of the souls that are going to burn for eternity because of the crime of pre-marital sex. I know I will be one of them.

Paul continues his rants against just about everyone, as there is only one more place where Paul indicates that homosexuality is a godless act. He uses the vague term "sodomites" to once again convict people of sexual sin.

> Now we know that the law is good, if any one uses it lawfully, understanding this, that the law is not laid down for the just but for the lawless and disobedient, for the ungodly and sinners, for the unholy and profane, for murderers of fathers and murderers of mothers, for manslayers, immoral persons, sodomites, kidnapers, liars, perjurers, and whatever else is contrary to sound doctrine, in accordance with the glorious gospel of the blessed God with which I have been entrusted. (1 Timothy 1:8–11)

Once again, Paul lumps "sodomy" in with an entire group of other sins. For additional effect, Paul once again hops on his high horse and announces that he alone is in charge of the spreading of the Gospel message. It is all pretty unfortunate.

Paul places himself on hallowed ground, not only when he declared himself the one and only prophet of Jesus Christ, but also when he became the patron saint of the conservative voyeur. We all know 'em. Those uptight white men who are concerned with everyone else's sex lives because theirs are so pathetic. The religious conservative has adopted the lifestyle of the sexually repressed Paul of Tarsus. Many of them are "serving" us right now in the halls of Congress. Lucky us.

Before we move on to what Jesus said about homosexuality, it is important to hammer home the point that, when Paul declared homosexuality a sin, he laid the groundwork for biblical justification of discrimination of a group of human beings. This is the third group that he has targeted for divine discrimination.

This is something that Jesus never did. Furthermore, in the times that Paul mentioned this "heinous" crime, just like God in the Old Testament, he lumped them in with a host of other evils.

The complete list of the people condemned by Paul are immoral people, idolaters, adulterers, sexual perverts, thieves, greedy people, drunks, revilers, robbers, murderers of fathers and murderers of mothers, manslayers, sodomites, kidnappers, liars, perjurers, and those engaging in pre-marital sex. Seriously, that literally covers almost everyone. Can we honestly regard homosexuality as worse than any of these offenses? It sure doesn't seem like it. But of course Paul orders us not to judge, "Therefore you have no excuse, O man, whoever you are, when you judge another; for in passing judgment upon him you condemn yourself, because you, the judge, are doing the very same things." (Romans 2:1)

Too bad Paul couldn't practice what he was preaching. According to Paul's own words, he must have been a homosexual because, by passing judgment on another, he (the judge) condemned himself for "doing the very same things"—sodomy, perversion, lying, stealing…

I really don't see what the big deal is. We let liars, murderers, thieves, drunks, and an assortment of perverts get married. We even let tax collectors take the plunge. Why not let gay people tie the knot? Homosexuality is just another one of man's transgressions that doesn't get punished with death, so why all the fuss?

Since Paul's teachings on homosexuality have been rendered meaningless, hypocritical, and even unethical, it is time to find out what Jesus had to say about homosexuals and other sexual perverts.

Searching High and Low

This task was a little easier than I thought it was going to be. However, the result is not all that surprising. Jesus did not say a word about homosexuality in any of the Gospels. Ye can look high. Ye can look low. Ye can seek and ye shall not find Jesus addressing the subject. You can read every word of the Gospels. You can search the most venomous anti-gay paraphernalia, pamphlets, and Web sites that you can find and you will find nothing about homosexuality from Jesus. You can even look at the most progressive pro-gay Web sites and, while they may have a quote about Jesus regarding tolerance, love, and forgiveness, there is not a single word to be found about gay people from the mouth of Jesus Christ. It simply doesn't exist. To Jesus and the writers of the Gospels, homosexuality was apparently a non-issue.

It is pretty sad that a topic that has inspired so much Christian zeal was so meaningless to Christ. I wonder how many Christians set out to find what their Savior said about the evils of homosexuality and came up empty handed? Unfortunately, this doesn't really matter because, after finding nothing from Christ, they went to the Old Testament and their conservative buddy, Paul of Tarsus, for biblical text that supports their discrimination.

Sex Crimes according to Jesus

The problem is that those of us who enjoy sex and even enjoy looking at attractive people are in a little bit of trouble in the eyes of Jesus. I am not a big fan of Jesus's words on this subject, but their meaning is undeniable—troubling for me, but undeniable.

Jesus was a hundred times more intelligent than His "Father." Jesus covered His bases by not being all that interested in specific sexual sins. He was more interested in people's attitudes as displayed by what exists in their hearts and souls. So when He says, "You have heard that it was said, 'You shall not commit adultery.' But I say to you that every one who looks at a woman lustfully has already committed adultery with her in his heart. If your right eye causes you to sin, pluck it out and throw it away; it is better that you lose one of your members than that your whole body be thrown into hell." (Matthew 5:28–29), Jesus isn't so much picking on people for a specific sin as much as He is pointing towards a universal problem. It is a problem that, as a horny guy, I struggle with on a daily basis. The problem is lust.

It is interesting that Jesus talks about lust only when a man is looking at a woman. In one of His only pronouncements about sex, Jesus directs His remarks to an audience of heterosexual males. He does not even recognize the idea that the lust could be committed from man to man. He doesn't do this because it is not all that important. What is important is that we respect each other.

The problem for me is that it is pretty difficult for me to live up to Jesus's words, and I am not going to pluck out my eye because I lust after a woman. But, at the same time, I am not going to go around saying that Jesus thinks it is all right if I imagine an attractive woman naked. If I am cast into the eternal fire for breaking this rule, I am cast into the eternal fire. That's the way the cookie crumbles.

While I agree with the sentiment of Jesus that it is probably wrong to look at women with lust in my heart, it is a command that I am unable to keep. I am also not interested in changing my life either. However, I don't run around telling everyone how religious and moral I am, like some people we know. So, while I may lust after women every now and again, at least I am honest with myself about my feelings and how they relate to His teachings. Hopefully, that's good for something. And if it isn't good for anything, I guess I am going to burn.

It's Unanimous! All of Our Biblical Heroes Hate Divorce

It is time to get off the "gay" issue and move on to the sanctity of marriage. It was George W. Bush, at the behest of Karl Rove, who made marriage an issue in the 2004 presidential election. Not only did he make it a political issue, but he made it a religious one as well.

Marriages are supposed to be legally binding contracts, but this legal contract got political and then it became religious. It became religious when George W. Bush and his conservative cronies added some choice adjectives to describe this institution. First, Bush is constantly referring to marriage as "sacred"—a word with heavily religious connotations. Likewise, people have repeatedly referred to the "sanctity" of marriage—another religious term. Bush says this himself in his official response to the Massachusetts Supreme Court's decision in the Goodridge case, "Marriage is a sacred institution between a man and a woman. Today's decision of the Massachusetts Supreme Judicial Court violates this important principle. I will work with congressional leaders and others to do what is legally necessary to defend the sanctity of marriage."11

Since George W. Bush and his conservative friends brought God into it, it is now important to see what He says about marriage. And, since some of our Christian leaders have been less than faithful in their marriages, it is also important to take a look at what God, Jesus, and Paul said about the destruction of the sacred institution of marriage: divorce. That is where things get real interesting, and the ugliness of Red State hypocrisy is exposed.

It is obvious that the God of the Old Testament is a pretty angry guy, it is no surprise that, while God condones marriage, He is no fan of divorce. It is becoming increasingly apparent that God hates just about everything, and He says as much about divorce in what must have been another angry revelation to a guy named Malachi. "For I hate divorce, says the Lord the God of Israel." (Malachi 2:16) 'Nuff said.

However, because He is a loving God, He also gives men some guidelines by which we should select our brides. Consider it God's form of pre-marital counseling. "They shall not marry a harlot or a woman who has been defiled; neither shall they marry a woman divorced from her husband; for the priest is holy to his God." (Leviticus 21:7) This is relatively reasonable stuff. Don't marry a whore. Don't marry a woman who, in what is a little more difficult prospect, has been "defiled." I agree with the not marrying a whore part, but it is pretty hard in this day and age to find a woman who still has her "files."

God delivers another blow to the already broken hearts of "used" women later in Leviticus. "And he shall take a wife in her virginity. A widow, or one divorced, or a woman who has been defiled, or a harlot, these he shall not marry; but he shall take to wife a virgin of his own people." (Leviticus 22:13) This is why the absence of a sexual law that determines the legal age at which to have sexual intercourse in God's list of sex crimes is a little troubling. There must have been young virgins running around everywhere back then. A man can only marry a virgin of his own "kind." God further eliminates widows and divorcees from consideration for marriage. It appears that these and other "defiled" women must die alone.

God's primary interest, besides the hating of divorce, is that a man must find the right woman. There is nothing wrong with this. If more people followed His orders, there would be less divorce. However, there would also be a lot less marriage, since God's people are only supposed to marry virgins of their own kind.

Unfortunately for women, God does not give them any marital advice, unless not being able to get married unless they are virgins is considered sound instruction.

Now Jesus was a pretty serious guy who had pretty serious rules. I think He probably agrees with God that it is not a very good idea to be flippant about getting married. He reiterates this on a few occasions. He does this, not by telling men to avoid certain types of women prior to marriage, but by telling men that divorce is forbidden unless a man's wife becomes a whore during the marriage. Under the rules of Jesus outlined in the Gospels, since divorce is off limits, a couple has to be real serious about getting married. According to Jesus, the only acceptable reason for divorce is infidelity. He says, "It was also said, 'Whoever divorces his wife, let him give her a certificate of divorce. But I say to you that every one who divorces his wife, except on the ground of unchastity, makes her an adulteress; and whoever marries a divorced woman commits adultery." (Matthew 5:31–32) It looks like millions and millions of Americans are in trouble.

He echoes this sentiment not once, not twice, not thrice, but four times. "And I say to you: whoever divorces his wife, except for unchastity, and marries another, commits adultery." (Matthew 19:9)

Again, "Whoever divorces his wife and marries another, commits adultery against her." (Mark 10:11)

And again, "Every one who divorces his wife and marries another commits adultery, and he who marries a woman divorced from her husband commits adultery." (Luke 16:18)

Jesus is not done yet and reiterates the importance of this "sacred" institution in a direct command not to violate the commitment of a marriage that is a contract made before God. "What therefore God has joined together, let no man put asunder." (Mark 10:9) I hear that one every time I go to a wedding. Divorce, if the applicable marriage was performed as a religious ceremony and in the eyes of God, is simply not allowed except in the case of infidelity! End of discussion.

It is also important to remember that adultery is condemned by death. Since divorce is adultery, and adultery is condemned by death. A lot of people are in trouble. That is if they were adhering to a strict literal interpretation of the Bible. Not even the Red State evangelical can follow these directives.

There is one way, and only one way, that a man can kick his wife to the curb, and that is if she is a slut. Fair enough. At least we know the rules before we take the plunge. It still seems a little rough on women.

There is no mention of whether or not a woman can divorce her husband if he is a man-whore. Also, remembering that adultery is punished by death, it isn't really fair that, when a woman is divorced, not only is she committing adultery, she is forcing a man into an adulterous relationship if she gets married again. Both would have to be put to death. It is too bad they can't just bear some iniquity.

Paul confirms all of this in one of the rare moments that he actually seems to be in the same ballpark as Jesus on an ethical issue. Paul reiterates Jesus's message that a man cannot divorce a woman and a woman cannot divorce a man. In another jab at the fairer sex, Paul does say that women can't get remarried to anyone but their husbands, "To the married I give charge, not I but the Lord, that the wife should not separate from her husband, (but if she does, let her remain single or else be reconciled to her husband)—and that the husband should not divorce his wife." (1 Corinthians 7:10–11)

I love it when Paul mentions that his words are directly from God's mouth. He does this all the time, as if he is trying to convince someone of a lie. So marriage is sacred. Now I get it. Marriage is sacred because, if it is done in the eyes of God, it is a promise that should not be broken. That makes sense. For what appears to be the first time, God, Jesus, and Paul all agree on something.

The Bible forbids divorce except in cases of adultery. The message is plain and simple. This underlies the notion that conservatives are right when they say that marriage is a "sacred institution."

A Sacred Institution? "Sex Romps" from the Friends and Family of George W. Bush

Since I am always looking for ways to uncover the hypocrisy of the Red State Republican and since their unequivocal leader is George W. Bush, it is interesting to note some of the personal sins and hypocrisy of the friends and family of George W. Bush. It does appear that marriage isn't all that sacred.

First of all, George Bush has a brother who is a bit of a philandering pervert. It turns out that Neil Bush, the younger brother of George W. Bush, was involved in a pretty messy divorce. Court papers revealed his "sex romps" in Asia, which included a woman showing up unannounced and giving him sex. Attorney Marshal Brown said, "It's a pretty remarkable thing for a man just to go to a hotel room door and open it and have a woman standing there and have sex with her." The Bush response, "It was very unusual."12

This is not so unusual if you are a Bush and your family is full of Red State religious hypocrites. You can do whatever you want.

Now, I don't give a crap about personal and private relationships, but, when a man declares himself the defender of an institution, it becomes funny when his relatives can't abide by the values that he wants to force on more than three hundred million people. For me, I wouldn't go on and on about an issue when members of my family make a mockery of it. It seems a bit "hypocritical." The great defender of marriage has a divorced brother who cheated on his wife. It isn't out of the realm of possibility that Neil Bush isn't the only Bush to violate the tenets of this sacred institution. It is also important to remember that in a country that follows the word of the Lord, adulterers are supposed to be killed.

Another Bush family friend and Bush appointee doesn't think too much of his marriage or his wife either. In December of 2002, Dr. W. David Hager was named to the Advisory Committee for Reproductive Health Drugs in the Food and Drug Administration. Not a bad appointment especially considering

Hager is a religious fundamentalist who authored a book titled, *As Jesus Cared for Women: Restoring Women then and now.* Under ordinary circumstances it would seem like Hager is a nice guy. He is also a self-anointed soldier of Christ who is being persecuted for his views at the FDA, "There is a war going on in this country. And I'm not speaking about the war in Iraq. It's a war being waged against Christians, particularly evangelical Christians. It wasn't my scientific record that came under scrutiny [at the FDA]. It was my faith…. By making myself available, God has used me to stand in the breach…. Just as he has used me, he can use you."13

Sounds like a great guy. He was appointed to a prestigious position by the president of the United States. He wrote a book about how much Jesus loves women. Dr. Hager is nothing short of an upstanding citizen and noble Christian man.

Alas, the revered Dr. Hager is also a divorced man, who has yet to be executed for this crime against God. Not only is he divorced, but as it turns out, he wasn't that great of a husband or a lover. It turns out that Hager likes sex, but it is a particularly violent and unnatural type of sex. Dr. W. David Hager, the man who wrote a book about how Jesus cares for women, likes anal sex, and apparently, he likes it rough, and he likes it without consent. According to his ex-wife, "I probably wouldn't have objected so much, or felt it was so abusive if he had just wanted normal [vaginal] sex all the time. But it was the painful, invasive, totally nonconsensual nature of the [anal] sex that was so horrible."14

That's right, Dr, Hager likes non-consensual anal sex.

Fortunately for American citizens, the great defender of marriage George W. Bush extended the appointment of this lover of "nonconsensual" anal sex fiend and "Soldier for Christ" through June of 2005.

Way to go, Mr. President.

Red State, Blue State: Exposing Red State Hypocrisy

So now we know that marriage isn't all that sacred to some Red State conservatives. Likewise, we have discovered that, while God and Paul have a long list of sexual sins, homosexuality really doesn't stand out from any of the others in terms of a special need for punishment. It also turns out that Jesus didn't give a hoot about homos.

Without further adieu, it is time for another game of *Red State, Blue State.* We need something to bring all of this nonsense together. I asked myself, "How do the conservative Red States fare against the liberal Blue States when it comes to divorce rates?" The answer to this question will tell us who makes staying married—a direct command of Jesus, God, and Paul—a priority. By comparing state-by-state divorce rates, we will be able to see if the pagan Blue

State liberals are casting their poor wives aside while Red State saints dedicate the remainder of their lives to their God-given soul mates. Or is the opposite true? Is it the Red State Christians who violate God's law against divorce while the Blue State heathens heed the call of our Lord and Savior? Let's find out.

First up, the states with the lowest divorce rates:

Lowest divorce rates by state

Rank	State	Divorce Rate	Red or Blue
1	Washington, D.C.	2.4	Blue
2	Georgia	2.5	Red
	Massachusetts	2.5	Blue
4	Illinois	2.9	Blue
5	North Dakota	3.0	Red
6	Pennsylvania	3.1	Blue
	Iowa	3.1	Red
	Minnesota	3.1	Blue
9	Rhode Island	3.2	Blue
10	Wisconsin	3.2	Blue

Source: Division of Vital Statistics, National Health Center for Health Statistics, CDC 2002.

It looks like it is the Blue States that respect the sacred institution of marriage. Not only do seven out of the top ten states belong to heathen liberal states, but also twelve of the first seventeen have the lowest divorce rates in the nation.

Because the majority of the Blue States are in the top twenty, most of the Red States are going to be in the bottom half. It is here that Red State hypocrisy shines bright.

The worst divorce rates in the country all belong to the residents of Red States. Yes, those same states, which are so hell-bent on defending the sacred institution of marriage, are the ones disobeying God and putting this institution "asunder."

Highest divorce rates by state

Rank	State	Divorce Rate	Red or Blue
49	Nevada	7.1	Red
48	Oklahoma	6.6*	Red
47	Arkansas	6.2	Red

46	Alabama	5.4	Red
	Wyoming	5.4	Red
44	Idaho	5.3	Red
43	West Virginia	5.2	Red
	Kentucky	5.2	Red
41	Tennessee	5.1	Red
40	Florida	5.1	Red

Source: Division of Vital Statistics, National Health Center for Health Statistics, CDC 2002.
* 1995 Data

Every member state of the bottom ten in annual rates of divorce voted for George W. Bush, the great defender of marriage, in the 2004 election. If we look deeper into the list, the next three states (Mississippi, Colorado, and Arizona) are also Red, meaning that the thirteen states with the highest divorce rates in the nation voted Red in the 2004 election that was at least in part defined by a moral crusade which had the intention of defending the sanctity of marriage. It may also be important to note that two Red States (Indiana and Louisiana) do not release divorce rates. I wonder what they have to hide. This Red State dominance on the breaking of a contract with God is the absolute height of hypocrisy.

Additionally, during the 2004 election, eleven states voted to amend their state constitutions and make same-sex marriages illegal. Not surprising, of these eleven states, nine of them were Red States that voted for George W. Bush and his crusade for moral values and upholding of God's mythical law.

Rank of states voting for amendment against gay marriage

Rank	State	Red or Blue
3	Georgia	Red
5	North Dakota	Red
21	Michigan	Blue
23	Ohio	Red
23	Montana	Red
24	Utah	Red
33	Oregon	Blue
37	Mississippi	Red
40	Kentucky	Red
47	Arkansas	Red
48	Oklahoma	Red

All told, only two of the eleven states voting for a ban on same-sex marriage are in the top third of state-by-state divorce rates. Only two of them voted Blue in the 2004 election. The two Blue States (Oregon and Michigan) should be ashamed of themselves. They betrayed the Blue State value of individual freedom.

Revenge of the Nerds: Divorce and the Conservative Christian Blowhard

To add insult to apparent injury, I have compiled a very incomplete list of conservative icons who love the idea of divorce. This list of people who, by getting divorced without cause, should have been sentenced to death because of their adultery includes haughty moralists like Newt Gingrich, Bob Dole, Phil Gramm, Ronald Reagan, John McCain, Henry Kissinger, Rush Limbaugh, Rush Limbaugh, Rush Limbaugh, and Bob Barr. Now, Bob Barr is hardly a famous politician, but he was one of the ones who sponsored the original act (DOMA) that started this mess in the first place. That hypocrite proposes an illegal law that defends an institution that he mocks.

It is also interesting that the great saint of New York, Rudy Giuliani, in his divorce proceedings, was accused of "notorious adultery." 15 Good for him.

I know why these kinds of guys get divorced. By looking at them, listening to them talk, contemplating their uptight ideas, it is obvious that they were hardly the life of the party while growing up. These guys were nerds. They were probably womenless geeks—except for Reagan—who married their first girl-friend. That, my friends, is a recipe for disaster.

Subsequently, after duping a bunch of conservative nerds like themselves and gaining fame and fortune, they became Red State heroes. After fame struck, they could no longer envision themselves with the same old "vaginer" for the rest of their lives. It is all perfectly reasonable to me. I avoided this midlife crisis by exploring the world of "poontang" in my teens, twenties, and thirties.

It wouldn't surprise anyone to discover that a fat loser like Rush Limbaugh has had only three girlfriends in his entire life, and they all became his wives and then ex-wives.

Phil Gramm, famous Texas hypocrite and divorcee, gave this sanctimonious pearl of wisdom regarding the sanctity of marriage, "The traditional family has stood for 5,000 years, Are we so wise today that we are ready to reject 5,000 years of recorded history? I don't think so."16 Yes, Mr. Gramm, you think you are "too wise." It was you who rejected 5,000 years of recorded history and the laws of our three most trusted biblical figures when you divorced your first wife and never accepted execution as your punishment for this crime against God.

The Oppressive Influence of Red State Morality

There are many reasons why the upstanding liberals in Blue States need to be worried about Red State values and hypocrisy invading our communities. It has happened in my beloved state of Washington. Even Washingtonians, filled with record numbers of heathens, must bear our evangelical burden. Following the "Christian" backlash caused by the 2004 national election, individual freedoms for law-abiding Washingtonians have been under attack.

A Red State evangelical has invaded the state of Washington and some lost souls are listening. Reverend Ken Hutcherson recently took credit for Microsoft distancing itself from a gay-rights bill that would have made it illegal to discriminate against homosexuals in the workplace. This measure lost in the Washington State House of Representatives 25-24. According to the reverend, when Microsoft stopped supporting this bill it was because of his threats of mass evangelical boycotts of Microsoft products.

Before I continue in this tale, I must address the background of the good reverend and his social and religious background. Blue State liberals hate to talk about race because by nature we feel guilty about the Red State sins of slavery and segregation. I am a little bit different. I don't feel bad. I wasn't there, so I don't mind addressing race.

Ya see, this guy is one of those odd black evangelicals who preach to a mostly white church. The primary reason I mention this is that in liberal Blue State like Washington, black people are given instant credibility. It is not malicious. It might even be a good thing. Liberals would rather be called child-molesters than racists. Sad but true. Black people in the United States have been targeted for discrimination and Americans need to be cognizant of the fact of Red State sins.

As a result of American racism, Hutcherson grew up in the very Red State of Alabama hating white people. He even used to play football so he could "legally" hit white people. Sounds good to me.

Now, he loves white people.

Reverend Hutcherson is the spokesperson for a mostly white religion. He married a white woman. His mentors—including Rush Limbaugh—are white. He lives in a white neighborhood. He has white hobbies (raising horses and restoring cars).

Yeeeee Hawwwww!

He also has that rare nerdy, white, evangelical sense of humor. He jokes about having "four German-chocolate kids." Get it. His wife is "German". He is "black". "Black" people are made of chocolate…get it…German Chocolate kids!

That's so funny, I forgot to laugh.

Ken Hutcherson became a "Soldier for Christ" in typical Pauline fashion.

Man gets in a motorcycle accident. Man is told he will never walk again. Man miraculously walks again. Man attributes this miracle to God. Man now believes he has been chosen by God. Man becomes spokesperson for the son of God. Meanwhile, man is still selfish and dumb so he simultaneously blasphemes and misinterprets the message he has anointed himself to send (See Chapter 5 Blaming Paul).

How does this Blue State devil know Reverend Hutcherson blasphemes Jesus? It turns out he has made quite the name for himself using the word of God to push his own agenda, the oppression of homosexuals. He has been self-anointed as the primary reason for the defeat of a bill that would have protected people from discrimination in the housing, insurance and employment based on their sexual orientation.

According to Hutcherson, "God became my coach. The Bible became my playbook. I run the plays the way they are written. That's my life. I have no personal agenda." He continues by calling people who say they are Christians but do not agree with him "evangelly-fish" because they lack a "spiritual backbone." This is a brilliant, evangelical metaphor. Get it…jellyfish don't have any bones.

Hutcherson's idiocy and blasphemy are shown when he brings Jesus into the equation by saying that homosexuals are "being disobedient to Him."17

Now a few minutes ago—I know it was a few minutes ago, because this book is so goddamn interesting you are flying right through it—I indicated that at no point in the Gospels does Jesus ever address the particular "sin" of homosexuality. Jesus addresses lust and even divorce, but never homosexuality. This makes Reverend Hutcherson either a liar or a moron. My guess is that he is a little bit of both.

Ken Hutcherson is being dishonest because he knows, just like we all now know, that Jesus never addresses homosexuality. Like all evangelicals, he does everything possible to avoid the words of Jesus and focuses on the words of Paul and the anger of the Old Testament.

In an interesting act of hypocrisy, it interesting to note that he includes Rush Limbaugh as a good friend and even has a football jersey autographed by Limbaugh on the wall in his office. If memory serves, Limbaugh is about to get divorced for the third time. If memory serves, God, Jesus, and Paul made very specific condemnations of divorce and even told us that divorce is adultery and that the punishment for adultery is immediate death. The good reverend hangs mementos of adulterers and divorcees (a crime condemned by Jesus) on his wall, yet he works like the devil to deny others of their rights when their lifestyle is an activity never even mentioned by Jesus.

Ken Hutcherson is kind of dumb because all of his Red State shenanigans are going to backfire since his evil activities are taking place in the very Blue state of Washington.

First of all, I don't think that Microsoft should have been very worried about an evangelical backlash. Imagine a bunch of evangelicals trying to figure out Linux. Considering their Red State education, this seems unlikely. They certainly wouldn't become Apple users since Macs are the computer of the extreme liberal. However, according to Hutcherson, Microsoft was shaking in their boots at the thought of a religious protest so they caved in to the threats of a pack of religious nuts.

After Hutcherson's arrogance, Microsoft recognized the error of their ways. CEO Steve Balmer has declared that Microsoft will actively support gay-rights legislation in the future. "After looking at the question from all sides, I've concluded that diversity in the workplace is such an important issue for our business that it should be included in our legislative agenda."18 It will be interesting to see if Hutcherson's lame protests can counter Microsoft's billions and the newfound activism of millions of newly inspired liberal activists.

Furthermore, Microsoft has dropped the notorious evangelical activist Ralph Reed from his $20,000 a year consulting job. Apparently, Microsoft now sees that there is no reason to seek the support of evangelicals. In declaring that he was the primary reason for Microsoft backing off an equal rights bill that lost by one vote, the self-involved and self-important Reverend Ken Hutcherson has helped lay the groundwork for the permanent defeat of his own cause.

In the end, Reverend Hutcherson is just like the segregationists of old in his Red State home of Alabama, where the white segregationists used the Bible in their pathetic fight against civil rights. It should be mentioned that once the equal rights were earned by the oppressed group, discrimination became the way of a backwards Red State past.

I could be wrong in all of this because according to Ken Hutcherson, just another in a long line of evangelical blowhards, "I think God has his hand on me and given me the gifts that I've developed and used for him. I always knew I was going to do things for the Lord if I just stayed faithful."19

Whatever you say Ken. Your lying, stupidity, arrogance, and big mouth just guaranteed the eventual passage of a gay-rights bill in the state of Washington.

Thanks for keeping Washington Blue.

It Was All about Discrimination and Bigotry

The biblical answer to the primary moral issue of the 2004 election is that Jesus never said that homosexuality was a sin. He never even addressed the subject. In addressing the issue of marriage, He said that divorce was a sin at least four times. Some of His supposed followers just aren't willing to take the log out of their own eye. Now, some citizens must suffer because of their indiscretions.

By discovering Jesus' lack of concern about homosexuality and finding out that God, Jesus, and Paul all vehemently condemn divorce; it appears that perhaps same-sex marriage isn't the religious and moral issue that some conservatives thought it was. Far too many politicians are notorious destroyers of this "sacred institution." This is hardly a "defense of marriage."

Additionally, the family, friends, and various Red Staters that support George W. Bush violate God's law against divorce at a higher rate than Mr. Bush's opponents. Thus, all of this nonsense about defending marriage is exposed for what it really is. The noble call to defend marriage was not about "religion," "values," or "morals."

I don't believe for a second that there was ever going to be a serious push for a national ban on same-sex marriage. Taking away a legal right from a citizen is unconstitutional, and Karl Rove and George W. Bush know it. This was an election year issue used to get Red State evangelicals to the ballot box. It worked.

Make no mistake about it, there was never going to be a constitutional amendment to ban gay marriage. Hell, it hasn't even been mentioned since the 2004 election. The proposed constitutional amendment against same-sex marriage was about creating a moral election year frenzy based on hypocrisy, and good old-fashioned discrimination and bigotry, traits mastered by the Red States.

8

Money Matters

Can a Millionaire Be a Public Servant?

Americans love to talk about money. It is our national obsession. This is apparent by our idolatry of the rich and famous. This love of celebrity is evident not only by our lust for information about our favorite Hollywood superstars and sports heroes, but also in our love and devotion to our political and religious leaders. In recent years, the two have become one and the same.

Politicians love to talk about God, and preachers love to talk about politics.

The thing that makes this phenomenon all the more disturbing is that many of the people sharing this "dialogue" about the nation's political and religious future are millionaires many times over. The rest of us are just poor saps. We don't covet our neighbor's wealth. We worship it.

An estimated one percent of Americans are millionaires. Compare this with our elected officials "serving" us in Washington, where more than a third of all senators and more than a quarter of members of the House of Representatives are worth in excess of one million dollars.

To be sure, this is not a "Republican" problem. Liberal fat cats John Kerry, Ted Kennedy, and John Rockefeller lead democratic millionaires in the halls of the Senate. Majority leader Bill Frist of Tennessee, who reported 45 million dollars in assets, leads the Republicans. In an interesting note, one of the poorest members of the Senate, Tom Daschle of South Dakota, who had earnings of less than a million dollars in 2003, lost his 2004 bid for reelection.

It is highly unlikely that a non-millionaire would be able to win a presidential election. In the 2004 election, all of the presidential and vice-presidential candidates were well-known millionaires. All four talked about the importance of religion in their lives. Evidently, God helped George W. Bush by blessing him with a politician and oil tycoon for a father and a callous old lady for a mother. God introduced John Kerry to Theresa Heinz. God helped Dick Cheney and Halliburton make millions. God inspired trial lawyer John Edwards to line his pockets as an "ambulance chaser" for the disinherited. On a variety of different levels, all four of these national political heroes are convinced they are doing God's work.

Bush, the millionaire who never had to work to earn a penny of his money, talks about his faith with pride, as if he has been anointed. There is little question as to whether his status as the King's son helps with his pompous attitude. John Kerry was at least a little humble about both his faith and his wealth. He made jokes about his wealth and only talked about his faith because a public obsessed with other people's religion forced him into it.

The financial and business résumé of George W. Bush hardly supports the idea that God has blessed His "chosen one" with an inordinate amount of financial sense and economic wisdom. From his dubious business dealings in Texas, which resulted in bankrupted companies and the trading of Sammy Sosa during his tenure as owner of the Texas Rangers, his decisions hardly seem inspired by an omniscient authority.

Currently, this man of God is leading the country into a national nightmare of mounting debt. During his first four-year term, the national debt has grown to over 7.5 trillion dollars. The debt is rising at a clip of 1.6 billion per day, and Congress has voted to raise the national debt ceiling by 800 billion dollars to 8.18 trillion.1 That is a pretty high ceiling.

Apparently, the way of the Lord is to spend and spend and not worry about paying anything back. The Bush administration is hardly an inspiration for financial success and spending discipline. This is all interesting because these millionaires, led by our president and vice-president, are doing the work of a God (Jesus) who was a homeless peasant while He was on Earth. The irony is not lost on this middle-class liberal.

Blessed Fathers and Fortunate Sons

But, as we all know in trying to figure out the biblical stance on wealth, we must go to the Old Testament first. It is here that God laid the groundwork for anointing His favorite subjects with riches and power beyond the reach of ordinary people. This whole idea of God blessing His chosen ones with obscene wealth begins with the notion that God has a special set of chosen people. It is these people who get to live lives of splendor. This wonderful life is achieved, at least in part, because of blessings sent directly from God.

Conservative icons of the Old Testament such as Abraham and Moses were particularly blessed with power and strength. There is not a great deal mentioned about glorious financial success sent from above. That particular phenomenon seems to be embodied by King David and his son, King Solomon.

The idea of God rewarding His followers with financial blessings is nothing new. The stories of King David and King Solomon that all of us learn in our religious upbringing definitely set the tone for our ultimate confusion. In Sunday school, we are constantly told about the riches and wealth of God's chosen people, as if they are rewards sent from above.

It is not surprising that people who are worshipped on Earth because of their fortunes start to develop some kind of God complex. The idea that a heavenly father has blessed these people with positive cash flow is difficult to dispute if we believe that God's servants are wealthy because of their devotion.

If we are to believe Old Testament text, two of God's chosen people, David and Solomon, were among the wealthiest people in the world during their time on Earth. In preparation for his son's ascension to the thrown, King David announces that a big, giant, gaudy temple that exalts the Lord is exactly what his son needs, "My son Solomon is young and inexperienced, and the house that is to be built for the Lord must be exceedingly great and famous and glorious in all the lands. Therefore, I must make provision for it." (1 Chronicles 22:5) King David is much like George Bush Sr., who knew that he had to make "provisions" for his son. King Solomon, like King George Jr., was born with a "silver spoon his mouth," a sign from God that all spoiled rotten brats are God's chosen people. It's great for them, but bad for the rest of us. King David continues bragging about his wealth, but this time he is a show off, as he lets everyone know just how much "stuff" he has: another sign that he is loved by God. "Notice I have taken great pains to provide for the house of the Lord— 3,775 tons of gold, 37,750 tons of silver, and bronze and iron that can't be weighed because there is so much of it. I have also provided timber and stone, but you will need to add more to them." (1 Chronicles 22:14) So King David is rich and likes to talk about it. King David was a braggart, desperately trying to prove his importance through a grotesque display of wealth. In the Old Testament, they are heroes. In real life, they are called "snobs.".

This is what makes rich people the world over some of the most boring people in the world. All they can talk about are their possessions, while seeking to impress those of us not blessed by God with wealthy parents or a God who "loves" us.

Eventually, the blessings of King David were passed on to the "fortunate son." It is here that we first are told that grotesque wealth equals infinite wisdom.

King Solomon is always noted as the wisest of the Old Testament bunch.

But this is only after he is identified as the richest of the pack. He uses his wisdom and riches to impress the beautiful Queen Sheba,

> And she said to the king, 'The report was true which I heard in my own land of your affairs and of your wisdom, but I did not believe

the reports until I came and my own eyes had seen it; and, behold, the half was not told me; your wisdom and prosperity surpass the report which I heard. Happy are your wives! Happy are these your servants, who continually stand before you and hear your wisdom! Blessed be the Lord your God, who has delighted in you and set you on the throne of Israel!' (1 Kings 10:6–9)

God has blessed Solomon not only with a big pile of gold and possessions, but he has wives, servants, and, most importantly, wisdom. King Solomon is a lucky guy. Not only does his cash flow surpass all inhabitants of the Earth, he has wisdom and more than one wife. It is apparent that he had a lot of people kissing his butt as well. The story of Solomon's embarrassment of riches and wisdom is reiterated for our benefit later in "the Good Book."

All King Solomon's drinking vessels were of gold, and all the vessels of the House of the Forest of Lebanon were of pure gold; silver was not considered as anything in the days of Solomon. For the king's ships went to Tarshish with the servants of Huram; once every three years the ships of Tarshish used to come bringing gold, silver, ivory, apes, and peacocks. Thus King Solomon excelled all the kings of the earth in riches and in wisdom. And all the kings of the earth sought the presence of Solomon to hear his wisdom, which God had put into his mind. Every one of them brought his present, articles of silver and of gold, garments, myrrh, spices, horses, and mules, so much year by year. And Solomon had four thousand stalls for horses and chariots, and twelve thousand horsemen, whom he stationed in the chariot cities and with the king in Jerusalem. (2 Chronicles 9:20–26)

This passage never indicates what makes Solomon wise. It only reminds us that, in addition to silver and gold, he is blessed with gifts from other people. It sounds a lot like the modern-day televangelist. It is also pretty neat that he has "apes and peacocks." God must be proud.

Our religious leaders and politicians are following the Old Testament model for wealth being the chief indicator of wisdom and blessings from God.

If it is true that an embarrassment of wealth and riches equals wisdom, why wasn't Jesus a multibillionaire living in a big Roman castle?

This would have been a very bad message for God (Jesus) to send, especially since it is apparent that many of our wealthy politicians didn't have to do a whole hell of a lot to earn their fortunes. Red State, right-wing, conservative, evangelical ministers, on the other hand, work like the devil.

Camels

There are numerous instances when Jesus gives His disciples the impression that being wealthy on Earth is not necessarily the best thing for a person's soul. It has always struck me as odd, hypocritical, and insane that so many rich people can claim a peasant as their Lord and Savior. Jesus was poor. He had no possessions; He lived a life of relative poverty. In so doing, He also gave us a pretty clear message on where He stands in regards to the possession of wealth and riches. It can't get any clearer than this. Unfortunately, members of the Religious Right do not recognize biblical metaphor unless it fits their own agenda and lifestyle.

> The young man said to him, "All these I have observed; what do I still lack?" Jesus said to him, "If you would be perfect, go, sell what you possess and give to the poor, and you will have treasure in heaven; and come, follow me." When the young man heard this he went away sorrowful; for he had great possessions. And Jesus said to his disciples, Truly, I say to you, it will be hard for a rich man to enter the kingdom of heaven. Again I tell you, it is easier for a camel to go through the eye of a needle than for a rich man to enter the kingdom of God. (Matthew 19:20–24)

It seems pretty simple. According to Jesus, rich people are going to have a real hard time getting into Heaven. Not only does Jesus give us an example of the futility of the man who loves his money more than he loves his God, Jesus actually makes an analogy about how difficult it is for a wealthy person to get into Heaven. How in the hell can a camel pass through the eye of a needle?

I have heard evangelicals get around this one by using metaphor and claiming that the "eye of a needle" is some kind of a gate at the entrance of Jerusalem where it was difficult to get a camel into the city, kind of like immigration post-9/11, for camels. This seems ridiculous. Jerusalem was in the desert for Christ's sake! Furthermore, didn't Jerusalem have more than one entrance?

The problem with all of this is that using metaphor does not follow the literal interpretation of the Bible defended by right-wingers everywhere.

Conservatives do not like metaphors in their religious texts, so why are they suddenly acceptable here? Second, whether it is the literal camel or the metaphorical camel trying to pass through the eye of a needle, this act is still, according to Jesus, a near impossible realization. His point is that it is difficult for a rich man to get into Heaven. All of the millionaires in government and all of the millionaire evangelists have a very convenient way around this one…They ignore it.

"The Gospel of Wealth"

It turns out that the message of the conservative, right-wing, Red State, evangelical minister is more insidious than I ever thought. I thought that these ministers were simply avoiding Jesus's messages against wealth. On the contrary, they actually use Jesus to support their selfish, money-grubbing behavior. There is a new, disturbing trend in conservative theology. Evangelical ministers everywhere are rewriting history and thousands of years of biblical study. Certain ministers actually portray Jesus as being a wealthy person, full of riches beyond imagination. It's hard to believe, but true.

Chief among these charlatans is the one and only Oral Roberts. Yep, the same guy who in a 1987 fundraiser announced that, if he was not able to raise eight million dollars for his City of Faith, God was going to "call him home." As absurd as this begging for money was, it is even more upsetting that he was able to scrape together more than the desired amount. Not surprisingly, a few months later Roberts announced that the City of Faith was closing down. Later in 1989, after the funds were secured, the plug was permanently pulled on the City of Faith.2 I wonder what happened to all that money he conned out of his parishioners? There is little doubt that the money that saved his life came from people with a lot fewer financial resources at their disposal than he had at his.

As bizarre as begging for millions in the name of the Lord was, Roberts' message regarding Jesus' wealth is even more insane. Oral Roberts spreads the word that Jesus wore designer clothes and lived in a mansion. He justifies all of this because of one lousy piece of scripture that announces that the infamous Judas Iscariot was Jesus' treasurer. According to Roberts, Jesus had a treasurer, so he must have been rich.

> According to John 13:29, a disciple by the name of Judas Iscariot was Jesus's treasurer. Now a treasurer is needed by a person who must deal with large sums of money that has to be accounted for, write checks, make purchases and pay bills, taxes and debts. You ask, 'Did Jesus have that kind of money?' Yes, or he wouldn't have needed a treasurer. He had so much that later Judas stole from the treasury.3

If we take a closer look at the chosen scripture, something Red State parishioners are not willing to do, we do indeed see that Judas was in charge of some money. As his lame justification, Oral Roberts uses a scene at the Last Supper where Jesus identifies Judas Iscariot as the one who would betray him.

It is he to whom I shall give this morsel when I have dipped it. So when he had dipped the morsel, he gave it to Judas, the son of Simon Iscariot. Then after the morsel, Satan entered into him. Jesus said to him, "What you are going to do, do quickly." Now no one at the table knew why he said this to him. Some thought that, because Judas had the moneybox, Jesus was telling him, "Buy what we need for the feast"; or, that he should give something to the poor. (Matthew 13:26–29)

Judas "had" a moneybox. This obviously means that Jesus is filthy rich. Talk about a wild imagination.

This all makes sense in the bizarre world of a man who is desperately trying to justify his wealth in the eyes of a peasant God. This kind of insane banter and selfish reading of the Gospels apparently helps convince an easily duped congregation into lining the evangelical ministers' coffers with their hard earned dollars. Bilking their conservative brethren out of their money is an important tenet of Red State theology. What a disgrace. And the "Bible Belt" Christians hate liberals! Give me a break.

But Mr. Roberts isn't done yet. Roberts insists that Jesus had a big house. He is convinced, like many other proponents of "The Gospel of Wealth," that Jesus lived in a mansion or at least a very nice condo overlooking Jerusalem. This is completely opposite of what Jesus says about his living situation. "And a scribe came up and said to Him, 'Teacher, I will follow you wherever you go.' And Jesus said to him, 'Foxes have holes, and birds of the air have nests; but the Son of man has nowhere to lay his head.'" (Matthew 8:19–20) Jesus had no place to live. According to the Gospels, Jesus may have been homeless. Having nowhere to lay his head is a far cry from living in a castle. I wonder who is telling the truth, Jesus or Oral Roberts?

After Oral Roberts's shameless whining for money in 1987, he lost all credibility and most people, with a brain, laughed at him. Today, he is a non-issue. I don't even know if he is still alive. However, he has influenced a new crop of disciples, who are actively spreading the message that not only is wealth a good thing and a blessing from God, but, like Roberts, they also tell their flock that Jesus was wealthy. Most of these clowns broadcast every day on the Trinity Broadcasting Network.

Troll-like evangelist, John Hagee, is at the top of the heap of these charlatans. He blasphemously declares that Jesus lived in the lap of luxury.

Jesus was not poor…Jesus had a nice house! John 1:38 says that Jesus turned to those that were following him and said, 'Come with me.' And they said, 'Where dwellest thou?' He said, 'Come and see.' And Jesus took that whole crowd home with Him to stay in His house. That meant it was a big house! Jesus wore fine clothes! John 19:23 says, 'He had a seamless robe.' Roman soldiers gambled for it at the foot of the cross. It was a designer original. It was valuable enough for them to want it! And then there are Christians that have poverty complex that says, 'Well, I feel guilty about having nice things.' Jesus didn't. 4

Since Hagee's followers are too dumb to read the Bible, it becomes important to address the chosen scripture used to support Hagee's fantastic claims. These claims say nothing about Jesus having a big house, only that He had a place to stay for the night. "And they said to him, "Rabbi" (which means Teacher), 'where are you staying?' He said to them, 'Come and see.' They came and saw where he was staying; and they stayed with Him that day, for it was about the tenth hour." (John 1:38) So Jesus had a slumber party. He could have had this party in a cave, in a tree house, in a homeless shelter, or on the street. There is no mention of a house, let alone a mansion. Hagee, to serve his own needs, takes a fairly innocuous piece of scripture and turns it into an out-and-out lie.

Like a blind man, Hagee conveniently ignores another seemingly harmless piece of scripture in which Jesus Himself once again indicates that He does not have a home. "They went each to his own house, but Jesus went to the Mount of Olives. Early in the morning He came again to the temple; all the people came to Him, and He sat down and taught them." (John 7:52; John 8:1) Jesus' friends go "home," and Jesus goes into the mountains. This is another piece of scripture forgotten by those who seek Jesus' blessing for their mansions. Hagee does the same thing with his declaration that Jesus wore nice clothes.

When the soldiers had crucified Jesus they took his garments and made four parts, one for each soldier; also his tunic. But the tunic was without seam, woven from top to bottom; so they said to one another, 'Let us not tear it, but cast lots for it to see whose it shall be.' This was to fulfill the scripture, 'They parted my garments among them, and for my clothing they cast lots.' (John 19:23–24)

So Jesus had a nice jacket; this obviously means he was rich and wore "designer clothes." Also, this was undoubtedly the first time a group of "honorable" Roman centurions took the clothes off the back of a crucified criminal.

"The Gospel of Wealth" is a dangerous and shameful Red State phenomenon. As proof, here are few more nuggets of "wisdom" from the money-obsessed evangelical:

Jesse Duplantis on "charitable" giving:
Cash is King! The hundredfold works. If I give $50, you mean God will give me $5,000? Yes! If you give $1,000 in the offering this morning, will God give you 100,000 by tomorrow? Yes!5

More on giving from Duplantis:
If I give $1,000 dollars, I deserve to get back $100,000 because I am just; that's not greed! 6

Fred Price on nice cars:
If the mafia can ride around in Lincoln Continental town cars, why can't the King's kids?" 7

John Avanzini on Jesus having "big" money:
Jesus was handling big money because that treasurer He had was a thief. Now you can't tell me that a ministry with a treasurer that's a thief can operate on a few pennies. It took big money to operate that ministry because Judas was stealing out of that bag.8

Kenneth Copeland on Jesus's poverty:
Some people say, "Well, Jesus' ministry was poor and He got along just fine." That's ridiculous. It would have been impossible for Jesus to be poor! All the way through the Old Testament, God promised material blessings to anyone who would walk perfect and upright before Him. If God had failed to bless Jesus financially, He would have been breaking His own word.9

As a warning, these clowns are on Trinity Broadcasting Network every day. While you may not recognize the names, any person with a remote control would recognize their faces

All of this is pretty absurd, even to some conservative Christians, but it is out there, and it is pretty sad. Christians living in Red States gobble it all up. These keepers of the faith hide out in the same areas that vote for George W.

Bush (Texas, Oklahoma, or any one of the states in "the Bible Belt"). The masses of evangelical parishioners give everything they have to people who are out to take advantage of them. The problem is, it is their own fault for being so stupid and gullible.

In my eyes, it is all pretty goddamn hilarious. If a bunch of screwball hillbillies and hicks are dumb enough to give a preacher their money in the hopes that their gift will be rewarded "tenfold," that is their decision. But the message is highly disrespectful to the liberal Jesus. And there are more than a few who are profiting from this blaspheming of Christ.

While this phenomenon doesn't really impact the life of the Blue State liberal, it is important that we know that it is out there and call it what it is: a wolf in sheep's clothing turning a House of God into a "Den of Thieves." Us intelligent and prudent liberals can laugh at it, but it is still kind of sad. The religious right in the pulpit and its ultraconservative friends in politics reap the benefits a "millionfold."

Where Does Your Treasure Lie?

In spite of the many evangelicals from the religious Right indoctrinating their flock into "The Gospel of Wealth," it is clear that Jesus and Paul were relentless in their condemnation of riches on Earth.

Jesus' repeated assertions that money is not good for the soul, like everything He says that is important, starts right at the start of the Gospels, during The Sermon on the Mount. It is here that Jesus first introduces us to the idea that we are supposed to take care of our souls and be concerned about eternity. The "earthly" needs of our bodies and the fleeting concerns of daily life pale in comparison to the health and well-being of the soul. Jesus says, "Do not lay up for yourselves treasures on earth, where moth and rust consume and where thieves break in and steal, but lay up for yourselves treasures in heaven, where neither moth nor rust consumes and where thieves do not break in and steal.

For where your treasure is, there will your heart be also." (Matthew 6:19–21) But I thought Jesus had a mansion, and designer clothes, and rode the Cadillac of all donkeys? Doesn't He have "treasures on earth"? I thought He had a dishonest treasurer who was stealing His millions?

The selfless message of Christ is quite a bit different from the selfish message of the modern-day conservative evangelical. Jesus seems to be telling us the exact opposite of anyone who believes that we are supposed to pursue riches on Earth. He believes they are a distraction to His message. "As for what was sown among thorns, this is he who hears the word, but the cares of the world and the delight in riches choke the word, and it proves unfruitful." (Matthew 12:22) It's interesting how people get to pick and choose the message they would like to believe. It is very convenient, if you're rich, to believe that Jesus had a big house and wants all of us to be financially successful. Unfortunately, Jesus says that riches take away from the Christian life, while some of His misguided followers say their riches add to His glory. Jesus is right; these followers are wrong.

It is also necessary to combine these words with the reality that Jesus was, in fact, a peasant. Jesus tells us He had no permanent home and tells us this by saying He has "no place to lay his head." He did not have great wealth and warned His followers against the accumulation of riches at the expense of their souls. He asks people to give away all of their worldly possessions to follow Him. The lesson seems crystal clear. Build your kingdom in Heaven, not on Earth. How could so many American Christians have missed the point?

It should be mentioned that, while evangelical Christians everywhere were virtually unanimous in their praise of *The Passion of The Christ*, while lining his conservative pockets, Mel Gibson did everything he could to make Jesus appear as poor as poor could be. Red State Christians, while enjoying watching the suffering of Jesus, never mentioned that He was a rich man who was getting His ass kicked. They enjoyed feeling the pain of an impoverished religious icon. This was very liberal of them.

This is just more of the same. Conservative evangelicals believe in a very self-centered religious doctrine that requires almost no work or sacrifice. Their precious Savior lives a life of poverty, and His most precious and anointed followers get to be rich in honor of a pauper. It defies logic.

It is pretty simple really. Conservatives everywhere have once again changed His message to fit their lives, rather than changing their lives to fit His message.

Finally, in a shocker, Jesus has the support of Paul. The words Paul of Tarsus and his description of the impoverished lives of his disciples confirm Jesus's attitudes towards the conflict between temporal wealth and the eternal soul. There were areas in which he confirmed Jesus's teachings. He needs to be congratulated for that. Just like Oral Roberts, John Hagee, the Bush family, etc. are proud of their prosperity on Earth, Paul seems to be equally proud of his intense poverty. Paul is not like the "trust-fund hippie" who plays the role of being poor. He is grounded in his beliefs and understands that he has chosen a vocation that is not going to result in the accumulation of a personal fortune. He is content with the spiritual life. Furthermore, he believes that this is the only way for him and the disciples to live. Paul's existence is a life of poverty and misery sanctioned by God. Paul describes the life of a Christian disciple as an earthly mess.

For I think that God has exhibited us apostles as last of all, like men sentenced to death; because we have become a spectacle to the world, to angels and to men. We are fools for Christ's sake, but you are wise in Christ. We are weak, but you are strong. You are held in honor, but we in disrepute. To the present hour we hunger and thirst, we are ill clad and buffeted and homeless, and we labor, working with our own hands. (1 Corinthians 4: 9–12)

One of the things that makes me admire Paul (only a little bit) is that he mentions that he works with his hands. He isn't even taking money for his ministry. This is a valid and important message. Paul was not one of the many religious leaders who got filthy rich by spreading the message outlined by a peasant. He spread the message of a poor man and lived like a poor, working-class citizen. He was not the role model of the modern-day evangelical, who gets a weekly manicure and a biweekly pedicure.

However, Paul does seem to be a bit of a glutton for punishment. He enjoys his status as a messenger who is suffering because of his devotion to his mission. "We put no obstacle in any one's way, so that no fault may be found with our ministry, but as servants of God we commend ourselves in every way: through great endurance, in afflictions, hardships, calamities, beatings, imprisonments, tumults, labors, watching, hunger." (2 Corinthians 6:4–5) The beatings, afflictions, and hunger do not sound like the chosen life of the modern-day minister or politician, liberal or conservative.

There is a clear difference between earthly riches and possessions and the soul. Paul agrees with Jesus that the soul is of paramount importance. He describes a life that is spiritually rich, yet economically poor. The followers of Christ are "sorrowful, yet always rejoicing; as poor, yet making many rich; as having nothing, and yet possessing everything." (2 Corinthians 6:10)

Evangelicals are the complete opposite. They are happy and always rejoicing about their prosperity, they are rich and make others poor by taking their money, and they have everything yet ultimately possess nothing. Paul is right when he indicates that we should be wary of these people. No worries for me, Paul. I am a Blue State liberal. There is no way in hell I am giving any of my money to a fluffy-haired, evangelical moron.

"The Crystal Den of Thieves"

But sometimes those of us in the cherished Blue States are forced to endure the pontifications of the arrogant religious Right and its messengers. The most obnoxious of these people is the esteemed Robert Schuler, who operates out of the liberal stronghold of California.

This clown broadcasts his drivel on Sunday mornings out of his own personal palace known as The Crystal Cathedral. It is pretty creepy. Jesus also warns us about those, like Mr. Schuler, who would turn his house into a "den of thieves."

As far as I can tell, The Crystal Cathedral is the gaudiest, most grotesque display of religious wealth in the United States. I was curious about all of this so I decided to go to the official Web site, crystalcathedral.org. What I found on the Web site was shocking but not very surprising. It was at this point that I realized that trying to defend the impoverished life of Jesus in modern—day America is pretty pointless. There are way too many people who have bought into "The Gospel of Wealth" and ignored The Gospel of Jesus.

The first thing I noticed on crystalcathedral.org was that Schuler has his picture plastered all over the Web site. He has really white hair. It also seems that he is a bit of an arrogant jerk.

The benevolent and humble Robert Schuler offers his flock the opportunity to donate their money and have their name inscribed on a marble wall. On this wall is a bigger than life painting of the grinning Mr. Schuler. He should be grinning, he is laughing all the way to the bank.

Then I noticed in the advertising section an ad for a book called *How to be an Automatic Millionaire* by David Bach. This book shows the followers of Christ an easy way to become a millionaire. "David has transformed his best-selling finish rich wisdom into a simple and compelling program that makes you rich automatically—without a budget, discipline or painful sacrifice."10 The price to financial security without work only costs a measly $19.95. Not too bad. Who knew that it was so easy to become a millionaire? The sequel, *Automatic Billionaire* must be on the way!

The shameless salesmanship of the Schuler family continues as more browsing through the Web site led me to a holistic online shopping experience of worthless crap. Among the items for sale on the "Hour of Power" Web site were the following: books, compact discs, Christmas ornaments, a ruby cross necklace, a "walk of faith" stepping stone, teddy bears, key rings, refrigerator magnets, and a $2,000 lithograph. The Schuler Family has made themselves "automatic millionaires" by blaspheming Christ.

The thing that I just can't figure out is how people can buy into all of this when Jesus so forcefully and literally warns us against this. There is another story that I remember from Sunday school in which Jesus goes crazy outside the doors of a synagogue. It always seemed to me that there was only one time that Jesus showed my favorite emotion, anger. It is the famous "den of thieves" diatribe in which He angrily cleared and tipped over all of the tables that were holding the objects that were being sold in the House of the Lord. "And Jesus entered the temple of God and drove out all who sold and bought in the temple, and He overturned the tables of the money-changers and the seats of those who sold pigeons. He said to them, "It is written, 'My house shall be called a house of prayer'; but you make it a den of robbers." (Matthew 21:12–14) I love it. That is anger. Jesus went on a rampage. Amen to that!

Robert Schuler and others have ignored this. It is remarkable that people who say they are Christians and say they read the Bible every fucking day are unable to see an occurrence like Jesus getting angry at people for selling a bunch of crap in His name when it occurs in their own lives and at their chosen place of worship. How does Schuler get around this? Is selling pigeons any different than selling a refrigerator magnet?

I need to contact the good Reverend Schuler and tell him that I have some product ideas for the "Hour of Power." What about the "Jesus Is My Rock" bowling ball? Maybe a "Jesus Is Lord" frisbee? How about a "Robert Schuler Cooler"? The possibilities to make millions of dollars mocking Jesus are endless. I am in the wrong profession.

So the life and message of Jesus are totally ignored by the proponents of the "Gospel of Wealth". The life of a pariah, a peasant, a poverty stricken man has been hijacked by a money-obsessed culture. The actions of the evangelicals and the religious Right as they beg for money on their way to amassing a personal fortune in the name of a peasant God is an egregious assault on the message and life of Christ.

Rendering Taxes

There is one more conservative financial obsession that needs to be addressed. Taxes. Taxes. Taxes. Conservatives in both Red and Blue States are forever bitching about paying their taxes.

The Bush solution for everything economic is the blessed tax cut. Being firmly entrenched in the middle class, I hear a lot about tax cuts going to the wealthy and, to be perfectly honest, I could care less.

I am more than happy to pay my taxes. I don't bitch, whine, and moan about it. I just pay. At times it seems a little excessive, but understanding that my tax money goes towards public schools, prisons, transportation infrastructure, the judicial system, libraries, parks, fire and police and other 911 services, and a litany of other things I can't think of, I can hardly complain. I do have some problems with running up the national debt to pay for a war in Iraq, but that is another story. Taxes go for some pretty good things. Maybe that is why Jesus insisted that we pay them without reservation.

At no point in the Gospels, or anywhere in the Bible for that matter, is there any encouragement to abstain from paying taxes. The whole conservative argument against paying taxes is ridiculous and a violation of Christian morality. While Jesus does not say anything about homos and abortions, He does say something about taxes…twice. And on each occasion, He tells His followers to pay them happily and dutifully.

> 'Tell us, then, what you think. Is it lawful to pay taxes to Caesar, or not?' But Jesus, aware of their malice, said, 'Why put me to the test, you hypocrites? Show me the money for the tax.' And they brought him a coin. And Jesus said to them, 'Whose likeness and inscription is this?' They said, 'Caesar's.' Then he said to them, 'Render therefore to Caesar the things that are Caesar's, and to God the things that are God's.' (Matthew 22:17–21)

If I am correct, the currency of the United States is issued by the government and has the "likenesses" of selected dead presidents. For this reason, it is not a stretch or even a metaphor to relate Jesus' biblical command to pay our taxes to our modern-day tax-collecting institution. In other words, we are to render to the IRS and the United States government what belongs to the IRS and the United States government. It is all seemingly pretty simple stuff without much room for misinterpretation. Jesus wanted His people to pay Caesar taxes, and Caesar was a jerk. I seriously doubt that the Roman Empire was putting as much money into the oppressed people of its protectorates as our government puts into our cities and counties. Yet, some of us, Red State Christians in particular, still complain in spite of the urgings of their supposed Savior. This story about Jesus encouraging His people to pay their taxes is repeated in Mark 12:14–17. See for yourself.

Jesus isn't the only New Testament icon that orders people to pay their taxes. Paul does so as well. "Pay all of them their dues, taxes to whom taxes are due, revenue to whom revenue is due, respect to whom respect is due, honor to whom honor is due. Owe no one anything, except to love one another; for he who loves his neighbor has fulfilled the law." (Romans 13:7)

It is unanimous. The Bible tells us to shut up and pay.

The Trickle over Theory

Now Mr. Bush and his conservative ilk are not advocating that people abstain from paying their taxes. They want people to pay their taxes. They have a war to fund. They just make it an issue because they think that some are paying too much—hence, the continual whining. The problem is that it is pretty unanimous that the tax cuts imposed by George W. Bush help millionaires more than they help the average American. Bush doesn't even shy away from this. It is kind of the continuation of the "trickle down" policies of the Reagan administration. To a certain degree, the Bush administration tax cuts are "trickling over" to his wealthy friends.

It is a little bit disturbing that Bush is supporting cuts for his friends in government, his friends in the oil industry, his friends at Halliburton, his family, and even his friends in the million-dollar industry of modern-day evangelism. In what seems to be a bit of a conflict of interest, all of those fat cat evangelical preachers (Billy Graham, Robert Schuler, Kenneth Copeland, et al.), who are making millions of dollars a year, are telling their parishioners that a vote for Bush is a vote for morality and a vote for God. What they are not telling their minions is that it is also a vote for a huge tax cut, for them.

It just doesn't seem very Christian that a bunch of millionaires get their taxes cut, while poor people continue to shoulder a burden, not just in the realm of paying taxes, but in an increase in gas prices, health insurance premiums, prescription costs, and other increases in the price of life's necessities.

Someone needs to tell the conservatives that it ain't all about taxes. Happily paying taxes seems the liberal way. As it turns out, fiscal insanity has become the conservative way.

It is obvious that, when a government cuts taxes, it must also cut services. Unfortunately, in the United States the services that will be cut undoubtedly impact poor children and their families more than these cuts impact wealthy children and their families. Combine a mounting national debt with a cut in services to poor, working Americans—this is the tax policy of a heartless Antichrist, not of a compassionate conservative. However, there is some good news for some very fortunate people.

It turns out George W, Bush and others in federal government have made it a priority to repeal taxes on inherited wealth. This insanity begins in 2005. "In 28 states, the estate tax will disappear in 2005 when the federal credit for state death taxes is phased out; in 18, death taxes will remain in effect despite the pending repeal of the federal estate tax; and in 4, there has been a temporary extension of their estate tax past 2005."11 This is of course a law made by rich people to defend the inherited money of rich people. It is nice to know that our friendly millionaires in the halls of Congress are looking out for themselves and their kids.

Cutting the taxes of the benefactors of massive inheritances probably was not a priority for Jesus. But who knows? Additionally, because of any tax cut, there will be a cut in services. These cuts usually come in areas that benefit the average American citizen. But hey, as long as the tax on inherited wealth for rich people is cut, everything is great! Earning money at the expense of family death is a noble occupation. This of course will lead to a few powerful and wealthy families of this country being obscenely wealthy until the end of time.

Now, I'm no economist but it is apparent that the Bush tax cuts reduced revenue at a time when Bush could not bring himself to reduce spending. The result is a mounting national debt. This is a nice fiscal policy for a man who inherited his money. But the anonymous American workers, who actually have to earn their money through hard work and long days, have learned through experience that they can't spend more money than they make. Most of us don't have Daddy and a pack of old crony friends to fall back on in a time of financial need. Bush has brought his personal financial policy into the White House. It is the American workers who will eventually suffer.

Red State, Blue State: the Fine Art of Sucking on the Government Teat

Finally, all of this does impact both the Red States and the Blue States. States have had to make a variety of cuts because of the national lack of revenue brought on by the unnecessary cutting of taxes. For example, in the United States, only fourteen states have not been forced to cut enrollment in Medicaid, SCHIP, or other state health insurance programs. Seven of these states are Red and seven are Blue. All told, between 1.2 and 1.6 million Americans are affected, with between 490,000 and 650,000 children having health care services interrupted.13 That is not very Christian of us. In addition, costs for post-high school education are soaring in every state.

Finally, in what is a shocking revelation, it has been discovered that Red States, while complaining about paying taxes, actually get more in federal funds than their tax-paying Blue State neighbors. That's right. Red States don't pay their fair share. Without further adieu, I think it is time for another little game of Red State, Blue State. It is here that we will see with ultimate clarity that the Blue States pay their keep and that it is the Red States who enjoy the sin of governmental handouts. That's right. While conservatives bitch about paying their taxes, they enjoy a plethora of government assistance. I believe that makes them economic hypocrites.

First of all, there are thirty-two states that received more money from the government than they paid to the federal government in taxes. The vast majority of these welfare states voted Red. These states are sucking at the government teat. Furthermore, seventeen of the twenty states that received the most in federal assistance in 2002 were Red States, while twelve of the fourteen states that received the least in federal assistance were Blue States.

It is here that, once again, the bizarre behavior from the conservative Red States indicates that they just can't seem to practice what they preach. Out of the ten states that received the most and paid the least, eight are Red.

States receiving the most in federal spending per dollar paid

Rank	State	Federal Dollar Received Per Dollar Spent	Red or Blue
1	Washington, D.C.	$6.59 per $1.00	Blue
2	New Mexico	$1.99 per $1.00	Red
3	Alaska	$1.89 per $1.00	Red
4	Mississippi	$1.83 per $1.00	Red
5	West Virginia	$1.82 per $1.00	Red
6	North Dakota	$1.75 per $1.00	Red
7	Alabama	$1.69 per $1.00	Red
8	Montana	$1.60 per $1.00	Red
9	Virginia	$1.58 per $1.00	Red
10	Hawaii	$1.58 per $1.00	Blue

Source: "Federal Taxing and Spending Benefit Some States, Leave Others Paying Bill" *taxfoundation.org*, October 7, 2004. http://www.taxfoundation.org/taxingspending.html

The whining Red States can't even pull their own weight. This is a total Red State phenomenon. The government handouts aren't confined to the backass-wards Bible Belt. It is a goddamn Red State epidemic!

Our national Red State welfare program continues, with seven out of the next eight states being Red (Kentucky $1.52 per $1.00, South Dakota $1.49 per $1.00, Oklahoma $1.48 per $1.00, Arkansas $1.47 per $1.00, Louisiana $1.47 per $1.00, South Carolina $1.36 per $1.00). Only Hawaii ($1.52 per $1.00), another vacation paradise, breaks the Red State logjam at the top of this dubious honor. All told, out of the top sixteen welfare states, fourteen are Red, and Washington D.C. isn't even a state! Besides Washington D.C. and Hawaii, only five of the other eighteen Blue States (Maine, Maryland, Pennsylvania, Rhode Island, and Vermont) paid less to the federal government than they received.

I also find it interesting and a little amusing that the only Blue entrants on the list of the top ten taxation hypocrites are the District of Colombia and Hawaii. One is the part-time home of the House of Representatives and the Senate. The other is a vacation paradise. Washington D.C. needs the extra cash because of an influx of millionaire lawmakers who invade the city a few months a year. While hard at work, they need to live a life of comfort that only mass government assistance can give. Life must be tough.

Conversely, it is the Blue States that pay taxes and are able to operate without excessive help from the federal government. Keep in mind that these states receive less than they are paying.

States receiving the least in federal spending per dollar paid

Rank	State	Federal Dollar Received Per Dollar Spent	Red or Blue
51	New Jersey	$0.57 per $1.00	Blue
50	New Hampshire	$0.64 per $1.00	Blue
49	Connecticut	$0.65 per $1.00	Blue
48	Minnesota	$0.70 per $1.00	Blue
	Nevada	$0.70 per $1.00	Red
46	Illinois	$0.73 per $1.00	Blue
45	Massachusetts	$0.78 per $1.00	Blue
44	California	$0.78 per $1.00	Blue
42	New York	$0.80 per $1.00	Blue
	Colorado	$0.80 per $1.00	Blue

Source: "Federal Taxing and Spending Benefit Some States, Leave Others Paying Bill" *taxfoundation.org*, October 7, 2004.
http://www.taxfoundation.org/taxingspending.html

Out of the ten states paying the most and receiving the least, nine are Blue. Furthermore, only four Red States paid more to the United States government than they received. These states are Nevada, Georgia, Indiana, and Texas. Furthermore, Nevada, the only Red entry that pays more than it receives that is in the top ten doesn't need any federal dollars because they are making billions from gambling and tourism profits.

It is pretty amazing that only four out of thirty-one Red States are able to pay their own way. The other twenty-seven Red States need government assistance to survive. Talk about the height of hypocrisy. To the contrary, it is the Blue States that have the dignity to pay more than they receive. Out of the twenty Blue States (including the District of Columbia), twelve paid more in federal taxes than they were given in federal government assistance.

Additionally, Oregon paid one dollar for every one dollar they received. This is much better than the poor performance of the Red States.

Conservatives say liberals aren't patriotic. Bullshit. Liberals happily pay more in taxes than we receive. That is the height of patriotism and love of country. Us kind-hearted liberals pay for the weaklings of our country. That, I might add, is very Christian of us Blue State liberals. As we remember the Christian ideal of giving more than people ask, liberals are able to keep the tenet of Christian philosophy. We happily give more than we receive. When someone asks Red State conservatives for a dollar, they cry like babies and reluctantly give seventy-five cents.

It all comes down to personal responsibility. Just like many other liberals, I don't mind paying my taxes. We pay taxes for services rendered. It is money that is considered well spent by responsible people. Conservatives, on the other hand, whine like little girls about paying taxes and then don't even have the dignity and honor to pay their fair share. What a joke!

This would all be pretty shocking if we were still under the assumption that the Red States actually follow the principles they so passionately espouse. They want taxes cut, but they still want more governmental help than everyone else. It is pretty pathetic. But, then again, they are Red States and pathetic is what they do best.

9

Moral Crime and Immoral Punishment

The Art of Judging Others

Conservative Christians have a pretty disturbing history of judging other people. Righteous indignation, in the name of Jesus, seems to roll right off their fork-shaped tongues. Whether it is judging the sexual behavior of other, more interesting people (George W. Bush), condemning other people to jail for crimes they also commit (Rush Limbaugh), or sentencing just about everyone in sight to an eternity in Hell (Red State evangelicals), this sinister reflection of Christian brotherhood makes itself heard in the most obnoxious manner by the most self-righteous and evil of all sinners.

There are three different areas in which God's people decide to judge others. First, our society has to judge others in terms of our legal culpability when we break laws. This seems reasonable because society must be protected from lawbreakers and criminals. Second, some people like to judge the morality of others. This is a sticky situation for people who are constantly bouncing between personal morality and immorality because of human folly. Finally, a smaller group people, who are mostly religious, like to put themselves in the lofty position of judging the souls of those who do not share their religious views. By most accounts, this mostly negative judgment sends the vast majority of people to Hell.

When George W. Bush warned all of us against picking at the speck in someone else's eye while ignoring the log in our own, he was not only using the metaphor of his "favorite philosopher," he was hinting at the peculiar instinct that plagues most human beings who think they know everything. People like to judge one another. It is hard to see that ever changing.

As I write this diatribe against the religious Right and the hypocritical Red States, I am well aware that I am judging my enemy. I have opinions about others, and I am making them known. I think right-wing, Red State, fundamentalist, conservative Christians are immoral scoundrels. In my own finite wisdom, I am making myself a judge of people with whom I disagree.

I am honest enough to admit that I am no better than they are in this area.

I want some of those miserable assholes to rot in Hell. Just like many conservatives believe that homosexuals, Muslims, and abortion doctors deserve a place in Hell, I would love to see George W. Bush, Jerry Falwell, Rush Limbaugh, Bill O'Reilly, Tom Delay, Bill Frist and a host of others burn for all eternity. It is what they deserve.

This liberal might even be for the death penalty under certain circumstances. The death penalty that I would endorse wouldn't be directed at low-income minority criminals. I would definitely condone locking them up and throwing away the key if they were a danger to society, but I wouldn't kill them. After all, I am a liberal, and I am against the death penalty. But when I see some of these pompous, sanctimonious windbags spewing their drivel, maybe, just maybe, I could change my mind, if only on a couple of special occasions. I probably couldn't condone it in the end. Life in prison would be funnier, and I am against the death penalty because I am a Blue State liberal.

The difference between the judgmental conservative who thinks that God is on his side and me is that I am not attributing my bitterness and distaste for those who are different or have a different set of values to God in a manner that suggests that I am His spokesperson. These are *my* opinions, based on my reading of scripture and my viewpoints regarding American culture. If I am wrong, and they are right, I will gladly accept eternal punishment and the eternal flame.

But as I think about it a little bit, my Hell would be a place where I was surrounded by a bunch of goody-two-shoes, smug conservatives. Imagine how boring that would be: no drinking, no smoking, no porn, no sex—except missionary style—no dirty jokes, no farting—just a bunch of boring nerds talking about God. How fun. If that is Hell, I had better change my ways. I don't wanna spend eternity in a second grade Bible study class.

Anyway, the problem with all of us humans judging other humans is that I am not entirely sure that we have the authority. Any one of us, including myself, could be wrong. Very wrong.

Law and Order

I understand that governments have the responsibility to protect their citizens from one another. It is for this reason that, especially in the United States, we have a judicial system that is actually pretty effective, unless you are poor. It is the task of this system to identify crimes and mete out the appropriate punishment. Our judgment—and crime-obsessed culture has literally thousands of crimes and thousands more punishments. In America, our blessed elected officials help us decide the difference between right and wrong. God bless them.

Obviously, there are things that are more wrong than others. Murder is worse than theft. Assault is worse than driving over the speed limit. Rape is worse than chewing gum in class. For the most part, this is taken into account by our legal system. Some laws are a little archaic and strange, like trying to enforce the marijuana laws when a shitload of responsible Americans smoke the stuff.

We don't really need marijuana anyway. It just makes people want to eat cookies and lie on the couch. We have alcohol, which makes people want to drive, fight, raise hell, punch their wives, and beat their kids. Alcohol is more a lot fun.

But whatever the crime, in the end, we need to judge other people when a crime is committed. A just legal system protects us from ourselves and from others. It is no surprise that God supports us in this area.

> You shall appoint judges and officers in all your towns which the Lord your God gives you, according to your tribes; and they shall judge the people with righteous judgment. You shall not pervert justice; you shall not show partiality; and you shall not take a bribe, for a bribe blinds the eyes of the wise and subverts the cause of the righteous. (Dueteronomy16:18–20)

This is pretty reasonable advice, even from an Old Testament tyrant who ordered a bear to kill forty-two children. At least He gave us a model, even if He had a difficult time following it.

For the most part, in the United States anyway, this model does a pretty good job of identifying violent criminals and putting them in prison, not just for punishment, but also to protect the rest of society. There isn't anything wrong with punishing people for their crimes against other citizens. Likewise, there isn't anything wrong with keeping these people off the street. However, there are differences in opinion in regards to the types and lengths of punishments and the right to competent defense. But nothing in this life is perfect. It is unfortunate that people with money get better lawyers, lighter sentences, and nicer jails than the rest of us. But anyone can avoid jail. People just have to avoid breaking the law.

The legal system we have in the United States is fine with me. Laws need to be on the books. While I am a liberal, I am no anarchist. So it is hard to argue with a government wanting to put away violent criminals, unless they are our family members.

Exerting Moral Authority

Legal judgment is not the primary focus of the religious Right. This group is obsessed with the crimes and punishments of other people in areas not necessarily within the boundaries of the law. Red Staters, evangelicals, and other conservative ilk are obsessed with judging others in regard to moral issues that are really none of their business.

A perfect case in point is the aforementioned reference that President Bush made when he paraphrased Jesus about judging others, homosexuals in particular. He was not addressing a crime (homosexuality is not a crime). He was judging a legal behavior. Even though gay sex is a bit odd and seems to be very painful, even to this diehard liberal, it would be hard to make the case that being gay is against the law. Mr. Bush was trying to make a legal relationship between two people illegal. He wants to make a moral issue into a legal issue. This isn't American, nor is it his business, even if he is the president. Is it our responsibility, as a society, to condemn non-crimes and mete out punishment? Keep in mind that the taking away of a right in a free society is a punishment. Some people, religious conservatives in particular, would like to punish people for behavior that is completely legal.

God gives us some instruction on this one when He says, "You shall do no injustice in judgment; you shall not be partial to the poor or defer to the great, but in righteousness shall you judge your neighbor." (Leviticus 19:15–16) We are to be impartial, which means we are not supposed to bring our oddball opinions and personal biases into our judgment and subsequent punishments.

I am judging the shit out of conservatives, but I don't want them punished. They do that to themselves. Life in a Red State is Hell on Earth.

At some point, we really need to ask ourselves whether or not it is honorable for us to condemn others who are different based on what we believe is right. People are fallible, and, when it comes right down to it, people don't know jack shit about right and wrong in the moral arena. Ultimately, it is all our opinion.

Consequently, problems arise when fallible humans dish out punishment in the name of morality. Those who behave wrong are ostracized by society. Those who do bad things are ridden with guilt because of pressure from family, peers, and members of the community. But this whole idea of what is "wrong" or "evil" can be very subjective.

Look no further than some members of the Catholic Church, who recently, in the name of judging others, decided to shift their allegiance from liberal Democrats to conservative Republicans. The members of the Catholic hierarchy can so easily convict, condemn, and riddle their parishioners into guilt plagued lives on the one hand, and yet they are so quick to hide child-molest-ing priests on the other. It is hard for any organization, religious or otherwise, to stand in judgment when such a horrendous crime is on their résumé. While I am well aware that only a small percentage of priests are child molesters, the behavior of the Catholic hierarchy in hiding, transferring, and defending child molesters should be considered an embarrassment to any Catholic. Furthermore, it is unconscionable that any member of the leadership of the Catholic Church attempts to stand in judgment of any person for any reason.

Making Heaven a Private Party

Unfortunately, our Christian brethren to the Right, in their finite wisdom and infinite arrogance, have an affinity for judging the souls of other people. It is they who are able to determine who goes to Heaven and who goes to Hell. Most of their ideas regarding eternal damnation or eternal salvation go right back to the Pauline doctrine of a faith that is triumphant over works. Say you're "saved" and, by golly, it happens. As if by magic, these children of God also know who is not "saved."

The strange thing is that, in the history of the world, only a small percentage of the Earth's inhabitants have ever been exposed to the doctrine and salvation of the Judeo-Christian faith. Why did an all-powerful God only reveal Himself to a small percentage of human citizens? What happens to the billions who have never heard of Christ when death comes a'knockin'? Do they all enter Heaven because they have never heard of Jesus? Or do they all go to Hell because they are not the chosen people? Either way, it is more bad theology with no logical answer. It just seems strange that God decided to originate his message in Jerusalem and not in Beijing or New Delhi. There are a whole hell of a lot more Asians in the world than Israelites.

This seems to be at the core of the "Christian" desire to judge everyone in sight. Religious extremists seem obsessed with making Heaven the place for themselves and their friends. This particular problem violently rears it's ugly head in the Judeo-Christian-Muslim world. All three of these religions have segments of conservative followers that condemn the rest of the non-believing world to Hell.

A few years ago, I had a fairly memorable conversation with a newly "saved" evangelical. So we were having one of those dumb conservative vs. liberal reli-gious discussions/arguments. The evangelical was espousing his second grade, fundamentalist beliefs on salvation. So I asked him, "Where am I going, Heaven or Hell?" It was kind of a trick question because I knew what his answer was going to be. I wanted to hear his answer because then I would blast him with my "biblical knowledge." When I got the answer I desired, I would retort as if I were some sort of religious genius.

It was all pretty silly. What can I say. I must have been real bored.

He responded with one raised eyebrow, and the answer I so desperately desired. He said something to the effect of this: "You can't go to Heaven if you're not saved." As a retort, I gave the same response as my favorite philosopher and religious icon...George W. Bush. I said that he should take the log out of his own eye before picking at the speck in mine. I thought I was brilliant.

The point here is not to prove whether I or Mr. Bush is right in our announcement that judging others is an ethical slippery slope, but to try to make the assertion that maybe people should not judge each other at all, especially when it comes to eternity. But with some people being so goddamn insecure, self-centered, and in many cases self-righteous, that seems to be impossible.

I and still have absolutely no idea why anyone would be concerned about whether or not a nudnik like me is going to Heaven or Hell. I don't care, so why anyone else. The only thing I can think of is that evangelicals want Heaven as their own resting place for themselves and their ilk. It must make them feel pretty good about themselves that they are exactly like God and everyone else is an infidel. The icing on the evangelical cake is that they belong to the one and only group that gets to go to Heaven for eternity. The rest of us aren't good enough so we get to spend an eternity Hell From my understanding, the billions of the rest of us are getting the short end of the stick.

An Angry God

At some point, it is necessary to address the idea that "God is an angry God, a vengeful God." I remember hearing something similar at one of the few evangelical church services I have been to. I don't recall who said it, but I do believe that I have heard it more than once. Since in my past I have tried to understand Jesus, I immediately tried to remember when he was angry and vengeful. He seemed like a pretty peaceful guy. I don't think of Jesus as an angry, thousand foot tall, muscular giant with flowing white hair and beard. We all know that is God, not Jesus.

But this is the reality of the Old Testament God. He is constantly bombarding His people with threats of destruction and earthly punishment if they disobey His different sets of rules and regulations. This image is assisted by different passages from the Old Testament in which He threatens His people with Hell, fire, brimstone, and mass murder. "For by fire will the Lord execute judgment, and by his sword, upon all flesh; and those slain by the Lord shall be many." (Isaiah 66:16) Scary stuff.

The threats continue. It isn't real difficult to see where conservative Christians get their zeal and lust for punishment. God gets pissed off at His people often, and He is lying in wait, ready to give appropriate recompense. Much of this retribution comes after God and His evangelical minions realize that some people just don't listen.

> And if in spite of this you will not hearken to me, but walk contrary to me, then I will walk contrary to you in fury, and chastise you myself sevenfold for your sins. You shall eat the flesh of your sons, and you shall eat the flesh of your daughters. And I will destroy your high places, and cut down your incense altars, and cast your dead bodies upon the dead bodies of your idols; and my soul will abhor you. And I will lay your cities waste, and will make your sanctuaries desolate, and I will not smell your pleasing odors. (Leviticus 26:31)

Now that is an angry God. He doesn't even want to smell our "pleasing odors." This is much like the banter of conservative ministers, seeking to transform the sinners into their brainless flock by threatening them with Hell, which, incidentally, is also the favorite hobby of the Red State Christian. The Old Testament God and the modern-day evangelical enjoy condemning people to eternal damnation

Some of God's eternal punishment for disobedience seems to have some magical and eternal consequences as well. "From new moon to new moon, and from Sabbath to Sabbath, all flesh shall come to worship before me, says the Lord. 'And they shall go forth and look on the dead bodies of the men that have rebelled against me; for their worm shall not die, their fire shall not be quenched, and they shall be an abhorrence to all flesh.'" (Isaiah 66:22–24) This is pretty scary stuff (sarcasm): dead people, eternal fire, unbearable pain...all suitable punishment for the lost follower of the great Jehovah.

This stuff just isn't very scary to the twenty-first-century American, especially since it is in prose. It may be only a tiny bit scary in various horror movies, children's books, and, sometimes, Harry Potter films. It just isn't very scary for a liberal adult. Promoting Hell as a punishment just isn't quite what it used to be.

God even has the ability to hate His poor followers. "And many of those who sleep in the dust of the earth shall awake, some to everlasting life, and some to shame and everlasting contempt." (Daniel 12:2) It must be really troubling to some of God's followers that His contempt can be everlasting.

There is no mention of forgiveness, no mention of understanding the folly of men, no mention of accepting people as being mistake ridden and worthy of redemption—just a whole hell of a lot of death and destruction. This is the Old Testament norm. The God of the Old Testament likes to punish His people. What tyrant doesn't? God might be an appropriate role model for some people. However, Jesus—the role model of the Christian—practices and preaches something a just a little bit different.

It is obvious that God pretty much cornered the market on His desire to judge His people. It was His job, not ours. Jesus and Paul agree, as they make it pretty clear that judging people isn't on the path to personal salvation. Jesus and Paul are right. Sometimes when people judge other people, they are wrong.

The true problem with the modern-day conservatives is that they seem to be consumed with judging others. It is a bizarre fascination born out of their belief that they know everything.

Red State Bigotry and German Hatred: Any Difference?

To that end, I decided to search for some outlandish quotes from the religious Right to prove my point. I found a gold mine. Some of the comments from these screwballs would actually be pretty funny if they weren't so goddamn scary. It is hard to believe people can be such morons. The panel of conservatives I found judging others consists of the following paragons of virtue: Adolf Hitler, Martin Luther, George Herbert Walker Bush, Anne Coulter, Jerry Falwell, Pat Robertson, Jesse Helms, Strom Thurmond, and Trent Lott.

Now, we all know that the Christians are the chosen people. It is still surprising that Christianity can be so bigoted and biased towards other religions. Adolf Hitler had a bug up his butt for the Jews. Is the irony lost on anyone that this genocidal "butt bug" was inspired by God, the Jewish God?

> I believe today that I am acting in the sense of the Almighty Creator.
> By warding off the Jews I am fighting for the Lord's work.[1]

Even most conservatives will admit that Hitler was a jerk. However, I was shocked to find out that the namesake of my family's Christian denomination (Martin Luther) was also a rabid anti-Semite.

> If I had to baptize a Jew, I would take him to the bridge of the Elbe, hang a stone around his neck and push him over with the words 'I baptize thee in the name of Abraham.'[2]

Disturbingly enough, there's more from the conservative father of Protestantism.

The Jews deserve to be hanged on gallows, seven times higher than ordinary thieves. We ought to take revenge on the Jews and kill them.3

I have always known that Pat Robertson has been highly critical of others. I just didn't know that some of his targets were various Protestants. This guy doesn't like anybody.

You say you're supposed to be nice to the Episcopalians and the Presbyterians and the Methodists and this, that, and the other thing. Nonsense. I don't have to be nice to the spirit of the Antichrist.4

So there is this guy named Anne, Anne Coulter, who is some kind of twenty-first-century, right-wing icon. He wants all red-blooded Americans to join him in his hatred for the A-rabs.

We know who the homicidal maniacs are. They are the ones cheering and dancing right now. We should invade their countries, kill their leaders, and convert them to Christianity.5

Man, that guy's mean. It also appears that he is very sad. He has a very long face.

The Bush clan loves to send out the perception that they are a group of fun-loving Christian folk from deep in the Heart o' Texas. Apparently, King George's father, the one-term Bush, doesn't know that atheists can be the life of the party.

No, I don't know that atheists should be considered as citizens, nor should they be considered patriots. This is one nation under God.6

That is one wacky family.

Our brothers on the conservative Right once again prove that there is only one true religion. This cast of conservative characters believes that Jews, Muslims, atheists, Episcopalians, Methodists, et al. are bound for Hell and not worthy of life on Earth. Judging other religions harshly probably isn't the best way to bring more disciples into the flock. It is also curious that I found it difficult to find very much conservative scorn for the Buddhists or any other Asian-influenced religion. The power of the Dalai Lama is everywhere.

Everyone loves the Buddhists. I wonder what in the hell they did to avoid conservative scorn.

The bigotry of the conservatives extends beyond religion to women as well. Every United States citizen who has taken a history class has been educated on the sins of the angry white Southerner. Likewise, everyone knows or should know that angry white men from the South fueled the conservative uprising over the past twenty years. It is here that my Red State brothers show that members of the fairer sex easily frustrate them.

The modern-day fundamentalist hates women, that is, unless they stay in the house and do what their man says. Jerry Falwell shows us what Southern hospitality is all about.

> I listen to feminists and all these radical gals—most of them failures. These women just need a man in the house. That's all they need. Most of the feminists need a man to tell them what time of day it is and to lead them home. They blew it and they're mad at all men. Feminists hate men. They're sexist. They hate men—that's their problem.7

Here's more about women from Pat Robertson, another Red State hero.

> [Feminism is] a socialist, anti-family political movement that encourages women to leave their husbands, kill their children, practice witchcraft, destroy capitalism, and become lesbians.8

I am starting to think that the infamous mouthpieces of the religious Right are somehow related. Falwell, Robertson, Limbaugh, Bill O'Reilly, and Pat Buchanan all have the same giant head, the same fat belly, the same gargantuan ears, and the same forked tongue. They sure as shit sound like their father, Satan.

I used to have a little bit of respect for Martin Luther. I understand that things were a little different hundreds of years ago, but come on! Some of this crap is ridiculous.

> Even though they grow weary and wear themselves out with childbearing, it does not matter, let them go on bearing children till they die, that is what they are there for.9

My dad, the die-hard Lutheran, is gonna hate me for exposing the bigotry of his Protestant hero.

It isn't even all that interesting to note that "the Bible Belt" was also "the Slavery Belt." It is here that America has found its most vehement racists. Some were legends of their backwards people; others had lasting careers in politics. It is all strange, very strange. Once again, it was the Red State white males who showed their true pallid color through their racism. The white men of the Old South had to somehow justify slavery; here's how Robert E. Lee did it.

> The blacks are immeasurably better off here than in Africa, morally, physically, and socially. The painful discipline they are undergoing is necessary for their further instruction as a race, and will prepare them, I hope, for better things.10

Robert E. Lee gave this rationalization for slavery more than a hundred years ago during the Civil War. He was giving slaves "painful discipline" for their benefit. What a guy. But some kept spewing their Southern hatred more than a hundred years later. Only it was even more vicious. At least Robert E. Lee was only patronizing.

> Strom Thurmond was downright evil. I wanna tell you, ladies and gentlemen, that there's not enough troops in the army to force the southern people to break down segregation and admit the nigger race into our theatres, into our swimming pools, into our homes, and into our churches.11

Even though Thurmond lost that battle and looked a bit humiliated in his never-ending fighting for bigotry, he was able to find some supporters in national politics. His defenders were Red State Republicans, and they obviously hailed from the South. One of his defenders was Trent Lott from Mississippi. He too has a forked tongue.

> I wanna say this about my state. When Strom Thurmond ran for president, we voted for him. We're proud of him. And if the rest of the country had followed our lead, we wouldn't have had all these problems over all these years either.12

Trent Lott is a funny guy. He is also lucky. That clown lives in the only state where he could possibly get elected. If that shithead moved to a Blue State, he would be laughed right back to the South. He is a caretaker of the most miserable state in our union, Mississippi. For proof, see repeated games of *Red State, Blue State.*

But there is more from our ancient Southern brothers. Jesse Helms hated Latins.

All Latins are volatile people.13

It is important to remember that Helms and Thurmond served about a hundred years a piece in the Senate—two more guys who would get laughed out of office if they lived in a Blue State. I say, disrespect the Southern vote. Not only did Helms hold the Latins in low esteem, he stands in judgment of homosexuals too.

Homosexuals are weak, morally sick, wretches.14

Now that is a surprise. Additionally, if a guy doesn't like Latins and doesn't like homosexuals, and he lives in the South, he must really hate black people. This is what the kind and compassionate racist said after the assassination of one of America's most beloved liberal heroes, Martin Luther King Jr.,

They should ask their parents if it would be alright for their son or daughter to marry a Negro.15

But Jesse Helms also has his support from the religious Right represented once again by Trent Lott.

For 30 years, Jesse Helms has been the conscience of our party.16

You know, I thought there were black people in Mississippi. Do they vote? How does Trent Lott keep getting elected? Is it possible to gerrymander a whole state?

While it may be true that Mr. Lott is the hero of the backward state of Mississippi, he seems to have lost some of his national power. His secret is out…he's dumb.

All of these guys, except for Anne Coulter, who escaped the very Blue state of Connecticut to another Blue State, New York, hail from Red States…or Germany. Shocking.

Maybe I am a little judgmental too.

A Lake of Fire for the Judgmental Hypocrite

The problem with all of this is that being judgmental is amazingly unchristian. Jesus leaves little doubt about that. Too many religious people operate under some kind of a superiority complex according to which they think they are better than everyone else. This confidence apparently comes from above. Now, while this idea may have support in the Old Testament and perhaps Islam or other religions I do not know about, it has no basis in the Christian religion. At least I can't find any.

The namesake of the Christian religion was a humble servant who espoused a very nonjudgmental line of social criticism. He knew that people should not judge one another, because He was smart enough to see that people are screwed up. People can be dumb. People can be biased. People can be selfish. People can be mean. These are not the qualities of a prudent and fair judge. Jesus knew this, so He commanded us not to judge one another. Unfortunately, some of His most dedicated and vocal followers refuse to listen.

Sadly enough, while Jesus does recommends that we do not judge others, He does in fact judge us. And He even plays the Hell card, the favorite card of the conservatives. This is unfortunate.

Jesus was a smart guy. He was God living on Earth. His laws and code of conduct are perfectly reasonable. But how could He miss the fact that people are not going to be afraid of the physical pain of Hell? The people running around talking about Hell disappeared years ago because it was an ineffective, childish message. The only ones left using it are the fundamentalists, and we see how every aspect of their lives violate the laws of Christ.

The beauty of the Christian message is that Jesus gives us the appropriate ways to behave because it is wise to live a just, peaceful, and correct life. The rewards are inherent. Obsessing about Hell only leads to the life of the false prophet or the hypocrite: the people who say one thing publicly and do another privately.

Jesus uses a couple of different scare tactics to get His ancient believers to live the ethical life. First, He threatens people by casting them into eternal fire, "But I say to you that every one who is angry with his brother shall be liable to judgment; whoever insults his brother shall be liable to the council, and whoever says, 'You fool!' shall be liable to the hell of fire." (Matthew 5:22)

It is interesting that he chooses a form of judgment—insults and revenge— as a sin punished with eternal flame. I like to think that the judgmental hypocrites that were constantly pissing Him off pushed Him a little too far at times. Jesus also tries to help us imagine the intense pain that can be associated with damnation. This is where He gives the noted "weeping and gnashing of teeth" form of punishment.

> Therefore you also must be ready; for the Son of man is coming at an
> hour you do not expect. "Who then is the faithful and wise servant,

whom his master has set over his household, to give them their food at the proper time? Blessed is that servant whom his master when he comes will find so doing. Truly, I say to you, he will set him over all his possessions. But if that wicked servant says to himself,' My master is delayed, and begins to beat his fellow servants, and eats and drinks with the drunken, the master of that servant will come on a day when he does not expect him and at an hour he does not know, and will punish him, and put him with the hypocrites; there men will weep and gnash their teeth." (Matthew 24:44–51)

It is profound that once again the individuals who are targeted by this painful punishment are the hypocrites. I really can't blame Jesus for condemning hypocrites to Hell. I think it is a great place for them, especially considering that hypocrites are sentencing other people to eternal damnation. Jesus knows it is what they deserve. Unfortunately, scaring people with Hell, fire, and brimstone isn't going to work with most liberals. Apparently, this doesn't work with evangelicals either, since it is the conservative Christian fundamentalists who are the biggest hypocrites in the world.

While Jesus, because He is God on Earth, decides He can judge others—His ruminations on the eternal hypocrite are endless—He does not want human beings to judge one another, and, if we do, we had better be careful.

In one of the more famous and profound moments in the Bible, Jesus comes upon a woman who is being condemned by the Scribes and the Pharisees for committing adultery. The Scribes and Pharisees, the conservatives of the day, wanted this women punished with a stoning. Jesus goes against the Law of Moses and gives the following liberal response.

And as they continued to ask him, he stood up and said to them," Let him who is without sin among you be the first to throw a stone at her." And once more he bent down and wrote with his finger on the ground. But when they heard it, they went away, one by one, beginning with the eldest, and Jesus was left alone with the woman standing before him. Jesus looked up and said to her, 'Woman, where are they? Has no one condemned you?' She said, 'No one, Lord.' And Jesus said, 'Neither do I condemn you; go, and do not sin again.' (John 8:7–11)

Here, we have a woman, in a time when women weren't exactly revered, being judged by a group of know-it-all sanctimonious religious leaders. This sure sounds familiar. Knowing that Jesus was a crazy liberal, they asked for His advice.

Because they were arrogant and stupid, like most Red State politicians and religious leaders, they were trying to get a man of peace to either violate Moses' law or expose Himself as the filthy liberal they knew Him to be. The answer of Jesus was brilliant. Since all people sin, not a one of us makes a competent, impartial judge. It is something we simply cannot do. People are too flawed.

Jesus requires compassion in judging others. He warns us that if we judge others with compassion, He will do the same for us. It sounds pretty fair to me. Right before Jesus tells His followers to take the log out of their own eye, He talks about the measure in which we should judge other people if we are in position to do so. "Judge not, that you be not judged. For with the judgment you pronounce you will be judged, and the measure you give will be the measure you get." (Matthew 7:1–2) People love to cite this quote when they are being judged, but seldom do they remember it when it is time to judge other people.

Prejudice with Deliberate Cruelty: the Red State Way

Jesus makes a lot of sense. It is His followers that continue to deceive. So far, I have documented some pretty hate-filled comments directed at people who are only guilty of being different. Adolf Hitler, Martin Luther, Anne Coulter, Pat Robertson, Jerry Falwell, and both editions of George Bush all claim Christianity as their foundation, and all judge other people in the harshest of manners. In some cases calling for death, these men are included: Coulter, Hitler, Luther, and Falwell. In the other cases, the harsh judgment only sought to deny other people of their basic human rights as citizens of a free country: Jesse Helms, Strom Thurmond, George H.W. Bush, George W. Bush, and Robert E. Lee. Maybe the problem of the modern-day fundamentalists is that they don't see all people as people.

This is the problem of the religious extremist. They use their views as the benchmark for classification into the human family of God. When some people don't meet the qualifications, they are shut out. Just about every group has been shut out of a holy family somewhere.

On every issue, the right-wing, religious, fundamentalist, conservative, evangelical expresses a deep, dark desire to conserve the old and put up an obstacle to the new, especially in the area of human rights. This is all based on the prejudgment of others. It has always been the liberal who worked for the freedoms of other, different people.

Religious conservatives have a bad history in the United States regarding the promotion of equal rights for people they deemed different. It was the Red State conservatives who wanted to preserve slavery and liberals who wanted to end it. It was the conservatives that wanted to protect segregation through state's rights politics and the liberals who wanted to extend rights to all people.

It was the conservatives who wanted to keep women from voting and the liberals who worked to ensure this fundamental principle of a democratic society.

It really is quite unbelievable that, on every human or civil rights issue ever fought for in the United States, conservatives came down against the promotion of these rights for more citizens. Then they call themselves Christian! Would a liberal vote against a civil rights issue? No way! We liberals support other people. We do not stand in negative judgment. When we are in a position to judge other human beings and determine whether they are worthy of equal status, we, the card-carrying liberals, say, "Hell yes! Come join the party!"

It has always been the conservative Christians who put up the "Do Not Enter" signs. It is the conservatives who are the ones who want to keep the party to themselves. And what a boring party it would be if liberals weren't around securing the rights of all people. There is no doubt about it. Some people judge others who are not like themselves with deliberate cruelty. These people have always been called conservatives.

Just as Hitler demonized the Jews, Luther ridiculed women, Helms and Thurmond hated the "'N' words," Coulter wants Muslims murdered or converted, and King George the First wanted to deny atheists the rights of an American citizen, modern-day Red State conservatives are back up to their dirty tricks. They continue to busy themselves sentencing a variety of nonbelievers, pagans, homos, and sinners to a life without equal rights and an eternity in Hell. It is clear that they just don't consider some people part of the human family.

My guess is that, in the same way the previous racists and sexists ran away from the personal embarrassments and their heroes of their pasts, people will some day be ashamed about their attitudes towards the new group of oppressed people.

Conservatives never learn.

491 Strikes and Yer Out!

Now there are quite a few times that Jesus gives us ways to avoid being so judgmental. It is almost like He is advocating a change in personality and personal philosophy. This is when He commands us to forgive. If we forgive, we can make some judgments against people but make peace with our souls. It is really kind of a splendid idea. This is another Christian virtue that humans have a difficult time practicing.

The personal salvation of the follower of Christ is one of the tenets that makes Christianity so attractive to the self-righteous windbags who love to talk about their justification in the eyes of God while sentencing everyone else to eternal damnation. Christians, especially the fundamentalists, love to accept forgiveness from Jesus...for themselves, and they love to deny the same forgiveness for others.

Jesus was just too nice of a guy. He comes to Earth, suffers at the hands of conservatives, and forgives the sins of His disciples. It is all part of the Eucharist and ritual of the Christian tradition of communion. "And he took a cup, and when he had given thanks he gave it to them, saying, "Drink of it, all of you; for this is my blood of the covenant, which is poured out for many for the forgiveness of sins." (Matthew 26:27–28) I don't want to be overly repetitive, but it is important to note that Jesus does the work and we reap the benefits. The problem with the conservatives is that they take the kindness of Jesus and not only take advantage of it, but also demean His existence. It is blasphemy in its worse form.

Paul takes a lot of the blame for this intriguing phenomenon, as he continually harps on what Jesus has done for us. We sin and Jesus forgives.

> He destined us in love to be His sons through Jesus Christ, according to the purpose of His will, to the praise of His glorious grace, which He freely bestowed on us in the Beloved. In Him we have redemption through His blood, the forgiveness of our trespasses, according to the riches of His grace, which He lavished upon us. (Ephesians 1:7)

It was pretty nice on Jesus's part to forgive our trespasses and bestow us with His grace. It would be nice if we would be more effective at doing for others what He does for us.

There's more from Paul: "And you, who were dead in trespasses and the uncircumcision of your flesh, God made alive together with Him, having forgiven us all our trespasses, having canceled the bond which stood against us with its legal demands; this he set aside, nailing it to the cross." (Colossians 2:13) It is interesting that Paul espouses a religion that gives and gives and does not require the same in return. This is not what either Jesus or, I suspect, Paul wanted. However, at least from Christians on the Right, that is exactly what Christianity has become.

On the surface, there doesn't seem to be any reciprocation necessary. Jesus does not need our forgiveness. However, rather than asking us for forgiveness on His own behalf, Jesus commands us—that's right...He commands us—to forgive others in the same way that He forgave us. It is here that Jesus's message differs widely from that of His homophobic, racist, misogynistic, right-wing, and holier-than-thou followers.

It is important to note that many of the ways that conservatives judge other people, by ethnic background, religion, sexual preference, gender, etc., are not sins. So when Jesus talks about forgiveness of sins and judgment, He is not telling us to forgive someone for being Asian, or forgive someone for being Jewish. Liberal religious leaders do not classify these things as sins. Regardless of what people deem a sin, we are ordered to forgive. Not only are we ordered to forgive, but also forgiveness is supposed to become a way of life. Jesus gives this lesson to Peter, "Then Peter came up and said to Him," Lord, how often shall my brother sin against me, and I forgive him? As many as seven times?" Jesus said to him, "I do not say to you seven times, but seventy times seven." (Matthew 18:21–22) Now, does this mean that we count up a man's transgressions and when they total four hundred and ninety-one, it is then that we can crucify him?

I don't think that is the point. We don't count; we forgive and we forgive without restriction because He forgave us without restriction. It really isn't that difficult…unless you are a Red State bigot or an angry German. All of this is missed because the Red State way is to make a harsh judgment based on personal bias and then to make a condemnation and determine appropriate punishment. When crime and punishment are established, they attribute all of their judgments to scripture and the life of Jesus. That is their way, but it is not the way of Christ.

Judgment from and Forgiveness for a Drug-Addicted Fat Lady

This kind of hypocrisy is no more evident in its hilarity than the recent drug troubles of the big mouthed, Red State conservative, Rush Limbaugh. In October of 2003, Rush Limbaugh was discovered to be a pill-popper. His drugs of choice were hydrocodone and oxycontin. These are the drugs of unhappy women everywhere. Even in his drug addiction, Limbaugh was a whining bitch.

It was all very funny. Since we all know the story, there is no real need to rehash his personal pain for our public pleasure. What is amazing is that, prior to his confession that he was a pathetic drug user, Rush Limbaugh was a rabid crusader against drugs and their users. He was very judgmental and did not follow the "love the sinner, hate the sin" model for modern-day Christians. He even made some of his attacks personal. The first victim, another dead fat guy, was Jerry Garcia: "When you strip it all away, Jerry Garcia destroyed his life on drugs. And yet he's being honored, like some godlike figure. Our priorities are out of whack, folks."17 It's interesting that, prior to being investigated for drug use, Rush derided Mr. Garcia and his fans for having the wrong priorities because they cared about a worthless junkie.

While I was scanning through Mr. Limbaugh's Web site, I found that, in his own arrogant way, he posted letters of encouragement from his supporters while he was away in a drug rehab center. It was the most obnoxious and self-serving crap I have ever read. These are available for online viewing at rush-limbaugh.com. Proceed to the section titled "E-mails of support pour into the EIB network."18 They are hilarious. Here are a few samples:

Rush,
Our prayers are with you. Our hearts hurt for you. Our brains already are stagnant without you.
Hurry back
Love Jane

Dear Rush,
I suspect you are in misery and pain and I want to send you a word of encouragement. We pray for your recovery every day. Please stay determined to beat this thing. We need you because you are our inspiration every day. We want you to be well, and we want you to come back to us stronger than ever.
I am on my knees praying for you. God will give you strength.
Love and prayers,
Gloria and Robert
Tucson, AZ

Rush,
We realize that this is not an easy time for you. Please know that we have added you to our prayer list. May these prayers and God's power strengthen you as progress on your journey.
Ed
Monroe, LA

Rush,
May the Lord protect you and give you a miracle healing. Our family loves you and is supporting you. We are praying for you twice a day. Hang in there and remember keep your eyes on Jesus. He is a healer.
Colleen
Bothell, Washington

Yes, there are actually human beings who occupy the United States whose brains are "stagnant" without Rush Limbaugh. It is a pretty disturbing world we live in.

These are only four of the thousands and thousands of letters of support that Rush Limbaugh received after he was exposed as a drug-using, feminine hypocrite.

It is just fine for him to receive acceptance, prayer, and forgiveness from his "Ditto head" fans. But when a "Deadhead" wants to revere Jerry Garcia, a more masculine drug user, Limbaugh arrogantly laughed at them as having no priorities. Limbaugh's hypocrisy and hubris are nothing short of remarkable. Of course, it continues. The following is a diatribe about an educator, probably a liberal, named Joe Fernandez.

All right. Joe Fernandez came to New York from Miami, ladies and gentlemen, to be schools chancellor...Now he is embattled—he's got a book that just came out, an autobiography that's soon to come out, I think, in which he admits that he was a mainliner as a teen-ager. This guy pest—shot up heroin. And people are praising him. He overcame the scourge. He triumphed over that profound obstacle in his life and has gone on to become this great schools chancellor...Reach out and try to help them, not give up on the kids, give them condoms and teach them about a bunch of stuff that is worthless in terms of preparing them for their future as adults in the greatest country on Earth, teaching them all this social gobbledygook. "Let's not forget about the kids." Whoa. The guy wants to be education secretary, folks. Watch out. Now why does he want to go to Washington? Probably because he's studied the case of Marion Barry. Here's a guy who got involved in drugs. You want to see my Marion Barry impersonation? Do you want to see that? All right. I'll do the Marion Barry impersonation. You put some stuff out here on the table and you go [pretends to snort cocaine]. "You tell Jesse to stay out of my town. This is my town, and Jesse—you tell him to stay out. [More snorting.] And I said no, no, no, no, I don't smoke it no more. Tired of ending up on the floor." [More snorting.] So what is he? He gets involved in drugs and ends up, ladies and gentlemen, as a newly elected official in Washington, D.C....So I'm sure Joe Fernandez is looking down there saying, "Hey, there's a future for, you know, drug users in Washington, D.C."19

Here are some more "e-mails of support" from his forgiving "Dittoheads"20:

Rush:
May the Lord bless you,

May the Lord make His face shine upon you,
May the Lord put His countenance upon you,
and give you His peace.
We're praying for you!
Mark and Donna

Dear Rush,
I've written a little poem for you:
"Rush is a Dear
He's full of cheer
And lively Optimism
He makes my day
In a special way
And if I could,
I'd kiss him/"
Note, with Marta's permission.
Sincerely,
Doris
Pompton Lakes, NJ

Dear Rush,
Me & my wife really miss you. You are the greatest man on earth. You have
helped us learn so much about politics. You are the greatest. Hurry back.
Roy
Okeene, OK

Rush,
My prayers and best wishes are with you and your family. You have made such
an impact on me and others I know. You have only grown stronger over the
years. Your self realization [sic] and personal battles only proves that. I anxiosly
[sic] await your return to the "golden microphone," and with God's good
graces, you will be an even more inspirational person than you are now to
those you touch daily.
Thank you and Ditto.
Bryan
Houston, Texas

People who live in Red States are weird, very weird. They are also pretty scary.

Finally, in spite of his sins, Limbaugh did give us a solution to the scourge of
drug use. "Send them all away, send the people who want to do drugs to

London and Zurich and let's be rid of them."21 I wish that guy would follow his own advice. We could get rid of him and millions of his fans, whose brains go "stagnant" without him. Unfortunately, as we all know, Limbaugh will never leave because right-wing, Red State hypocrites seldom follow their own advice.

The point here isn't necessarily to pick on Limbaugh. Wait, yes that is part of the point. Addicted to painkillers, what a bitch! The point is also to expose Limbaugh's sanctimonious judging of others. It is amazing that he shows a complete lack of forgiveness for others and showers himself in the forgiveness of other people when he sins. We all deserve lenient judgment and forgiveness, not just those with the biggest mouths. Limbaugh and his conservative ilk need to extend to others what they want for themselves.

A Lesson from Jesus about Forgiveness

In stark contrast to the judgmental rants of Limbaugh, Jesus continues on His same line of thinking throughout the Gospels. People aren't supposed to judge; they are supposed to forgive. He outlines this in the Lord's Prayer, a ritual practiced by good-hearted Christians everywhere, "And forgive us our debts, as we also have forgiven our debtors; And lead us not into temptation, But deliver us from evil. For if you forgive men their trespasses, your heavenly Father also will forgive you; but if you do not forgive men their trespasses, neither will your Father forgive your trespasses." (Matthew 6:12–25) In spite of reciting this once a week during church liturgy or private prayer, people manage to forget it every day.

Finally, it should always be remembered that not judging others and forgiving others are inextricably linked. When Jesus gives His famous "judge not" order, He followed it with His own capacity for grace, "Judge not, and you will not be judged; condemn not, and you will not be condemned; forgive, and you will be forgiven." (Luke 6:37) It seems like a pretty simple message, but it sure is hard to follow, even for liberal windbags like me, which leads us to another installment of *Red State, Blue State*.

Red State, Blue State: Crime and Punishment

We all know that judging others is not only our favorite pastime, but for some it is an occupation. The legal system in the United States is bogged down by a variety of different criminals guilty of a variety of different crimes. Some are doing time as punishment for breaking a law and will be soon released, while others will rot away forever because they are a threat to society. I am all for protecting society, but, being a liberal, I understand that punishment in the form of jail time only makes for harder criminals and exacerbates the problem of the lifelong criminal. After all, most prisoners are released at some point.

To that end, I thought I would do some state-by-state research regarding incarceration and crime rates. It is useful research for anyone interested in providing a safe environment for his or her kids. Once again, the answer is clear. The more I play Red *State, Blue State*, the more I am extraordinarily thankful that I live in a Blue State.

First of all, Red States tend to have more male prisoners than Blue States.

Highest Number of male prisoners with sentences averaging more than one year per 100,000 residents

Rank	State	Inmates per 100,000 residents	Red or Blue
1	Louisiana	801	Red
2	Mississippi	768	Red
3	Texas	702	Red
4	Oklahoma	636	Red
5	Alabama	635	Red
6	South Carolina	551	Red
7	Georgia	539	Red
8	Missouri	529	Red
9	California	525	Blue
10	Delaware	501	Blue

Source: Prisoners in 2003, Bureau of Justice Statistics, United States Department of Justice

Since Red States dominate the top, Blue States will equally dominate the bottom.

Lowest number of male prisoners with sentences averaging more than one year per 100,000 residents

Rank	State	Inmates per 1,000 residents	Red or Blue
51	Maine	149	Blue
50	Minnesota	155	Blue
49	North Dakota	181	Blue
48	Rhode Island	184	Blue
47	New Hampshire	188	Blue
46	Vermont	226	Blue
45	Nebraska	228	Red

44	Massachusetts	233	Blue
43	Utah	240	Red
42	West Virginia	260	Red
41	Washington	260	Blue

Source: Prisoners in 2003, Bureau of Justice Statistics, United States Department of Justice

Eight out of eleven of the lowest rates of incarceration signals more good news for the Blue States.

Now, we know that conservatives have an ugly history on women's rights issues. As noted, Jerry Falwell and Pat Robertson have criticized women in some of their more offensive comments. Likewise, Rush Limbaugh has repeatedly referred to successful women as "feminazis." Consequently, it is no surprise that female incarceration rates in Red States are far higher than the female incarceration rates of the liberal Blue States. Once again, I am proud to be a Blue State liberal.

Highest number of female prisoners with sentences of more than one year per 100,00 female U.S. residents

Rank	State	Inmates per 100,000 residents	Red or Blue
1	Mississippi	134	Red
2	Oklahoma	127	Red
3	Louisiana	104	Red
4	Texas	98	Red
5	Montana	91	Red
6	Idaho	86	Red
7	California	85	Blue
8	Nevada	79	Red
9	Colorado	77	Red
10	Georgia	71	Red

Source: Prisoners in 2003, Bureau of Justice Statistics, United States Department of Justice

Only California, with its numerous urban centers, disrupts Red State dominance in this area. The bottom ten in this area are even more impressive than the rates of Blue State male incarceration. Each of the bottom nine states is Blue. Only North Dakota breaks a Blue State stranglehold, holding firm at number ten.

Lowest number of female prisoners with sentences of more than one year per 100,00 female U.S. residents

Rank	State	Inmates per 100,000 residents	Red or Blue
51	Rhode Island	10	Blue
50	Massachusetts	12	Blue
49	Minnesota	17	Blue
48	New Hampshire	18	Blue
47	Maine	18	Blue
46	Vermont	27	Blue
45	New York	29	Blue
44	Pennsylvania	29	Blue
43	New Jersey	34	Blue
42	North Dakota	34	Red

Source: Prisoners in 2003, Bureau of Justice Statistics, United States Department of Justice

This is pretty impressive stuff. Blue States don't like to send their women to prison. We prefer them to be either in school, at work, or being good parents. The female criminal is a little bit upsetting.

Everyone knows that judgmental conservatives love to play God and kill the infidels. They also like to make murder legal. Before we review this one, it is important to remember that Jesus ordered us not to judge and God ordered us to be impartial.

Therefore, it is not very surprising that Red States are in one hundred percent complete control of the top states in executions. I even continued and went past the top ten.

Highest number of executions by state since 1976

Rank	State	Number of Executions	Red or Blue
1	Texas	337	Red
2	Virginia	94	Red
3	Oklahoma	75	Red
4	Missouri	61	Red
5	Florida	59	Red
6	Georgia	36	Red
7	North Carolina	34	Red
8	South Carolina	32	Red

9	Alabama	30	Red
10	Arkansas	26	Red
11	Arizona	22	Red
12	Ohio	15	Red

Source: Number of Executions by State and Region Since 1976, *Death Penalty Information Center,* January 4, 2005.
http://www.deathpenaltyinfo.org/article.php?scid=8&did=186

It is probably important to underscore the shortsightedness of the death penalty and to show how, because of human folly and bias, it can be tragically unfair to certain groups. The Death Penalty Information Center tracks executions for interracial murders. The results are nothing short of astounding, but amazingly believable since virtually all executions are performed in Red States, which have an ugly history or racism and bigotry.

Since 1976, there were 192 executions ordered for black defendants who were convicted of killing a white victim. Conversely, there were only 12 executions ordered for white defendants who were convicted of killing a black victim. That's right: 192 to 12. This troubling statistic is even more disturbing when it is taken into account that this lopsided total was compiled after the Civil Rights movement rendered forced segregation illegal.

This would indicate to any rational person that the death penalty is unquestionably tainted with racism. But, then again, Red States have always had problems with racism, and, since the death penalty is only an issue in Red States, it only stands to reason that racism would occur.

Now, you would think that all of this imprisonment and death might result in safer, more peaceful Red States, wouldn't you? You would be wrong. Red States tend to be the most violent places to live, in spite of their aggressive form of judgment and lack of forgiveness. Violent punishment does not lead to law and order.

Red States dominate the rankings in the highest rates of violent crimes despite their emphasis on judgment and incarceration. The Federal Bureau of Investigation considers murder, rape, robbery, and aggravated assault as violent crimes. It is not a source of state pride to be at the top of this list. I can see the advertisement now, "Welcome to South Carolina, the most violent state in America" or "Welcome to Florida: Home of Murder, Rape and Robbery."

Highest rates of violent crimes per 100,000 U.S. residents

Rank	State	Violent Crimes per 100,000 residents	Red or Blue
1	South Carolina	882	Red
2	Florida	770	Red
3	Maryland	770	Blue
4	New Mexico	740	Red
5	Tennessee	717	Red
6	Louisiana	662	Red
7	Nevada	638	Red
8	Illinois	621	Blue
9	Delaware	599	Blue
10	California	593	Blue
11	Texas	579	Red
12	Alaska	563	Red
13	Arizona	553	Red
14	Michigan	540	Blue
15	Missouri	539	Red

Source: Crime in the United States, Federal Bureau of Investigation fbi.gov
<http://www.fbi.gov/ucr/ucr.htm#cius>

While this list is not completely controlled by Red States, there are still more Red States (ten) at the top of the violent crime list than Blue States (five). It is clear that, while Red States have more prisoners and more executions, they still have more violent crime. Neither their judgment nor their subsequent punishment does anything to ensure a safer society and culture for Red State residents.

A Hypocritical Disclaimer for My Habit of Judging Others

There is no question that, in this diatribe against Red States and conservatives in general, I am making harsh judgments. This makes me a hypocrite. I am condemning the act of judgment, yet I am judging others. I may be petty. I may be selfish. I may think I know everything, but I am honest. I believe that conservatives such as Jerry Falwell, Rush Limbaugh, George W. Bush, Pat Robertson, and all of their minions are blasphemous, hypocritical morons. That is judgment.

But there is a difference between what I do and what they have been doing. I don't claim Heaven as the personal dominion for my friends and me. And, even though I acknowledge Christ as a genius with an astounding and rare liberal message, I am not making a public declaration of Christ as my personal savior, not here anyway; those decisions are personal and private. Furthermore, if because of my sins I go to Hell, my guess is that I will deserve it, and I accept it.

10

Revenge

I Love Japanese Electronics

The United States has only been attacked on its own soil by a foreign invader twice in history. The first was Pearl Harbor, and the second was on September 11, 2001, when the World Trade Center towers in New York City were attacked by Islamic terrorists.

The response of the United States to the attack on Pearl Harbor was to seek revenge against Japan. Eventually, we found our retribution by dropping two atomic bombs on Hiroshima and Nagasaki. This marked the end of the conflict. By attacking the United States, the Japanese awoke a sleeping giant and ultimately paid the price. In many ways the economy and lifestyle of the average American has benefited from these unfortunate events.

Now, the Japanese are our best friends. I say, "Thank God for the Japanese." Anything electronic, I buy from Sony, a Japanese company. That shit works. Would I buy an American electronic product? Yeah right, I may be a liberal, but I'm not stupid. I have also driven a Japanese car for my entire adult life. Whether it is Honda, Nissan, Toyota, or Mazda, those cars run forever. Would I buy an American car? I don't think so. I am a Blue State liberal with a long commute. The good ol' U.S. of A. got its revenge, and I have directly or indirectly benefited from it. Since I am trying to advocate liberals not being wimps anymore, I dare say that revenge can be sweet. But it is only sweet if the revenge is placed upon the person or entity that deserves it.

This brings us to the September 11 attacks and the United States' current dilemma of being involved in what appears to be an endless war against a country that may not deserve our retribution. Such is the blindness of revenge.

Oh by the way, we got slew of electronics and efficient cars from Japan, when do we get the cheap oil from Iraq?

A Trip to a Red State Sunday School Class

Whether or not we are in fact God's chosen people is up to debate. The Old Testament is littered with instances of God destroying cultures and people who offended either Him or His people. God sent locusts, plagues, frogs, magic tricks, and even bears to defeat those who stood in the way of His chosen few. But it was God who initiated this revenge, and not man. This indicates that our desire to punish others for their crimes against us might not be our job. It is the job of the Almighty. At least, that is what He says.

The calls for Old Testament revenge are literally endless. There are far too many to mention here. But most of the characters in the Old Testament, from Adam and Eve to Cain and Abel to Samson to Jeremiah and Isaiah, were either calling for revenge from God or were the victims of God's brutal vengeance. Because of the nature of the conflict between the literal and metaphorical interpretations of the Bible, it appears that, in both respects, God does the smiting and that His people are the agents. In the area of revenge, people are not acting alone. God is on their side, and He is the one committing the act. God is omni-everything.

Whether an angry and, perhaps, a little bit of an arrogant God wants the glory and the power to Himself or wants His people to remain innocent of the sin of murder and mayhem is another question that has no answer. All we know is that, when there was death and destruction in the Old Testament, it was God who was doing it. He may be doing it through people, but it was always His idea.

An example of this occurs with one of the favorite Old Testament Bible tales of my youth, the story of Samson. I love this guy. His story has been cast aside as nothing more than a meaningless children's story. I love it because there is a lot of death, destruction, sex, and violence. I will do my best to tell the story with the wonder and spirituality of a Red State Sunday school teacher. Here it goes.

"Before Samson was born an angel came to his mother and told her that she was going to have a very special son. The angel also told Samson's mother that she was not to cut her son's hair. It was here that Samson held all of his strength. Cut Samson's hair and Samson becomes a normal man.

"Samson grew up and became a very strong man. He was a man who was able to kill a lion with his bare hands. He was so strong that he was able to kill one thousand Philistines with the jawbone of a donkey. He did all of this with the help of the Lord. God told Him that he would keep his strength as long as he would stay obedient to the Lord and never cut his hair.

"Then one day, he met a woman named Delilah. She was an evil Philistine whore. She seduced the great Samson with her beautiful brown eyes, soft skin, and supple bosom. She became Samson's girlfriend. Apparently, Samson liked "dark meat." The leaders of the pagan Philistines told Delilah that it was her job to find out Samson's secret. Why was he so strong?

"Because Delilah was a Philistine and an ungodly slut, she did what her evil leaders told her. The Philistines were agents of Satan. This treacherous woman found out Samson's secret and told the Philistines that his strength was in his hair. Cut his hair and Samson loses his strength.

"One night, Samson awoke to find that his hair had been cut. All of his strength was gone. God was not happy. He never should have told a Philistine his secret, no matter how seductive and pretty she was. Remember children, something similar happened to Adam and now all of us live in sin.

"Samson was going to pay for his mistake.

"The Philistines captured Samson, took out their sharpest knife, and cut out his eyes. With his eyeballs rolling in the dirt, the bloody and newly blind Samson was sent to prison. All seemed lost for the once great Samson.

"For some time, Samson was in prison. But it was during this time that a miracle happened. Samson's hair continued to grow and he regained some of his strength. But being blind, Samson found revenge difficult. He was going to need the Lord.

"One day, the Philistines became boastful and paraded the blind Samson in front of the Philistines at one of their pagan, devilish, satanic celebrations. While the Philistines cheered and mocked the once great Samson, God became very angry. As luck would have it, the Philistines placed Samson right between two great pillars that were holding up the palace.

"Samson asked God for one more act of strength so he could destroy all of the Philistines. Samson said, 'O Lord God, remember me, I pray thee, and strengthen me, I pray thee, only this once, O God, that I may be avenged upon the Philistines for one of my two eyes.'

"The Lord answered Samson's prayers and gave him all of his strength back. Samson, still standing between the two pillars, pushed them with all of his might. The Philistine palace began to shake, rattle, and roll. All of the Philistines began to scream in fear and trembling. The leaders of the Philistines had worry on their faces.

"Samson begged to God, 'Let me die with the Philistines.' Samson's prayer was answered as the building shook and crumbled to its foundation. Everything was destroyed. All of the heathen Philistines were killed. Samson killed more Philistines on that day than he killed in his whole life.

"Unfortunately, Samson was killed also. His brothers came to the temple, found his body, and took his corpse home. They buried him with honor and sadness.

"The lesson, little children, is this: Don't mess with the Lord…and don't have sex with Philistines.

Anyone want a cupcake?"

I bet Delilah was smokin' hot…a dishonest Philistine woman, Oh man! She probably had dark, sultry eyes, luscious lips, nice cans, and a firm butt. She must have looked like Jessica Alba or that Mexican lady from *Desperate Housewives*.

I'm a little like Samson. I've always had a thing for Philistines.

But I digress. Samson destroys a city and gets his revenge, but it is with God's help. The only real problem is that Samson died while taking down his enemies. I wonder if there is some sort of message in that? Even though Samson got his revenge, he died anyway. What the hell was the point?

Now, God got His revenge, and we need to believe Him when He says that vengeance is His. Unfortunately, God does leave some wiggle room for humans to enact revenge on their own.

There is so much violence, punishment, and retribution in the Old Testament that it becomes difficult for people to know where the orders for revenge come from. For example, in the famous "eye for an eye" order to humans in Leviticus, "When a man causes a disfigurement in his neighbor, as he has done it shall be done to him, fracture for fracture, eye for eye, tooth for tooth; as he has disfigured a man, he shall be disfigured" (Leviticus 24:19–20), God does not make it clear that, if a man does get his eye plucked out and he plucks out the eye of his eye plucker outer, is it God doing it or if it is the man doing it? Who is enacting the revenge, God or man? It is hard to say.

Blindness

This is why Jesus brought a new way. His way lessens the confusion. Jesus is pretty direct when it comes to things like this. His message is clear: as people, we are to build our kingdom in Heaven and not bother with "earthly matters." There is little doubt that revenge is an earthly matter. Retribution is not eternal. So when Jesus is confronted with the law of His Father, "an eye for an eye" as appropriate revenge, He takes a step back and not only ignores this law, but changes it. His words, known by all who have ever been to church, are pretty straightforward. This, once again, is right at the beginning of the New Testament in the book of Matthew, one of the most liberal rags ever written. Jesus says, "You have heard that it was said, 'An eye for an eye and a tooth for a tooth. But I say to you, do not resist one who is evil. But if any one strikes you on the right cheek, turn to him the other also." (Matthew 5:38) Jesus doesn't just make a strong statement against revenge; He renders the law of the Old Testament virtually meaningless. People should not, under any circumstances, exact revenge. It is that simple. Jesus, the most radical liberal of all time, continues by saying that not only are we supposed to avoid revenge, but we are also supposed to love our enemies.

You gotta be frickin' kidding me!

> You have heard that it was said, 'You shall love your neighbor and hate your enemy.' But I say to you, Love your enemies and pray for those who persecute you, so that you may be sons of your Father who is in Heaven; for He makes his sun rise on the evil and on the good, and sends rain on the just and on the unjust. For if you love those who love you, what reward have you? Do not even the tax collectors do the same? And if you salute only your brethren, what more are you doing than others? Do not even the Gentiles do the same? You, therefore, must be perfect, as your heavenly Father is perfect. (Matthew 5:43–48)

This doctrine of loving your enemies, is the most radical in religious history. In a world dominated by religious strife, warfare, and death, Jesus tells His people to avoid all of it. Revenge on Earth is the path to spiritual destruction. We are supposed to love our enemies. We are supposed to pray for those who do us harm. We are supposed to strive for perfection on Earth so we can be with our perfect Father for all eternity.

There cannot be any misunderstanding of this instruction. It is simple. It is honest. It is beyond misinterpretation. People simply ignore it. Revenge is better. Revenge feels good. Revenge makes us happy on Earth. However, it leaves us blind just like our aggressors, blind just like Samson and dead just like Samson. Yep, Jesus had a new way and, as with so many of His other teachings, we choose to ignore it.

The problem for our leaders in government, who want to claim Christ as their God, is that it is nearly impossible to have a doctrine of nonviolence and operate a nation in a very violent world. Governments not only need to defend the interests of their people, but they also must oppress and enact revenge on those who threaten them. This is not the Christian way.

When the nonviolent philosophy of Jesus was practiced en masse during the twentieth century, it was used against a government, not by a government. The two most famous governments embarrassed into submission by nonviolence were the colonialist British Empire in India and our very own United

States government during the Civil Rights movement. Jesus inspired this movement and Gandhi practiced it in India. It was here that the nonviolent movement as a way to subdue oppressors got its start.

Martin Luther King Jr. brought it to the United States as part of the Civil Rights movement, and, low and behold, it worked. An entire area of the country, (Red State governments in the South) was attacked by a bunch of liberal Christian pacifists. And the liberal Christian pacifists won. They shamed the Red State conservative segregationists! How do ya like them apples? Jesus was right, again. The Brits left India. They left it a mess, but they stopped colonial rule. Likewise, the South was integrated. It was Gandhi who elaborated the message of Christ, "An eye for an eye makes the whole world blind." The evangelical Red State Christians probably think Gandhi is burning in Hell because he wasn't "saved." But he was right, and he did lead his people in a very radical Christian manner.

Hell, Paul even agrees with Jesus on this one. Paul says,

> If possible, so far as it depends upon you, live peaceably with all. Beloved, never avenge yourselves, but leave it to the wrath of God; for it is written, 'Vengeance is mine, I will repay, says the Lord.' No, if your enemy is hungry, feed him; if he is thirsty, give him drink; for by so doing you will heap burning coals upon his head. Do not be overcome by evil, but overcome evil with good. (Romans 13:18–21)

Paul starts off on the right track, but eventually he misses the point once again. Paul cracks me up. Any time there is a profound Christian message, Paul is right there to help us screw it up. In a stroke of comic genius, Paul doesn't quite get the full impact of Jesus' message about avoiding the pitfalls of revenge. While Paul might be speaking in metaphor that, by being good to our enemies, we are causing them discomfort, he still has to insert the element of divine revenge into the equation. He is too good to be true. He wants us to be good to our enemy now, so God can get him later. "Give him drink" now; "pour burning coals on his head" later. What is he talking about? Why not just be like Jesus and repay evil with good? That is the message. Forget about cosmic revenge. Paul always has to contradict Jesus.

Bush Family Revenge: the Good Son

So how does the "blindness of revenge" impact our modern-day situation of being involved in a war we can't seem to get out of? It is important to remember that we are in this situation because God's choice for the presidency made the decision to invade Iraq based on his faith. It seems a bit absurd, but it is the situation that we are in. It doesn't look too good for our collective soul. It is hard to understand how a man (George W. Bush) can claim Christ as his savior and invade another country (Iraq) for suspect reasons. This shows his (George W. Bush's) lack of faith in His (Jesus Christ's) teachings. It is unfortunate for the soul of Mr. Bush, but tragic for the American soldiers and the Iraqi civilians.

So let's start at the beginning of this mess. The United States is invaded in the form of hijacked airplanes flown into the World Trade Centers in New York. Al Qaeda, led by Osama Bin Laden, proudly claims responsibility. Afghanistan, led by the conservative Taliban, has been harboring Bin Laden and his crew of assholes for years. Ultimately, after repeated warnings, the United States attacks Afghanistan, seeking to destroy the Taliban and bring Osama Bin Laden to justice. So far, this Blue State liberal is with the Commander-in-Chief. Turning Afghanistan upside down and capturing Osama Bin Laden was fine with me.

While I acknowledge the message of Jesus to turn the other cheek, it is something that under certain circumstances I am unwilling to abide by. Again, I don't declare Heaven as my ultimate destination. There are quite a few things that Jesus says, that I can't enact in my life although I understand the morality of them. This whole notion of "loving our enemies" is one of them. I was one of the people understanding the need to turn Afghanistan into a parking lot on the way to finding Bin Laden and bringing him to justice.

The only problem is, somewhere along the way, like Jesus says, our lust for revenge made us blind. Out of nowhere, the fortunate son (George W. Bush) decided to seek his own personal revenge on the enemy (Saddam Hussein) of the father (George Bush. Sr.). So the United States of America invaded Iraq. Those people who think that the invasion of Iraq was not a Bush family act of revenge should ask themselves one question and answer it honestly. If Al Gore had been president and the World Trade Centers had been attacked in the same way, would he have invaded Iraq? There is no f'in' way.

The dutiful son, George W. Bush, as a tribute to his father, went after Saddam Hussein's head. He got it. Now, more than three years after the World Trade Centers fell, the Taliban is gone, but Osama Bin Laden is still on the loose. Saddam Hussein is in an Iraqi prison, and we are stuck in an Iraqi quagmire.

The Lies of the Chickenhawk

A lot has been written and discussed by liberal pundits suggesting that we were led into the Iraq War by a pack of cowardly "chickenhawks." This is undoubtedly true as the Bush administration is filled with people who did everything possible to avoid serving their country in times of war. Now, years after avoiding service they call upon the patriotism of others to do their dirty work.

During the 2004 presidential campaign, we all became aware of George Bush's flight from the National Guard and John Kerry's apparent cowardice in Vietnam. Kerry's dutiful service was somehow twisted into something less than noble by noted chickenhawk and coward Karl Rove. While Kerry did serve, our leaders in the Bush administration did not.

For example, Dick Cheney a man who continually challenges the patriotism of anyone against the Iraq War took four student deferments during the Vietnam War. After two drunk-driving convictions cancelled these deferments, he was granted a paternity deferment. John Ashcroft who successfully fought to take away the freedoms of innocent Americans with the Patriot Act took a deferment to teach business school. Karl Rove, yes the same Karl Rove who slang enough conservative mud to successfully brand both John Kerry and John McCain as war serving cowards, did not request any deferments; he was able to avoid the conflict entirely.

Requesting deferments to avoid military service is not against the law. The fact that these men requested deferments would be acceptable if they were not at the forefront of our present situation which has us in the middle of a war without an end. Simply put, many Americans would have applied for multiple deferments to avoid serving in a war just like Cheney, Ashcroft, Paul Wolfowitz (school deferment), Dennis Hastert (medical deferment), Bill Bennett (school deferment), Rush Limbaugh (ingrown hair on his butt), Bill O'Reilly (College Deferment), Newt Gingrich (graduate school deferment), and Trent Lott (hardship exemption).1 But, most of these Americans would not abuse their power and promote a war that puts hundreds of thousands in harms way.

The lies and mismanagement of this war are obvious and as bit players in this conflict many people in the Bush administration have been able to avoid the scrutiny that comes with being a lying chickenhawk. George W. Bush, because he is the president and constantly in the public eye has left a trail of inaccurate statements in support of the Iraq War.

President Bush used the myth of "Weapons of Mass Destruction" (WMD) as his justification for invading another country. He declared to the United Nations, "Iraq is the central front in the war on terror."2 Other evidence does not support this assertion. For example, Fox News, of all places, cited a study by the Jaffee Center for Strategic Studies at Tel Aviv University which says, "instead of striking a blow against Islamic extremists, the Iraq war 'has created momentum for many terrorist elements, chiefly Al Qaeda and its affiliates.'"3

Furthermore, numerous authorities have completely debunked the myth that Iraq had WMD, which was our strongest reason for invading Iraq.

Let's start with a bit of a presidential timeline following the claim by the Bush presidency that Iraq was loaded with WMD. This was the reason the Bush administration gave for the invasion of Iraq, which led us down the slippery slope of "blind man's revenge." On counterpunch.com, there is a timeline of quotes called "Who said what When" regarding WMD.4 It is some pretty interesting stuff. These are only a few of the entries:

September 12, 2002: Right now, Iraq is expanding and improving facilities that were used for the production of biological weapons. **(George W. Bush)**

February 8, 2003: We have sources that tell us that Saddam Hussein recently authorized Iraqi field commanders to use chemical weapons—the very weapons the dictator tells us he does not have. **(George W. Bush)**

March 18, 2003: Intelligence gathered by this and other governments leaves no doubt that the Iraq regime continues to possess and conceal some of the most lethal weapons ever devised. **(George W. Bush)**

April 24, 2003: We are learning more as we interrogate or have discussions with Iraqi scientists and people within the Iraqi structure, that perhaps he destroyed some, perhaps he dispersed some. And so we will find them. **(George W. Bush)**

May 3, 2003: We'll find them. It'll be a matter of time to do so. **(George W. Bush)**

May 6, 2003: I'm not surprised if we begin to uncover the weapons program of Saddam Hussein—because he had a weapons program. **(George W. Bush)**

May 12, 2003: The United States never expected that "we were going to open garages and find" weapons of mass destruction. **(Condoleeza Rice)**

May 27, 2003: They may have had time to destroy them, and I don't know the answer. **(Donald Rumsfeld)**

May 28, 2003: For bureaucratic reasons, we settled on one issue, weapons of mass destruction (as justification for invading Iraq) because it was the one reason everyone could agree on.
(Paul Wolfowitz)

March 25, 2004: Those weapons of mass destruction have got to be here somewhere.
(George W. Bush, joking at the 60th annual dinner of the Radio and Television Correspondents' Association)

March 26, 2004: If George Bush thinks his deceptive rationale for going to war is a laughing matter, then he's even more out of touch than we thought. Unfortunately for the president, this is not a joke.
(John Kerry)

September 9, 2004: I recognize we didn't find the stockpiles [of weapons] we all thought were there.
(George W. Bush)

There are more George Bush contradictions. This time he is found trying to link Saddam Hussein to the World Trade Center bombings. His efforts were in vain.

September 2002: You can't distinguish between Al Qaeda and Saddam when you talk about the war on terror...they're both equally as bad, and equally as evil, and equally as destructive.5

Two years later, President Bush "waffles" on his once confident assertion.

September 2004: We've had no evidence that Saddam Hussein was involved with September 11th.6

With some prompting and two years without any evidence to support his claims, George W. Bush was actually able to tell the truth. But it was too late. His lies and incompetence caught up with him. Our "Christian" president, with God at his side, let all of us down. He became the evil dictator, pursuing a personal agenda in the name of revenge. And we, with the help of the Red States, reelected his sorry ass.

The problem is that the deception never stops. Most liberals, at least to some degree, are familiar with the Downing Street Memo. This report was a transcribed meeting with the Prime Minister of England eight months before the Iraq War started. This document includes the following "impressions" of the closest ally of the United States.

> Military action was now seen as inevitable. Bush wanted to remove Saddam, through military action, justified by the conjunction of terrorism and WMD.

> No decisions had been taken, but he thought the most likely timing in US minds for military action to begin was January, with the timeline beginning 30 days before the US Congressional elections.

> And...

> The intelligence and facts were being fixed around the policy.7

This is quite disturbing. If we are to believe this memo, the Bush administration knew they were going to attack Iraq and with or without evidence linking Saddam Hussein with the 9/11 attacks or with or without evidence supporting the claims of WMD. It is even more troublesome that the conflict was set to begin in conjunction with congressional elections. All of the lies of this administration would lead a normal American to give the Downing Street Memo some credence.

There is a trickle down effect to all of these lies as well. This occurrence was no more evident than in the tragedy surrounding American hero and former professional football player Pat Tillman, whose death was manipulated by a branch of the military struggling under the pressure of a failing war.

Immediately following the death of Pat Tillman, the Army told a story of a brave soldier dying in combat. Tillman was declared an American hero who was killed by the unforgiving enemy. As it turns out, soldiers who knew the truth about his death at the hands of friendly fire, were under orders to keep silent Tillman's funeral was used not only as a recruiting tool but as a reminder of the battle against and increasingly evil enemy.

After the truth about this accidental death was told, Tillman's mother Mary was outraged and went public with her displeasure and heartbreak telling the Washington Post, "The military let him down. The administration let him down. It was a sign of disrespect. The fact that he was the ultimate team player and he watched his own men kill him is absolutely heartbreaking and tragic. The fact that they lied about it afterward is disgusting."8

The lies of the Bush administration have been mounting since before the Iraq War even started. Should anyone really be surprised? Chickenhawks, unless they are religious dictators, should never be put in charge of a military conflict. Perhaps this is the reason Colin Powell, a decorated military hero, stepped down from his position as Secretary-of-State. His replacement, Condoleeza Rice, is just another in the long line of people willing to participate in the dishonesty and incompetence of the George W. Bush administration and his effort to exact personal revenge.

Guilty Man and Guiltless Society

About ten years ago, when I was trying to be an intellectual—it didn't work, I read a book regarding the difference between individual morality and group morality. The title of the book was *Moral Man, Immoral Society* by Reinhold Neibuhr. In it, Neibuhr makes the strong case that, when acting alone, human beings tend to be moral and ethical creatures. The opposite is true when it comes to the morality of the group. The result is a mob mentality. This is an oversimplification of his thesis, but he makes some strong points in defending this notion.

The reason why I bring this up here is that I think it is interesting to note how much in the name of government, politics, and war that a group is able to get away with in the name of revenge. If we take the actions that George W. Bush used while pursuing his personal agenda during "the War on Terror" and assigned similar actions to an individual pursuing personal revenge, it becomes clear that the actions of Bush are completely unethical and beyond misguided. These blind acts of revenge are absolutely evil and, by the standards of our legal system, totally illegal.

The judicial system in the United States is the envy of the world. While it is not perfect, our system strives to afford all of its citizens equal rights and equal protection under the law. Since our system is so respected, I think it is appropriate to relate the way that our nation has acted under our president and compare it to a similar situation of an average American citizen whose family has been attacked by an unfriendly outsider.

Let's say that my brother was killed in a violent attack. I know the culprit and I am going after him. The problem is that he left the country and my government is not willing to extradite him and bring him to justice. I then make the decision that I must pursue revenge for this attack and loss of life on my own. Nobody else is going to help me, so I decide to track down my nemesis.

After a few months of looking in vain for the man that I know killed my brother, I get frustrated. However, in a stroke of luck I identify his second cousin. I know him to be an evil scumbag because in the past he publicly humiliated my father. Losing sight of my original mission of tracking down my brother's killer, I seek revenge on his second cousin, my father's nemesis.

I enlist the help of some friends by telling them that the second cousin of my brother's killer knew about the murder and is planning more murder against my family. My friends and I attack his house and imprison him. We even kill some of his family. All the while, the perpetrator of the original crime continues to hide successfully, and I don't even worry about looking for him anymore. I am busy with his second cousin and his family. Later, some of my friends tell me that they heard that the guy who killed my brother hates his second cousin and he thinks it is funny that we attacked the wrong guy.

A few months after that, some of my friends become disgruntled and find out that, while the second cousin was an evil man, he did not murder my brother and that he barely knew my brother's true killer. They now believe that they are in way over their heads. They have the blood of innocents on their hands and they don't want to help me clean up the newly razed house of my father's former enemy. My friends go to the authorities and turn me in. I am arrested for the murder and property damage against the second cousin of my brother's murderer.

What would the defense be at my trial? True, I lost a loved one, but in the United States, we have laws against taking revenge into our own hands. It is illegal. Furthermore, the authorities are going to be totally confused at my course of action. If my only mission was the revenge of my brothers' death, why did I attack the house of the second cousin of my brother's murderer? My defense of saying that it was because he is the enemy of my family and might have attacked me at some point is more than a little presumptuous. In my criminal trial, the prosecutors may agree with me that the second cousin was a criminal. However, my fate would be sealed when the prosecutors make it perfectly clear to the judge and jury that the second-cousin of my enemy was not going to attack anyone because he wasn't strong enough.

All the while, because of my misguided lust for revenge, some of my friends are dead, and some innocent bystanders who just happened to be in the wrong house at the wrong time have also been killed. The prosecutors tell me that, if I had just gone after my brother's killer, found him, and turned him in, I would have been a hero. Now, they tell me that my poor judgment in pursuit of my personal blind revenge has led to deaths of innocent people and a house that needs to be rebuilt. They also tell me that I am to be charged with multiple counts of first-degree murder.

I am pretty sure that my actions would put me in the category of Charles Manson or some other psychopath who, while not having the balls to kill anyone themselves (George W. Bush, Dick Cheney, Donald Rumsfeld), convinced other people to do the killing for them (the United States military and the coalition forces). It's pretty shameful behavior.

The result would be that I lost some of my friends and family, my brother's killer is still on the loose, and I am headed to jail for a pretty long time. My sentence would, at the very least, be life without parole, like Charles Manson, another psychopath who convinced others to do his insane dirty work for him. Furthermore, if I lived in Texas, the home state of the Bush family, I certainly would be executed.

Tragically, in my efforts to exact revenge, I went from being a heroic avenger of the death of my innocent brother to a misguided lunatic. Jesus and Gandhi were right: "an eye for an eye" does leave the world "blind." In the case of the war in Iraq, the mob (our governmental leaders led by George W. Bush) invaded a country that was not involved in the original attack on the World Trade Center. Now we are in the middle of a war. But what the hell! The men who declared the war are safe and sound. Neither Bush, nor Donald Rumsfeld, nor Dick Cheney, nor John Ashcroft, nor Karl Rove, nor Condoleeza Rice, nor Bill Frist, nor Bill O'Reilly are actually fighting in the war. It is really no big deal...for them.

Neibuhr was right. The group not only acts differently than the individual, but the leaders of the mob are also held to a different standard. They get away with murder.

Lame "Soundbites" from a Lying Sack of Crap

Before I get into some casualty reports and the next game of *Red State, Blue State*, it is important to address the justification by George W. Bush, Dick Cheney, and Karl Rove for invading a country that had nothing to do with the attack on American soil.

Ever since it was discovered that there were no WMD in Iraq, the Bush administration has had to come up with other reasons for sending American soldiers and citizens off to another country to fight and die in a suspect war for suspect reasons. George W. Bush isn't going to admit that this was revenge for his father's failures. He isn't going to admit that he went to war without some kind of political or moral justification. So beyond the production of weapons, Bush chose two other reasons to justify his war.

The first reason was that Saddam Hussein is an evil dictator who was oppressing his people. There is little doubt that George W. Bush is right on this one. Saddam Hussein is a bad man, and the people of Iraq were struggling during his leadership. But does that justify a mass invasion that has cost thousands of American and Iraqi lives? There are dictators all over the world destroying their countries in the name of selfishness, and we don't invade every one of them. If we go after dictators, why not invade and oust Kim Jong-il of North Korea, Fidel Castro of Cuba, Than Shwe of Burma, Hu Jintao of China, Robert Mugabe of Zimbabwe, or Crown Prince Abdullah of Saudi Arabia? The list of dictators destroying their own countries is literally endless. Yet, we only chose to go after only one. Is it a coincidence that, instead of invading Iran, Saudi Arabia, or Syria, we chose Iraq? George W. Bush had his choices of dictators to remove from power and he picked one. He chose the one who embarrassed his father. He could have just left well enough alone and continued to pursue Osama Bin Laden. President Bush would have been a national hero for all time. Instead, the good son chose to exact retribution in the name of the incompetent father.

The second George W. Bush battle cry is the cry for world freedom. This, after his WMD fiasco and his concerns about removing dictators from power fell on deaf ears, became his favorite reason for starting a war. Yep, the good ol' U.S.A. needs to spread freedom throughout an oppressed and unhappy world. President Bush provided us with some great, deceptive, and hypocritical sound bites on this issue.

In the 2004 State of the Union address, Bush insists that the invasion of Iraq was in the defense of the strongest nation in the history of the world.

> Our greatest responsibility is the active defense of the American people.9

I didn't know we had to be protected from a Third World nation. Since we are the freest country in the world, we must spread our most prized asset throughout the world, even if we need to use force to do it.

> We are serving in freedom's cause—and that is the cause of all mankind.10

This is a nice sentiment. But is it necessary for thousands of United States citizens to die fighting for another county's freedom when its citizens never even asked for our help?

Bush invokes a call for personal responsibility in the fight for freedom.

> History has called America and our allies to action, and it is both our responsibility and our privilege to fight freedom's fight.11

Notice that George W. Bush says that it is our responsibility and privilege to fight. Let's get this shit straight. George W. Bush isn't fighting anyone. He is and always will be a coward who has other people fight his battles for him. President Bush is safe and sound in the White House, surrounded by millions of dollars in personal security and millions more in fine china. This was his war, and he is not fighting in it. There is a big difference between living life in the lap of luxury, protected by others, and being on the front lines in the middle of a desert.

Here George Bush invokes the name of God to support his view of the world. Americans are a free people, who know that freedom is the right of every person and the future of every nation.

> The liberty we prize is not America's gift to the world; it is God's gift to humanity.12

Using God to justify a bad war that is costing two nations thousands of lives is blaspheme in its worst form. This is truly reminiscent of Hitler invoking the name of God while murdering Jews and trying to control all of Europe.

However, President Bush wants to make sure that people in other countries do not consider the United States a religious bully.

> We have no intention of imposing our culture—but America will always stand firm for the non-negotiable demands of human dignity.13

The fact is that George W. Bush *is* trying to impose our culture on another culture. It isn't working, because that part of the world is becoming more and more anti-American every day. Even though we have a better way, that doesn't give us the right to force it down another nation's throat. And remember, according to the first quote, this invasion was supposed to be about defending America, not about spreading freedom.

It's hard to believe, but a man who wants to take rights away from American citizens tries to promote freedom to countries struggling under the yoke of religious oppression.

> Whenever people are given a choice in the matter, they prefer lives of freedom to lives of fear.14

This is another nice thought, but, in a time of invasion, everyone is in fear. Is the fear different if a foreign aggressor or a homegrown dictator imposes it? Needless to say, Iraqi citizens are living in just as much fear now as they were under Saddam Hussein. Who knows? It might even be worse.

Here is some more on freedom from the man who does not want all freedoms extended to all people in his own country.

> We believe that freedom can advance and change lives in the greater Middle East as it has advanced and changed lives in Asia, in Latin America, in Eastern Europe and Africa.15

Bush is now so desperate and delusional that he thinks a poorly planned war is going to spread freedom. This war is making America look like an incompetent bully. Last time I checked, bullies don't inspire freedom.

Our increasingly delusional president tries to put a positive spin on a war that even he knows was a mistake.

> My fellow citizens, the dangers to our country and the world will be overcome. We will pass through this time of peril and carry on the work of peace. We will defend our freedom. We will bring freedom to others and we will prevail.16

Here's a news flash for President Bush! Attacking another country for suspect reason can never be considered "the work of peace." Furthermore, the war in Iraq is going much worse than anyone ever expected. Iraqi civilians are still living in fear and do not have any more freedom now than when we arrived. American soldiers are being forced to stay in Iraq beyond their original deployment. This is like a kidnapping. Coalition members are looking for ways out. This is hardly a decisive victory that is bringing freedom to others. Both nations are losing hope that this quagmire will ever end.

Finally, President Bush blames Iraq for all of this mess. Remember, we attacked them.

> Our enemies in Iraq are good at filling hospitals, but they don't build any. They can incite men to murder and suicide, but they cannot inspire men to live in hope and add to the progress of their country.17

Does anyone remember what Jesus said about all of this? "But I say to you, Do not resist one who is evil. But if any one strikes you on the right cheek, turn to him the other also." (Matthew 5:39) Jesus doesn't say, "If someone strikes you, chase him, and, if you can't catch up with him, get an army of innocents to attack someone else and their innocents." Talk about a blind, arrogant man missing the point!

George W. Bush continually attacks Saddam Hussein and Osama Bin Laden as evil, murdering, terrorist dictator scum. How about a little self-evaluation in this area? George W. Bush talks about the evil that Iraqi citizens had to face under the reign of Hussein. He talks about terrorists attacking innocent people for reasons of hate. Bush talks about the children—suffer the children; they need to be saved.

According to iraqbodycount.org, it has been estimated that 30,000 Iraqi citizens have died during this war.18 Other reports including one from the Washington Post put that figure closer to 100,000. Never forget that it was the United States who started it. Saddam Hussein did not attack us and was not going to attack us. We attacked him. Now, the paragon of virtue and freedom (the United States of America) has blood on its hands, to the tune of what may be 100,000 dead Iraqi citizens.

I have no doubt that many of these people were evil scumbags. Likewise, it is obvious that thousands of others were innocent men, women, or children. Now, they are dead because of a war George W. Bush and Dick Cheney started, a war started in the name of self-defense, WMD, eliminating a dictator, spreading freedom, blah blah blah. It is all bullshit. My point here is that it is better for Saddam Hussein, or any other dictator for that matter, to kill his own people rather than having America do the killing for him. This diminishes our democracy and condemns our soul.

The John McCain Presidential Campaign Begins

Since this particular act of revenge is going badly, it is no wonder that many patriotic Americans are jumping off the George W. Bush war bandwagon. However, now it is the Red State conservatives who are starting to question the direction of our military invasion of Iraq.

The hypocrisy of the Red State Republican politicians knows no bounds. In the build up to the November election, Republicans everywhere were unanimous in their patriotic and consistent cries that George W. Bush was the man who would lead us to victory in Iraq.

One month after the election, he began losing support—not from Blue State Democrats, but from Red State Republicans. The lightning rod seems to be the poor old Bush family servant, Donald Rumsfeld. It is he who will be the fall guy for the failed act of Bush family revenge.

There are three Republican senators leading the criticism of the embattled Secretary of Defense: John McCain, Red State Republican from Arizona; Trent Lott, Red State Republican from Mississippi; and Charles Hagel, Red State Republican from Nebraska.

First up is John McCain. Here is what he thinks about poor Mr. Rumsfeld.

"I said no. My answer is still no. No confidence."19

McCain continues.

I have strenuously argued for larger troop numbers in Iraq, including the right kind of troops—linguists, special forces, civil affairs, etc. There are very strong differences of opinion between myself and Secretary Rumsfeld on that issue.20

Now it is Chuck Hagel's turn.

I have no confidence in Rumsfeld. The fact is, we're in deep trouble in Iraq…and I think we're going to have to look at some recalibration of policy.21

Amazingly enough, Trent Lott was able to defend a couple of notorious Southern racists. However, he cannot find it in his heart to stand up for the embattled Donald Rumsfeld.

I don't think he listens to his uniformed officers. I would like to see a change in that slot in the next year or so.22

In spite of all of the controversy, George W. Bush defends his man.

I know Secretary Rumsfeld's heart. I know how much he cares for the troops. He's a good, decent man. He's a caring fellow.23

Liberals never had confidence in Rumsfeld. Why does it take Red State politicians so much time to figure out the obvious?

I believe they knew it all along.

Everyone, politicians included, is entitled to an opinion. The problem here is that we just went through a national election in which the people in the Republican Party hailed George W. Bush as the only man that could be successful in Iraq. If memory serves me correctly, a decorated military hero—not

John McCain, but John Kerry—was consistently ridiculed as waffling on the issues surrounding this war. He was in support of the war; then, as the Bush administration lies started to expose themselves, he came to the conclusion that we were fighting a losing battle. He was ridiculed for a change of opinion based on his intelligence and morality. The conservative response to Kerry's change of heart and criticism was to brand a past military hero as both un-American and weak.

Now after the election, Republicans are telling us that we are in trouble. Isn't that convenient? Why now? Why didn't Red State politicians declare their lack of confidence in Rumsfeld earlier? Blue State liberals knew Rumsfeld was mishandling this operation for a long time. The answer is obvious. If they would have declared a lack of confidence in Donald Rumsfeld in October, a month before the election rather than a month after it, George W. Bush might have lost the election.

These dishonest Red State politicians couldn't break ranks before the election, so they broke ranks after the election. They had to have a Republican victory, even if it cost more American lives overseas. These guys expect their followers to believe that they are political heroes who are busy protecting the interests of the American soldier serving overseas. Bullshit. They are serving themselves and their political affiliation, and then they have the audacity to call themselves patriots.

When we leave Iraq, if we ever leave, there will not be a pristine, shining example of democracy inspiring Middle Eastern nations. Iraq and the Middle East are going to be a mess, just like they were when we got there.

Remember Jesus, your Savior, who said, "An eye for an eye leaves the whole world blind"? These guys played party politics and supported God's man so they could get another four years in the White House for their political party. Their dishonesty is sickening.

Finally, and make no mistake about it, by criticizing Donald Rumsfeld, John McCain has started his run for the White House in 2008. He knows he can't win the presidency unless he starts to criticize a floundering Republican president and his confused administration. The problem for us liberals is that it's going to work.

John McCain is using the struggles of the United States military effort in Iraq to further his political career. There is no doubt in my mind that, in three years, John McCain will announce that he is running for the presidency. His platform will be anti-Bush, just like the 2004 platform of John Kerry. He will be going after the vote of Blue State liberals and other moderates.

Because McCain knows the Bush administration and the effort in Iraq will be failures, he is immediately distancing himself from the Bush presidency.

This is just another example of Red State hypocrisy and lies, from the next president of the Untied States, Red Stater John McCain. Blue State liberals and Democrats better wake up now, or this shit will never end.

All of this leads us to another game of *Red State, Blue State*. This edition of the now famous game does not deal with Iraqi deaths—they don't count—but with the deaths of United States citizens fighting for another country's freedom.

Red State, Blue State: Over Two Thousand Reasons Why We Have already Lost the War

When contemplating my revenge issue of this game, I could only come up with one thing. Is it possible to discover whether there is a trend regarding American casualties and what states these American citizens come from? Will there be an answer to whether or not one group of states is bearing more of the burden of casualties than another group of states?

First of all, as of November 13, 2005, the Department of Defense has confirmed that 2056 Americans have been killed in Iraq. Additionally, there have been 190 people from other coalition countries who have been killed during the war. Obviously, America is shouldering the vast majority of the burden not only of fighting the war, but also in surrendering lives. It was our idea, so I guess we must bear the burden.

Iraq War casualties by state as of November 13, 2005

Rank	State	Number of Fatalities	Red or Blue
1	California	217	Blue
2	Texas	183	Red
3	Pennsylvania	105	Blue
4	Ohio	98	Red
5	New York	97	Blue
6	Florida	89	Red
7	Illinois	81	Blue
8	Michigan	65	Red
9	Georgia	61	Red
10	Virginia	59	Blue
11	Arizona	51	Red
12	Louisiana	48	Red
	Wisconsin	48	Blue
14	Tennessee	46	Red

15	North Carolina	44	Red
16	Indiana	41	Red
17	Washington	40	Red
18	New Jersey	38	Blue
19	Alabama	34	Red
20	Oregon	33	Blue
	Mississippi	33	Red
	Oklahoma	33	Red
23	South Carolina	32	Red
	Kentucky	32	Red
25	Maryland	31	Blue
	Massachusetts	31	Blue
27	Missouri	30	Red
28	Arkansas	29	Red
	Colorado	29	Red
30	Minnesota	26	Blue
31	Iowa	24	Red
32	Kansas	20	Red
	Nebraska	20	Red
34	Connecticut	18	Blue
35	New Mexico	14	Red
	West Virginia	14	Red
	Vermont	14	Blue
38	Idaho	13	Red
	Nevada	13	Red
40	South Dakota	11	Red
41	Montana	10	Red
	North Dakota	10	Red
43	Maine	9	Blue
	Utah	9	Red
45	Delaware	8	Blue
	Rhode Island	8	Blue
47	New Hampshire	7	Blue
48	Wyoming	6	Red
	Hawaii	6	Blue
50	Alaska	5	Red
51	Washington D.C.	3	Blue

Source: Iraq Casualty Count, 13 November 2005 icasualties.org
<http://icasualties.org/oif/ByState.aspx>

The Web site icausualties.org also lists the following casualties from the United States forces from the following countries or protectorates (American Samoa 5, England 1, Guam 1, Guatemala 1, Northern Marianas Islands 3, Puerto Rico 17, and Virgin Islands 3). These numbers are changing just about every day. It is also very disturbing to note that there have been two months that had significantly higher rates of casualties than other months. The most recent of these two months was January, the month that preceded the Iraqi elections. During January 2005, 127 American soldiers were killed in Iraq, an average of 4.1 casualties per day.

The other month with a high number of American casualties was November of 2004. That's right, the month that George Bush was elected president of the United States, which signaled our continued occupation of Iraq. During November 2004, 141 Americans were killed, an average of 4.7 per day.

There are some trends that can be detected between Red State and Blue State casualties. Five of the top ten are Red States and the other five are Blue States. Likewise, five of the bottom ten states are Red and the other five are Blue. However, out of the 1756 total casualties as of November 13, 2005, 1138 (55.5%) are from Red States, 885 (43%) are from Blue States, and 32 (1.5%) are from the protectorates. The conclusion: Red States are losing more soldiers than Blue States.

After the recent Iraqi elections, I was one of many Americans who got all warm and fuzzy inside and, for about a day, I thought that maybe the war could be justified because of the election. As I continued to hear reports of more suicide bombings, more attacks on Iraqi police and military, more American deaths, more mounting national debt, more proposed cuts to services in America, and more insanity from other countries (North Korea and Iran to name only two), I came to my senses. Iraq, and much of the world, is still in a state of chaos, and one act of Bush family revenge, even if it results in one election, isn't going to change any of that. The warm and fuzzy feeling went away pretty quickly.

Now, I am well aware that it is difficult to make a game out of a casualty report. But, without getting overly liberal, war is not a game. I don't know what my plan of action would be if I had a child that was draft age and this particular war continued to spin out of control. Being wary of the politics and religion of George W. Bush, being somewhat of a military pacifist by nature, and understanding that an election in Iraq hardly impacts my life, I don't think I would allow my child to fight in a war of Bush family revenge. The life of one of my family members simply wouldn't be worth it. I am sure that the entire Bush clan, all of the Cheneys, and even all of the Rumsfelds, Roves, Ashcrofts and Frists would agree.

George W. Bush Should Leave Jesus out of Acts of Personal Revenge

George W. Bush and his buddies like to talk a lot about religion...the Christian religion. There is a level of criticism associated with the behavior of a blowhard, cowardly, egomaniac, millionaire politician seeking to enforce his values on other countries. But the actions of George W. Bush and his warmongering conservative friends rise to a new level of evil and hypocrisy never really seen before in the United States.

George W. Bush has brought a notorious liberal pacifist into the mix. He invaded another country in the name of God. Since he claims Christianity, he invaded another country in the name of Christ. The words of Christ do not in any way support bloodshed. They support peace, brotherhood, and love. To some, this makes George W. Bush the Antichrist. He is murdering innocent people in the name of Jesus. Worse yet, he is having other innocents, American infantrymen in Iraq, do the killing for him. In what should be considered a national embarrassment, a Christian nation has authorized him to continue his policies. Now the United States is in a murderous mess of blind revenge for the long haul.

One last message to George W. Bush and his Red State devils: if you are going to try to justify your barbarity, leave Jesus out of it. Furthermore, if you believe in your cause so much, maybe you should send some of your family members over to fight in your war. This was, after all, an act of Red State family revenge.

I am sure I wasn't the only person who thought that it was just a little bit pretentious and disturbing to see the Bush twins partying like rock stars during the inauguration while other less fortunate twenty-somethings, both male and female, have died or are currently wasting away in an Iraqi desert for what must feel like an eternity.

What a disgrace.

PART IV

Blue State Pride, Red State Shame

11

Red State, Blue State Part II

Hammering It Home

When I started this little project, my primary desire was to prove beyond a shadow of a doubt that Red State religion is a fraud. I wanted to make it crystal clear that the Red States and the religious movement that placed George W. Bush and a host of others in office did so on a faulty and blasphemous interpretation of Christian theology. I hope I was successful in this effort.

The moral issues of the religious Right that are protected by Red State values and culture are not supported by the Gospels. As I moved on to learn more about Red State culture, I also learned that Blue State culture is much more positive, much more Christian, and that it promotes the values of liberty and freedom in a much more significant and meaningful way than I originally thought. The truth is that, while, just like everyone else, I tell hillbilly jokes every now and then, I had no idea that life in a Red State was so much different than the life I live in a Blue State.

So what started as a condemnation of religious attitudes and behaviors became something more. In addition to learning and proving that Red State conservative Christians are hypocrites who have changed the message of Jesus to fit their own backward and prejudiced lifestyle, I learned that it is the Blue State values that are most in line with the teachings of an extraordinarily liberal Jesus.

I also was able to expose what I have heard in different religious circles, that conservative Paul has permanently harmed the message of the liberal Christ. Evangelicals everywhere have modeled their lives, morals, and ministry based on the teachings of Paul and not on the teachings of Jesus.

I also understand in my discoveries about Red State hypocrisy and Blue State morality that by giving only the top ten in each category, these results lend themselves to generalizations. My point is to indicate a trend that suggests the existence of values that lead to the definition of a culture. There is no doubt that Red State culture is much different than Blue State culture.

I was also a little bit surprised to find out some things about scripture and the popular conservative issues of the day. I don't want to be too repetitive, but I do think it is important to summarize my findings in the areas of abortion, same-sex marriage, taxation, crime and punishment, and the reality of our involvement in a war.

Regarding Same-Sex Marriage
- There is nothing in the Bible that says gay people should not marry.
- Homosexuality is no greater a sin than adultery.
- According to scripture, divorce is a sin that is unanimously condemned.
- Red States, which are desperately trying to defend marriage, have higher divorce rates than their Blue State counterparts.

Regarding Abortion
- The God of the Old Testament does not value life.
- The God of the Old Testament only issued a fine for the murder of a fetus.
- In the New Testament, Neither Jesus nor Paul ever addresses the issue of a fetus or of abortion.
- Consequently, abortion cannot be considered a religious issue.
- Blue States take much better care of their living children than Red States.

Regarding Taxation and Monetary Issues
- Jesus tells us to build our kingdom in Heaven and not on Earth, indicating that financial success is not a high priority.
- The Bible consistently tells us to pay our taxes without reservation.
- Blue States pay more than their fair share in federal taxes.
- Red States are welfare states because they pay less to the federal government than they receive.

Regarding Crime and Punishment
- The Bible tells us that we are not to judge others.
- Red State culture has an ugly history of prejudice.
- Blue States have always been far more tolerant than Red States.
- Red States, in spite of having more prisoners and more executions than Blue States, continue to have higher rates of crime.

Regarding a Lust for Revenge
- The God of the Old Testament wants revenge left to Him.
- Jesus instructs us to never offer violence as a resolution, but non-violence as a solution.
- Jesus tells us that an eye for an eye makes us blind.
- The blind family-motivated revenge of the Bush administration has led us into a war that is now a quagmire.
- Red State and Blue State troops in Iraq are suffering equally.

I have proven these points with numerous biblical references. I tried to find points in the Bible that would justify the Red State perspective. When I found them, the justification for conservative values never came from the mouth of Jesus.

The stance of the Red State conservatives is wrong on all of these issues, yet they are the ones who have monopolized the Christian religion for themselves. Liberals have been bullied into silence and have refused to claim their liberal God. I have said it once and I will say it again: liberals are wimps.

Proof That Red States Need Big Government

It has also been very interesting to discover that, while conservatives have historically been the ones who consistently moan about "big government," it is their Red State values that inevitably lead to more government intervention in all aspects of life.

-**Red State conservatives need "big government"** to defend marriage by preventing law-abiding citizens from enjoying a legal right. Ironically, it is the Red State marriage that fails.

-**Red State conservatives need "big government"** to outlaw abortion. They want "big government" to control a woman's body and protect the unborn. Ironically, Red States do a poor job of taking care of their living children.

-**Red State conservatives need "big government"** to house and punish all of their criminals. Ironically, it is the Red States that struggle in vain to control their crime.

-**Red State conservatives need "big government"** to execute people they deem evil. Ironically, as Red States end these lives, they quote a nonviolent religious leader.

Red State conservatives need "big government" to offer them a handout by giving them more tax dollars than they pay. Red States are fat, sloppy, lazy welfare mothers.

The last one really makes me sick. Just remembering Newt Gingrich and other like-minded conservatives picking on welfare mothers and discovering the reality of Red State handouts is disgusting. The truth is that it is the Red Staters that sit around and complain about paying taxes while they are getting fatter and fatter and lazier and lazier living off of government handouts. Then they complain like petulant little children about putting in their fair share. Furthermore, they criticize others for being bloated and lazy just like they are.

It is nauseating.

Blue States liberals don't want "big government." Sure, we might be for a tax increase, but it is only because we are well aware that the government needs more money, because our "big government" needs to take care of the Red States, because they simply cannot take care of themselves.

In Praise of the Blue State Liberals

Make no mistake about it, the Blue State liberals save democracy from the Red State conservatives. Without the liberals, the values that are cherished by the citizens of the United States would have been gone a long time ago. The truth is that, without the liberals, the United States never would have had a constitution. This liberal constitution protects citizens from people with Red State values. It is the conservatives who seek to destroy democracy. It is the liberals that saves it.

Here is proof.

Without Blue State liberals, we would still be under the rule of a king.

Without Blue State liberals, slavery would still be legal in the Red States.

Without Blue State liberals, there would have been no Civil Rights Act of 1964 and southern states would still be segregated.

Without Blue State liberals, women would not have secured the right to vote.

Without Blue State liberals, there would be no mandatory public schooling of our children.

Without Blue State liberals, the gates of this country would have been closed to immigrants a long time ago.

Without Blue State liberals, we would have lost our "freedom of speech" long ago.

Without Blue State liberals, there would be no unions to defend worker's rights.

Without Blue State liberals, we would not be able to worship who and how we choose.

Without the hard work, dedication, and bravery of the Blue State liberals, we would be living under a theocratic form of government that forces its religion down its people's throats.

There is no doubt about it, without the Blue State liberals, this country would be living under a dictatorship, because that is what Red State values and hypocrisy promote.

The list of what liberals have done for this country literally goes on and on. It has always been the work of the Blue State liberals to defend the rights of the individual unto their death. It has always been the Red State conservatives that have worked tirelessly to place restrictions on individual freedom and personal growth.

I still don't understand why liberals are so goddamn ashamed of themselves. We have bowed to the pressure of the diehard, obnoxious conservatives that continue to work at taking away our individual freedoms because of their belief in a God that does not exist. Liberals need to wake up.

Alert: Fascists Are against Public Education

Before I move on to the final editions of *Red State, Blue State*, I must show everyone a couple of quotes about public schools. I might as well do it now, since I just went on a tirade that accused Red State conservatives of working tirelessly at moving this country towards a theocratic dictatorship.

I am a public school teacher. As a public school teacher, I believe that a free education for all citizens is the backbone of our democracy. I am going to present two quotes, one from noted dictator and fascist Adolf Hitler, and one from noted minister and fascist Jerry Falwell. See if you can figure out who said which.

> I hope I live to see the day, when, as in the early days of our country, we won't have any public schools. The churches will have taken them over again and Christians will be running them.1

> Secular schools can never be tolerated because such schools have no religious instruction.2

They are both pretty similar in nature because they both call for the destruction of the backbone of freedom and democracy, the public school, and seek to replace this free education with religious institutions and instruction. At the end of one of these quotes, Falwell says, "O, What a happy day that will be!"

Now, since everyone knows that Hitler was a unhappy jackass, we know he would have never said something like that. Hitler was not a jolly fat guy. On the other hand, Jerry Falwell is very fat and very jolly. Falwell's full quote reads:

I hope I live to see the day, when, as in the early days of our country, we won't have any public schools. The churches will have taken them over again and Christians will be running them. O what a happy day that will be!3

What a dork.

If Jerry Falwell and other Red State religious leaders had their way, this country would not be anywhere near as free as we are now. We wouldn't even be recognizable. The Red State Bible thumpers would have maintained slavery, never allowing people their freedom, let alone the right to vote. They would have promoted a national religion and persecuted anyone different. They would have closed our borders to immigrants except for the purposes of slavery. They would have made sure that women would be seen, in the kitchen, and not heard. Does any of this sound familiar?

I just described a religious dictatorship, and that is what America would be if not for the Blue State liberals who have consistently defended our freedom from the Red State religious conservatives.

Red Staters who love whatever freedoms they have need to thank the Blue State liberals. We have worked tirelessly to defend the freedoms of all citizens. To that end, we certainly shouldn't be taking any Red State shit.

Red State, Blue State: Fat, Dumb, Irresponsible…and about to Have a Heart Attack

It is time to get off of my moral high ground and get down and dirty. Once again, it is time for a little more *Red State, Blue State.*

Since I'm now in a bad mood, I think it is time to be a little mean. The first topic for the new edition of this fun game is: who is fatter, people living in Red States or people living in Blue States? Since we have already proven that Red State culture promotes the lifestyle of a big, fat pig that takes handouts from its government, could it be true that the average Red State citizens are fat, sweaty hogs just like the state that they call home?

We will start at the bottom. The lower ranking means that the state has more obese residents. Because I am in a particularly nasty mood, I am going beyond the bottom ten.

Percentage of the population estimated to be obese

Rank	State	Percentage of Obese People	Red or Blue
50	Alabama	28.4	Red
49	Mississippi	28.1	Red
48	West Virginia	27.7	Red
47	Indiana	26.0	Red
46	Kentucky	25.6	Red
45	Michigan	25.2	Blue
44	Georgia	25.2	Red
42	Tennessee	25.0	Red
41	Arkansas	25.2	Red
40	Ohio	24.9	Red
	Louisiana	24.9	Red
38	South Carolina	24.8	Red
37	Oklahoma	24.4	Red
36	North Carolina	24.0	Red
	Delaware	24.0	Blue
34	Nebraska	23.9	Red
33	Iowa	23.9	Red

Source: Behavioral Risk Factor Surveillance System, Centers for Disease Control and Prevention.

If it weren't for those lard asses in Michigan, the fattest fifteen states would have all been Red. As it stands, fifteen out of the top seventeen fattest states voted for George W. Bush in the 2004 election. Shit, if it wasn't for the liberals, not only would we be living under a religious dictator, we would all be fatsos.

Thank God for the liberals. Can I get an Amen?

There are some skinny Red States. They didn't perform too badly. But this exercise wasn't to praise the healthy Red States as much as it was to ridicule the fat ones.

Percentage of the population estimated to be obese

Rank	State	Percentage of Obese People	Red or Blue
1	Colorado	16	Red
2	Hawaii	16.4	Blue
3	Massachusetts	16.8	Blue
4	Rhode Island	18.4	Blue

5	Montana	18.8	Red
6	Connecticut	19.1	Blue
7	Vermont	19.6	Blue
8	Florida	19.9	Red
9	Maine	19.9	Blue
10	Arizona	20.1	Red
	Michigan	20.1	Blue

Source: Behavioral Risk Factor Surveillance System, Centers for Disease Control and Prevention.

The results are not too bad for either side: seven to four. The Blue States still win.

Right after the election, there was an Intelligence Quotient chart that was floating around the Internet. I thought it was kind of funny. This was actually the place where I first developed the idea for the game of *Red State, Blue State*. Anyway, this chart shows state-by-state IQ scores. Conveniently, it also makes the old Red State or Blue State declaration. I believe all of this to be true. However, the chart that I came across had an disclaimer.

The IQ numbers were originally submitted to the book *IQ and the Wealth of Nations*, though they do not appear in the current edition. The tests and date were administered via the Raven's APT and The Test Agency, one of the UK's Leading publishers and distributors of psychometric tests. This data has been published in the *Economist* and the *St. Petersburg Times*, though this does not mean it should be taken as fact.

I believe it, but, then again, I am a jerk, and I hate Red State culture.

Average population IQ by state

Rank	State	Average Population IQ	Red or Blue
1	Connecticut	113	Blue
2	Massachusetts	111	Blue
3	New Jersey	111	Blue
4	New York	109	Blue
5	Rhode Island	107	Blue
6	Hawaii	106	Blue
7	Maryland	105	Blue
8	New Hampshire	105	Blue
9	Illinois	104	Blue
10	Delaware	103	Blue
11	Minnesota	102	Blue

12	Vermont	102	Blue
13	Washington	102	Blue
14	California	101	Blue
15	Pennsylvania	101	Blue
16	Maine	100	Blue
17	Virginia	100	Red
18	Wisconsin	100	Blue

Source: *I.Q. and the Wealth of Nations*.

It took seventeen states before there is a Red State on a national state-by-state IQ chart. That is some pretty pathetic shit. It gets funnier though.

Average population IQ by state

Rank	State	Average Population IQ	Red or Blue
25	Alaska	98	Red
26	Florida	98	Red
27	Missouri	98	Red
28	Kansas	96	Red
29	Nebraska	95	Red
30	Arizona	94	Red
31	Indiana	94	Red
32	Tennessee	94	Red
33	North Carolina	93	Red
34	West Virginia	93	Red
35	Arkansas	92	Red
36	Georgia	92	Red
37	Kentucky	92	Red
38	New Mexico	92	Red
39	North Dakota	92	Red
40	Texas	92	Red
41	Alabama	91	Red
42	Louisiana	91	Red
43	Montana	91	Red
44	Oklahoma	91	Red
45	South Dakota	91	Red
46	South Carolina	90	Red
47	Wyoming	90	Red
48	Idaho	87	Red

49	Utah	87	Red
50	Mississippi	85	Red

Source: *I.Q. and the Wealth of Nations.*

Ladies and Gentlemen! We have another "Sea of Red"!

The twenty-six states with the lowest average IQ all voted Red in the 2004 election. That is incredible. This, at the very least, supports my belief that the values and cultures of the Red States would eventually lead to a dictatorship. These people don't value education, freedom, or democracy. If they did, they would do a better job of educating their children.

Since this IQ card may not be the most reliable of my statistical tables, I searched high and low for some test scores to prove that Red State children are not as educated as they should be.

Now, I know that IQ tests aren't everything, but I do believe that IQ does signal, at the very least, a lack of emphasis on literacy and education. To further this point, each state has children in particular grade level take the standardized tests that everyone loves to hate in different subject areas. In this case, we will look at the state by state Reading and Math scores of eighth grade students.

As it turns out, there are quite a few Red States that are below the national average in eighth grade Reading and Math scores.

States with eighth graders below the average mathematics scale score of 276

State	Score	Red or Blue
Mississippi	261	Red
Alabama	262	Red
New Mexico	263	Red
Arkansas	266	Red
Hawaii	266	Blue
Louisiana	266	Red
California	267	Blue
Nevada	268	Red
Tennessee	268	Red
Georgia	270	Red
Arizona	271	Red
Florida	271	Red
West Virginia	271	Red

Oklahoma	272	Red
Rhode Island	272	Blue
Kentucky	274	Red

Source: "The Nations Report Card: Mathematics" *National Center for Educational Statistics*, 2003.

Not surprisingly, Red States did not fare much better on the standardized Reading test. Once again, there were quite a few Red States that were below the national average.

States with eighth graders below the average Reading scale score of 261

State	Score	Red or Blue
Hawaii	251	Blue
California	252	Blue
Nevada	252	Red
New Mexico	252	Red
Alabama	253	Red
Louisiana	253	Red
Arizona	255	Red
Mississippi	255	Red
Florida	257	Red
Arkansas	258	Red
Georgia	258	Red
South Carolina	258	Red
Tennessee	258	Red
Texas	259	Red
West Virginia	260	Red

Source: "The Nations Report Card: Reading" *National Center for Educational Statistics*, 2003.

These two tables provide us with some interesting information.

First of all, there were four states that were on one list but not on the other (Texas, Rhode Island, Kentucky, and South Carolina).

Only three out of nineteen Blue States appeared on at least one of these lists. To the contrary, fourteen out of thirty Red States made it on a scale with below average Reading or Math scores. Eleven of these fourteen Red States scored below the national average in both Reading and Mathematics.

The only two Blue States scoring below the national average in both Reading and Math were Hawaii and California

The eleven Red States scoring below the national average in both Reading and Math were Nevada, New Mexico, Alabama, Louisiana, Arizona, Mississippi, Florida, Arkansas, Georgia, Tennessee, West Virginia.

Since education for most Red State citizens stops after high school, these scores are not going to improve as people get older. Going back to the very first game of *Red State, Blue State* that involved the "Percentage of Residents with at Least a Bachelor's Degree," if Red and Blue State adults were to take these tests, the results would probably be the same as the scores of fourteen year olds. A national average for adults would be established. Blue States would tend to be above the national average while Red States would not only be below the national average, but would in fact bring down this average in both Reading and Math scores. The result: a dumber nation. A nation that votes for conservatives against their own interests.

Thanks a lot!

We already know that Red States tend to have more children living in poverty, and now there is some evidence that they are not learning as much as they should. Additionally, there is a movement led by George W. Bush and other fascist lunatics who are seeking to undermine the influence of public education. To this end, it is appropriate to compare state-by-state rates of annual educational spending to see if Red State culture values education. This is at the very least a partial indicator of the funding priorities received by public educational institutions.

It is also important to remember that Red States get a lot of tax money from the federal government, so the funding of schools shouldn't be a problem.

States below national average of $6,835 in spending per student

State	Spending per pupil	Red or Blue
Utah	$4,331	Red
Arizona	$5.033	Red
Mississippi	$5,014	Red
Idaho	$5,218	Red
Tennessee	$5,343	Red
Oklahoma	$5,394	Red
Arkansas	$5,470	Red
South Dakota	$5,521	Red
Alabama	$5,601	Red
Louisiana	$5,652	Red

Florida	$5,691	Red
Nevada	$5,736	Red
New Mexico	$5,748	Red
North Dakota	$5,830	Red
Kentucky	$5,922	Red
North Carolina	$5,990	Red
South Carolina	$6,114	Red
Missouri	$6,143	Red
Texas	$6,145	Red
Colorado	$6,165	Red
California	$6,298	Red
Kansas	$6,211	Red
Montana	$6,214	Red
Washington	$6,394	Blue
Georgia	$6,417	Red
Nebraska	$6,422	Red
Hawaii	$6,487	Blue
Iowa	$6,547	Red
New Hampshire	$6,742	Blue

Source: United States Bureau of the Census, 2001.

There are twenty nine states that are below the national average of spending per student. Of these states, twenty six are Red and only three are Blue.

Pathetically, only five Red States exceed the national average in spending per student (Alaska, Ohio, West Virginia, Wyoming, Virginia). At the same time, fifteen out of nineteen Blue States exceed the national average.

Statisticians, Red State politicians, and even educators will say that spending does not necessarily equal a quality education. However, it should be noted that there were only two states West Virginia (Reading and Math) and Rhode Island (Math) that were below the national average in eighth grade test scores but above the national average in per student spending.

In the Chapter 11 edition of *Red State, Blue State*, statistics were given for rates of male and female incarceration. It is interesting to note that, all states with the highest numbers of male and female prisoners serving a sentence of more than one year, with the exception of Delaware, are below the national average in educational spending.

Furthermore, ten Blue States pay more than their fair share in federal taxes, yet still manage to exceed the national average in educational spending per student (New Jersey, New York, Minnesota, Illinois, Massachusetts, Connecticut, Oregon, Wisconsin, Delaware, and Michigan.) Only one of these (Delaware) was listed in the top ten of male incarceration rates. Likewise, none of these ten were in the top ten of female incarceration. Additionally, all of these states, except Delaware again, scored above the national averages scores in both Reading and Math.

It gets worse for the Red States. Out of the states receiving more in federal tax dollars than they received, Indiana is the only Red State that receives more than they give to the national government and is still able to exceed the national average in per students pending.

What the hell do Red States do with their tax profits? They certainly are not spending them on students.

In what probably is not too much of a shocker, they aren't spending their tax profits on their teachers either.

Here are the states with the highest rates of teacher pay.

Average teacher salary in 2002–2003, by state

Rank	State	Average Annual Teacher Salary	Red or Blue
1	California	55,963	Blue
2	Michigan	54,020	Blue
3	Connecticut	53,962	Blue
4	New Jersey	53,872	Blue
5	Washington, D.C.	53,194	Blue
6	New York	53,017	Blue
7	Rhode Island	52,879	Blue
8	Massachusetts	51,942	Blue
9	Illinois	51,496	Blue
10	Pennsylvania	51,425	Blue
11	Maryland	50,410	Blue
12	Delaware	49,821	Blue
13	Alaska	49,694	Red

Sources: American Federation of Teachers, annual survey of state departments of education, Early Estimates of Public and Secondary Education Statistics 2001–2002, U.S. Department of Education, April 2003. National Occupational Employment and Wage Estimates, U.S. Department of Labor, Bureau of Labor Statistics May 2002,May 2003.

I listed the rankings until I came upon a Red State. In this case, the top twelve states in average teacher salary were all Blue States. Conversely, the bottom sixteen, and twenty-four out of the last twenty-five states with the lowest annual average of teacher salaries, are Red States. Only Maine snuck into the bottom twenty-five.

Unbelievable.

Average Teacher Salary in 2002–2003, by State

Rank	State	Average Annual Teacher Salary	Red or Blue
51	South Dakota	32,414	Red
50	Oklahoma	33,277	Red
49	North Dakota	33,869	Red
48	Mississippi	35,135	Red
47	Montana	35,754	Red
46	New Mexico	37, 054	Red
45	Louisiana	37,116	Red
44	Arkansas	37,536	Red
43	Missouri	37,641	Red
42	Wyoming	37,789	Red
41	Nebraska	37,896	Red
40	Iowa	38,000	Red
39	Kansas	38,030	Red
38	Utah	38,268	Red
37	Kentucky	38,486	Red
36	West Virginia	38,497	Red
35	Maine	38,518	Blue
34	Tennessee	39,186	Red
33	Alabama	39,582	Red
32	Idaho	39,784	Red
31	Arizona	39,955	Red
30	Texas	39,972	Red
29	Florida	40,281	Red
28	South Carolina	40,362	Red

Sources: American Federation of Teachers, annual survey of state departments of education, Early Estimates of Public and Secondary Education Statistics 2001–2002, U.S. Department of Education, April 2003. National Occupational Employment and Wage Estimates, U.S. Department of Labor, Bureau of Labor Statistics May 2002,May 2003.

Because I am a liberal, I find all of this kind of sad. I have been harping on education as a way out of poverty and as a way towards a successful and happy life throughout my entire teaching career. The problem here isn't that teachers are low in salary in Red States. The problem is that teacher salary can be an indicator of what kind of emphasis governments place on their schools.

Education as a low priority is a Red State trend. This isn't a problem only in the South. It is a problem in the Heartland, the Southwest, anywhere where Red State culture rules supreme. If a state is Red, education is not a high priority. Conversely, the average Blue State liberal thinks public education is the backbone of a democracy. I guess I am living in the right state.

It is actually pretty disturbing that the states, which receive more from the federal government than they pay, are short on the funding of education. I guess this is acceptable because Red State blowhards like Mr. Falwell and Adolf Hitler want public schools eliminated. Now, that is a Red State value. It sure as shit isn't what we want in the freedom-loving and well-educated Blue States.

Red States seem to be in a bit of trouble, with high rates of obesity, low IQ scores, low eighth grade Reading and Math scores, and low rates of spending on education, it does seem that Red States, particularly those in the South, are truly "Fat, Dumb, and Irresponsible."

It also appears that many Red States residents are about to have a heart attack.

States with the highest rate of cardiovascular deaths per 100,000 residents

Rank	State	Cardiovascular Deaths per 100,000	Red or Blue
1	Oklahoma	411.6	Red
2	Mississippi	411.0	Red
3	West Virginia	393.3	Red
4	Kentucky	390.1	Red
5	Tennessee	386	Red
6	Arkansas	379	Red
7	Alabama	377.5	Red
8	Missouri	370.5	Red
9	Michigan	365.3	Blue
10	Louisiana	361.8	Red
11	Georgia	361.3	Red
12	Indiana	361.7	Red
13	Ohio	359.4	Red
14	Texas	351	Red
15	South Carolina	349.5	Red

Source: *Center for Disease Control and Prevention*, 2001

Apparently, a lack of activity, a lack of education, and squandering excessive tax profits also leads to stress.

Bummer.

Purple Sucks

The Red State and Blue State phenomenon is a collision of cultures. We liberals in the Blue States should not be putting up with any Red State bullshit. If they want to underfund schools, take away rights from their citizens, throw everyone possible in jail, that's their problem, and that is their way of life. We do things differently in the Blue States, and we should be proud that we do things the right way.

That is why it makes me sick to my stomach to hear liberals express the need to cater to the Red States and pursue some kind of loving compromise. This is unacceptable! Red States need to stay Red States if they want. Likewise, Blue States need to keep their values untainted by Red State conservatism. Millionaires like Ted Kennedy and Bill Clinton want us to reach out to the Red States. Even Howard Dean, the new leader of the Democratic National Committee, wants to reach out to our Red State brothers. We need to reach out to them alright. We need to reach out to them with closed fists and punch 'em in the nose. Forget compromise. Do you think Red States are going to compromise with Blue States? Hell, no! And when only one of two groups wants to compromise, the battle is a slaughter. Liberals have been compromising too long. It is time to launch an attack.

To that end, I was doing some grocery shopping a in January of 2005 and I experienced an impulse buy. I bought the January 3rd edition of *Newsweek* magazine. I bought it because on the cover was the smiling face of a new liberal hotshot named Barack Obama. He was grinning over a very disturbing headline that read, "Seeing Purple." According to *Newsweek*, Mr. Obama is "A Rising Star Who Wants to Get Beyond Blue vs. Red."

Purple is not what America needs. I must defend Mr. Obama from an almost slanderous headline. I read the article about him, and nowhere does Obama mention the word "purple." He does want liberals to explore a renewed connection to liberal religion. Obama says, "This shouldn't be hard to do. Martin Luther King did it. The abolitionists did it. Dorothy Day (of the Catholic Workers) did it. Most of the reform movements that have changed this country have been grounded in religious models."4 I completely agree with him, as long as the religion is liberal, which means it isn't forced down any citizen's throat.

All of which leads to another shining star featured in *Newsweek*. This guy doesn't see purple, he sees Red, and he would like the "Sea of Red" to expand. His name is Rick Santorum. He is a SHCAK (Self-Hating Catholic against Kerry). This prick is so Red that he believes that "evolution should be taught in public schools, but only as a still-controversial scientific theory that 'has holes.'"5 Perhaps one of Mr. Santorum's "holes" is that evolution does not make our incestuous roots clear enough.

He also thinks that the constitutionally protected "right to privacy" laws are unconstitutional. This fits right in with the Red State notion that we need a theocratic dictator invading our private lives. He does believe in states' rights, which is a good thing. However, this Blue State conservative hypocrite doesn't believe in states' rights when it comes to same-sex marriage.

It sure doesn't seem to me like he is in a mood to compromise, which is the problem. *Newsweek* portrayed Obama as the new guy extending an olive branch to his enemies. All the while, conservatives like Santorum, who enjoys the protection of the democracy that life in a Blue State (Pennsylvania) has afforded him, will push a Red State agenda. He will not compromise. Neither should we.

A Plan of Action from a Blue State Know-It-All

Everyone needs a plan. Conservatives have had a demented plan of action for years. They have already ruined Christianity; now they are threatening Blue State democracy. We let them take a liberal Jesus and turn Him into a conservative lunatic without ever quoting scripture. Listen to their religious rants. They can't quote Jesus, because He was a liberal. Liberals stood by and let them destroy His message and blaspheme it to their own ends. We can't let them ruin democracy.

For this reason, I have some advice for Blue State liberals everywhere. Liberals need to aggressively promote Jesus as a liberal in an effort to assert moral authority. Liberals need to bring this argument to the conservative. When a Red State "Jesus Freak" says that we are a "Christian Nation," don't argue with them. Agree with them. Then note that Jesus does not support their values or their arrogant attitudes towards their religion. Jesus condemns the boastful attitude of the religious braggart on a consistent basis. He endlessly refers to them as hypocrites and false prophets. He makes it crystal clear that His message is not for them. He stresses that it is the vain, self-confident, arrogant "Christian" that will destroy His message.

Without further adieu, here are a few things that liberals can do in an effort to stop the flow of Red State crap down our Blue State throats.

1. Liberals need to aggressively defend the message of Jesus

If liberals ever get in religious discussions with conservatives, we should be confident. Tell them to bring it on. When Red State evangelicals who have never read the Gospels start pontificating about God and using the Bible to prove their points, we must make them quote Jesus. Remind them that we are a Christian nation and that Jesus was God. Ask these buffoons to quote Jesus to support their views on same-sex marriage, abortion, war, or any of our individual rights that they want to take away. They will be stunned into silence.

Here is a sample conversation. The antagonist and protagonist are Tom (a Blue State liberal) and Billy Joe (a Red State conservative).

Tom: Christianity does not teach us to hate gay people and Jesus was not against same-sex marriage.

Billy Joe: Oh yes it does. It does it says so right in the Bible.

Tom: Where?

Billy Joe: I don't know where; I just know.

Tom: Alright, Billy. I am going to do you a favor. I am going to show you where God says that homosexuality is a sin.

Billy Joe: Thanks.

Tom grabs a Bible out from underneath a stack of newspapers, magazines, and novels. He thumbs through the pages and stops at Leviticus. He points to a passage in the Bible. He hands the Bible to Billy Joe.

Tom: Read.

Billy Joe: "If a man lies with a male as with a woman, both of them have committed an abomination; they shall be put to death, their blood is upon them." See, I told you so.

Tom grabs the Bible.

Tom: Read this.

Billy Joe: "If a man commits adultery with the wife of his neighbor, both the adulterer and the adulteress shall be put to death."

Tom: Ya see, Billy? God hates adulterers just as much as he hates homosexuals. Just about everyone commits adultery. So what is the big deal? Anyway, that is the Old Testament. Jesus never says anything in the Gospels about homosexuals or same-sex marriage being a sin.

Billy Joe: Yes, he does.

Tom: No, he doesn't.

Billy Joe: Yes, he does.

Tom: Show me.

Billy Joe: I don't have to show you; I know it's in there.

At this point, the argument ends because Billy Joe, your average Red State conservative, has no intention of reading his Bible and doing some research about this or any other issue. What he will do is ask his evangelical pastor, who will direct him to the teachings of Paul.

The tale continues. A couple of days later, Billy Joe takes the argument to Tom. Billy Joe, with his Bible in hand, confidently confronts a surprised Tom.

Billy Joe: I found it.

Tom: You found what?

Billy Joe: I found where Jesus says that homosexuality is a sin.

Tom: Really? I'd like to see that.

Billy Joe has his Bible bookmarked in two places. He opens the Bible to the first and begins reading.

Billy Joe: "Their women exchanged natural relations for unnatural, and the men likewise gave up natural relations with women and were consumed with passion for one another, men committing shameless acts with men and receiving in their own persons the due penalty for their error."

Tom: Where is that from?

Billy Joe: Romans, Chapter 1.

Tom: Billy Joe, do you know who wrote Romans?

Billy Joe: Ummm. God?

Tom: No. God didn't write Romans. That's not Jesus. that's Paul. I asked you to show me where Jesus states that homosexuality and same-sex marriage are wrong. You showed me something from Paul. Paul was not Jesus.

Billy Joe: It doesn't matter; it's in the Bible.

Tom: No, Billy Joe. It does matter. I am a Christian. I follow Jesus.

It is possible for liberals to use this kind of an argument on just about any conservative issue. The truth is that, if conservatives want to declare Jesus as their rock, foundation, and inspiration, they will be unable to support their wacky, bigoted views with scripture from the Gospels. Jesus never supports their bigoted views. In fact, He usually says the opposite. Shit, I listed all of the quotes that conservatives are going to use to support their bigotry and they aren't from the Gospels. Likewise, I have provided liberals with Gospel quotes that indicate Jesus is diametrically opposed to the teachings of the evangelical Red State-influenced church.

Now, I am fully aware that the Red State Christians are not going to change their minds. Evangelicals are self-righteous nerds who have been brainwashed by more powerful self-righteous nerds. The point is not to convert them. The point is to establish Jesus as a liberal and to establish Jesus as the liberal's guide. The liberal does not follow "God." The liberal does not follow Paul. The liberal follows Jesus, and His teachings are in the Gospels.

2. Liberals need to stop playing with their votes.

I learned this one the hard way. I did not vote in the 2000 election. At the time, I was dating a woman who was heavy into Ralph Nader. She and her friends were off-the-chart liberals and the stupid-ass message of Nader inspired them. They were off to support the Green Party.

So one night I was having a political argument with them. They were saying that there was no difference between the Democrats and the Republicans. That was about the dumbest thing I had ever heard, especially coming from a pack of environmentalists. My point was that, while politicians from both sides are probably the same (a lot of arrogant millionaires), there was going to be a huge difference in policies and appointments. They disagreed and voted for Nader. I was an apathetic, liberal voter. I didn't even go to the polls. I can admit my culpability as an apathetic liberal voter who threw away his vote by not going to the polls.

We all know what happened next. Gore wins the popular vote and Bush won the presidency. It was all the fault of the liberal non-voter and the Ralph Nader voters who were trying to make some kind of point while casting a ballot. Had there been no Ralph Nader and no Green Party, it would have been a Democratic landslide. Al Gore would have increased his popular vote victory and added Florida and New Hampshire to his list of Blue States. Gore would have had almost 300 electoral votes to around 250 for George W. Bush.

As I was doing some Christmas shopping in downtown Seattle in 2003, it was with some anger and sarcasm, that I noticed an anti-war march. It was without reservation that I told my wife, "Looks like the same group of idiots that I saw at Ralph Nader's presidential campaign rally a couple of years ago." Are liberals and conservatives the same? I don't think so. Liberals brought this shit on themselves, and they still haven't learned their lesson.

The gubernatorial race in Washington State lingered on for months. After three counts, Democrat Christine Gregoire was certified as governor on December 30, 2004. She won the election by a little more than one hundred votes. What the statistics don't tell you is that 63,346 residents, mostly liberals, threw their votes in the trash when they voted for a Libertarian candidate. The election should never have been this close. And if it hadn't been for the constitutionally protected right for a hand recount of all ballots, my beloved Blue State would have elected a governor with Red State values. It makes me sick to my stomach thinking about that. In the end, all of us liberals in the Blue state of Washington would have kept his Red State ass in check.

Nationally, even after the Nader fiasco of 2000, more than 400,000 retarded liberals voted for him in the 2004 election. Liberals need to stop making statements with their votes or it is going to cost us…again.

Now, this is all Monday morning quarterbacking of the election variety, but Bush only won Ohio by less than a hundred thousand votes; 25,000 residents of Ohio played games with their votes and voted for a Libertarian and a candidate from the Constitutional Party, whatever that is. I don't know too much about it, but, based on previous trends, most of these voters were probably liberal, which makes the state election in Ohio, the state that decided the election, even closer than it was.

3. Tell Your Friends! A vote for a Republican in 2006 or 2008 is a vote for Dubya and Red State culture.

After we have stopped throwing away our own votes, it becomes time to help turn the votes of moderates and other proponents of common sense into a new bloc of Blue voters. The way things are going, this shouldn't be too difficult.

First of all, there is a difference between the old school Reagan Republican and the new school George W. Bush, evangelical Republican. The old-school Republicans may have different ideologies than the Blue State liberal, but they are reasonable people. The problem is that in national politics, the old school Republican has either been transformed into or capitulated to the new school Republican. These people are not reasonable. They are evil. And they need to be removed from office.

Obviously, liberals will vote Blue in the upcoming 2006 and 2008 National elections. However, Blue and Red State liberals are going to need help in both these elections. Red States have the White House until 2008. They don't need to have both the House and Senate in 2006.

Liberals have plenty of ammunition in their effort to turn undecided voters Blue. This is what five years of Red State religious conservatism has wrought on our country.

The Economy
- An out of control national debt (approaching $8,000,000,000,000)
- Tax cuts for the wealthy.
- Service cuts for the poor and middle-class.
- Outrages gas prices.

An Oppressive and Freedom-hating Social Agenda
- A ban on stem cell research.
- Governmental intervention in personal issues (same-sex marriage, abortion rights, and the right to die with dignity).
- Attack on so-called "activist judges" (any judge that is not conservative).
- Two new conservative judicial nominees and lifetime appointments to replace Sandra Day O'Connor and William Rehnquist.

The Current State of National Security
- Osama bin Laden still on the loose four years after the September 11 attacks.
- "Scooter" Libby assisting in the "outing" of a CIA agent.
- Constant "Terror Alerts" that keep Americans in fear.

The War in Iraq
- Over 2,000 American troops killed.
- Over 25,000 Iraqi citizens killed.
- More than 7,000 American troops wounded.
- No end to the conflict in sight.
- Hints at an upcoming Iraqi Civil War with American troops caught in the middle.

Politicians, both Red and Blue, have been bullied into accepting these and all of the other circumstances that currently plague our nation. Since we are a Democracy, we can vote these Red State bums out of office—especially if they call a Blue State their home. Now if people like the direction the United States ahs taken since Bill Clinton left office, they should vote Red. For those citizens who do not like the Red State direction of this country (unstable economy, oppressive social agenda, decrease in national security, and our current involvement in a war) should vote Blue.

A Red vote in this political climate is a vote for George W. Bush and an evangelical Red State nation. We cannot trust a Republican in national politics to do anything but capitulate to the Bush administration and the religious Right. For example, my own state of Washington has a Democratic senator (Maria Cantwell) that is up for re-election in 2006. Her Republican opponent, no matter who he or she is, should be seen as a pro-Bush activist and should never be allowed to represent a Blue State.

Furthermore, the following Blue State Republicans are up for re-election in the Senate in 2006: Lincoln Chaffee (Rhode Island), Rick Santorum (Pennsylvania), and Olympia Snowe (Maine). Obviously, keeping all of the Blue seats Blue is a priority, but bouncing these Red State expatriates out of office in 2006 should be a no-brainer for any freedom-loving Blue State resident.

After all of the shit that has happened in the United States over the last five years, it is hard to believe that anyone in their right mind would vote for a Republican. But, people will. It is time to reduce that number to a national minority.

Ultimately, history will judge George W. Bush as one of the worst presidents in the history of the United States. My guess is that history isn't going to be too kind to the 2004 electorate either.

4. Screw Florida.

In the weeks prior to the 2004 election, I would read some newspapers and look at Web sites to check out different polling information in the effort to get a better idea of who might win what was turning out to be a very tight presidential race. One item that I stumbled upon, that was repeated over and over, was that whoever won two out of three battleground states was going to win the election. The three sates were Ohio, Florida, and Pennsylvania. If I knew this, why didn't the Kerry campaign catch on? Kerry was not going to win Florida. After the shenanigans of 2000 and a Bush brother in the governor's mansion, Kerry shouldn't even have tried. He should have gone after Ohio and Pennsylvania and said, "Screw Florida."

Earlier I mentioned that, in my not so humble opinion, John Kerry made a mistake when he selected John Edwards as his running mate. This was undoubtedly an attempt to swing at least one Southern state (probably Florida) by putting a Red State Democrat on the ticket. As we all know, this did not work.

Now, all of us Blue State Democrats must imagine what would have happened if Kerry had selected someone like General Wesley Clark. Imagine what Clark, a decorated four-star general, would have been able to do to Dick Cheney, a man who requested multiple deferrals from military service, in a debate. A four-star general would have had an impact in states like Ohio and Iowa.

Even though John Edwards hails from a Southern Red State, he did not help the cause of Blue State liberals one bit. Maybe two Red State Democrats (Clinton and Gore) can win a national election. A Blue State candidate needs to select a Blue State running mate.

It is also important to make note of what Florida really is. Blue State liberals become confused because Florida has some college towns and big cities that vote Blue. What we don't want to acknowledge is that beyond these cities, Florida is filled with steaming piles of white trash. And hot, steamy piles of white trash always vote Red.

Furthermore, there are more than enough states that typically vote Blue to win the presidential election in any year without the help of the South. The 2004 election was the first time Ohio or Iowa voted for a Republican since 1988. Securing these two states in 2008, in addition to the states that voted Blue in the 2004 election, would mean 279 electoral votes. Furthermore, states like

New Mexico (Bush won by 6,000 votes) and Nevada (Bush won by 20,000 votes) could easily go Blue in 2008 because they are growing and diversifying. That is, of course, if Democrats and liberals pull their heads out of their asses and stop capitulating to the South and pay more attention to other areas of the country.

At any rate, by ignoring Florida and bombarding Ohio, John Kerry may have turned Ohio and the United States Blue. Instead, he wasted his time with Florida and capitulated to the south by choosing John Edwards as a running mate and did much worse than Al Gore did in 2000. It's pathetic.

5. Liberals need to start being advocates for states' rights.

It doesn't matter whom the goofballs in this country elect president as long as my state stays Blue. Hell will freeze over, or we will be taken over by a theocracy—we are closer than we think—before my beloved state of Washington and other liberal strongholds turn Red.

During the days of slavery and segregation, the Red States in the South were harping on states' rights as a way to continue to enforce their policies of government—enforced bigotry. After begging, pleading, and invading, both with violence and non-violence, Red States in the South gave up their history of discrimination and racism. For decades, they used their bigoted rally cry of states' rights to deny other human beings of their individual rights.

There is nothing wrong with Blue States using states' rights as a way to protect our individual rights and freedoms. Keeping in mind that Blue States grant rights to others, while Red States want to take them away, America is supposed to respect freedom and individual rights. Our cry of Blue States' rights is much different than past Red Staters' hollerin' to respect the rights of states.

They continue in their efforts to deny citizens of their rights, while we are trying to extend rights to as many human beings as possible. That is why I thought it absolutely outstanding that voters in California voted in favor of Proposition 71. This proposition granted more than three billion dollars for embryonic stem cell research.

Even the Republican governor was for it.

Not only will this promote scientific efforts to help cure various illnesses and diseases, but it will also be a boon to the California economy and infrastructure.

Scientists will move en masse to California. There will be funding for the construction of labs. It will be a haven for scientific discovery and academic freedom. California has moved to the forefront of modern science. This is a great example of how states can be independent of an oppressive federal government.

There are a variety of ways Blue States can buck the totalitarian wishes of our theocratic national government, and it all starts with Blue Staters being independent thinkers. Now, we need to act on our principles. Our beloved Blue States need to stay Blue by continuing to be independent thinkers that are able to create, innovate, and continue to be successful states and safe places to live without massive intervention from the federal government. The Red States need and want federal government intervention in every aspect of their lives in everything from mass government assistance to crazy cases like the situation with Terri Schiavo. Red States cannot survive without the paternalism of the federal government. The Blue States are different. We neither want nor need the constant moral chirping from the feds.

We are Blue State liberals. We enjoy freedom, democracy, and our individual rights. We are the protectors of these noble ideals. If some citizens don't like freedom. They can move to or stay in their favorite Red State, where the federal government will continue to tell them what to do and how to do it.

6. Liberals need to stop being such big, giant wimps. It is embarrassing.

I hate to be overly negative to my Blue and Red State liberal brothers and sisters, but we are a bunch of sissies. We have let Red State politicians and religious figures run roughshod over our values and religion for too long.

If Red Staters are going to be dicks to us, we need to be bigger dicks to them. They are nothing to be afraid of. Look at their leaders: George W. Bush, Karl Rove, Dick Cheney, John Ashcroft, Rush Limbaugh, Newt Gingrich, Jerry Falwell, Pat Robertson, Ralph Reed, Tom Delay, Bill Frist, and Bill O'Reilly. Has anyone ever seen a bigger collection of nerds and dorks in their lives?

These guys aren't intelligent. They aren't brave. They aren't physically strong. They are fat, soft, gooey punks who are constantly running their mouths. They are the heroes of Red State conservatism. They are a bunch of geeks who have hijacked America!

We let them do it because we thought they were a joke. We thought, and I know that I am guilty of this, that there was no way in hell that the United States would follow a pack of fat, arrogant, brainless, Red State clowns. But we did, and it is our own fault, because for years we have been in the middle of a cultural war between Blue State liberalism and Red State conservatism and we have been fucking around enjoying our freedom. While we were laughing at their idiocy, these Red State freaks stole our country in the name of our liberal God!

There is some good news on the horizon. Because of the tireless effort of the Blue State liberals, things will get better. The nation will wake up and realize that eight years of Red State *morality* was a national disaster. We should keep in mind that, while life for Blue State liberals will always be comfortable, we should not lapse into another pattern of political laziness and irresponsibility. The laziness and irresponsibility of the Blue State and Red State liberals put George W. Bush and his form of blasphemous Christianity in the White House. Freedom, democracy, and the liberal message of Christ have been paying for it ever since.

Afterword

You know, when I started this book I hated all of those goddamn Red States that elected George Bush to a second term and established a majority in both the House of Representatives and the Senate. I compiled all of the fucking information to make them look bad, and I think I was pretty successful. In my not so humble opinion, not only have Red State conservatives totally blasphemed Christ in the name of bad theology and a very self-serving religion, but their whole way of life is threatening our democracy.

Being the good liberal that I am, I now kind of feel sorry for them in a patronizing and condescending sort of way. This is what good-hearted liberals do. It is our identity. We try and help the unfortunate sad-sacks of the world because we think we are better and have a healthier lifestyle. We actively promote this lifestyle by trying to convince others that they deserve more, that they deserve to be like us. It is pretty arrogant behavior

But because I am a bit of a jerk and I am quite selfish in my own right, this whole experience has caused a bit of a revolution in my attitude towards a culture that is quite a bit different than mine. I am a Blue State liberal to the bone, and when all of this started, I despised Red State culture. Now, I think I love it.

Red Staters, I think I love you.

As symbol of my love, I should probably to tell you that I am sorry. That's right, it is time for me to apologize for being so mean and nasty to my Red State neighbors.

Here it goes.

Dear Red States Conservatives,

From the bottom of my heart I apologize for my most recent behavior, words, and attitude towards you. I have been very mean. I have laughed at your culture and your backwards religion and made money doing so. This has been horrible of me. Please forgive these regrettable actions.

Now that I have apologized, I would like to extend an olive branch (biblical metaphor) of sorts. Us Blue Staters will leave you alone, if you agree to leave us alone. I have learned to love and respect your culture and I wouldn't want it changed for all of the tea in China. I hope that in time you feel the same way towards us Blue State devils and our culture up North, back East and out West.

I believe that it is time for the Red States and Blue States to be allowed the freedom to practice and promote their own culture and values without intervention.

For example, the Blue States will let the Red States lead the free world in male and female incarceration rates and executions as long as the Red States let the Blue States lead the free world in providing a free education to each and every one of our children. To be perfectly honest, I think you might be right about jailing and executing Red State criminal scum.

In the Blue States, we try and prevent children from becoming criminals in the first place. Crazy liberals like me think it is wise to dump endless funds into programs that try to aid in the prevention of the criminal life. In order to do this, we ask you to help us allow our children have high expectations. We beg of you to let our children go on to college. We want our children to position themselves for stable adult employment. Please don't stand in our way.

In return, we will not only continue to pay more than our fair share in federal taxes, but we will allow you to continue to under fund public education in your states. You are free to underpay your teachers and retain your low test scores in your Red State hope that your children will continue to avoid satanic, liberal institutions (colleges and universities). We will allow you to continue to prepare your children for life in a $10 an hour job at Walmart. There is nothing more noble than preparing your children for a job that earns $12,000 a year, while each of Sam Walton's children remain firmly entrenched in the top ten list of wealthiest Americans. I am sure Mr. Walton is grateful. Maybe someday the Walton's will repay your loyalty with a penny an hour pay raise.

Better yet, we will continue to allow you to send the important message to your youngsters that there is nothing wrong with flippin' burgers at McDonalds or pancakes at Aunt Bev's greasy spoon. That may not be good enough for our children, but it is good enough for yours.

I also beg you to let us do what we need to do to provide better health care to our Blue State residents. Granted, it appears that we are a bit healthier than you, and may not need the great health care we desire, but for some dumb reason we still want more. So please don't deny us our misguided goal of universal and affordable health care. We want our people insured. If a quarter of your population remains uninsured, we respect this as a valued way of life and an important part of your culture. We do not wish to deny you of your God-given right to ignore the health and well-being of your children and people.

We also hope that you will allow our homosexual citizens get married. If you don't want to allow gay people to become married in your state that is fine with us. In return for this favor, we will take all of your married homosexual couples and bring them up and over to the Blue States. We will find them jobs.

We will order them to pay their taxes. We will even let them adopt some kids because we really don't believe that they are going to force their new children into a life of sodomy and perversion. Methinks we have a better impression of homosexuals than you do. What could be better than a happy, healthy, financially secure couple adopting a pair of impoverished and neglected kids?

After all of the married homosexuals have moved to the Blue States, you will be free to reinstate the unconstitutional sodomy laws of your past.

We also want to continue to be honest about our Blue State sexuality. You can continue to keep all of your perverted secrets in your evangelical closet hidden from everyone except your victims.

As noted by one of my games of *Red State, Blue State*, the Blue States also like abortion. The truth is, we love abortion. We soften this immoral attitude by saying that we are for a woman's "right to choose." What a crock! That, my Red State friends, is all smoke and mirrors. We really do love abortion. We want to continue to have abortion as an option, not only for horny teens who are not prepared to be parents, but for the victims of rape and incest, and in those rare situations where a mother's life is at stake. We want these fetuses out of the womb and out of our personal lives forever. However, it would be nice if we could transfer these fetuses from the womb to a Petri dish where they can be studied in the effort to help conquer disease and other infirmities. I believe scientists call this practice stem-cell research.

For you, we will let your teens, rape and incest victims, and dying mothers have all of the babies that they want. And if these offspring struggle with poverty, we will try not to be sanctimonious liberals who move into your neighborhoods with communistic social programs that seek to eradicate poverty. No sirree Jim Bob! We won't do that anymore. If your kids want to have kids, your kids should be taking care of them. There is no need for Blue State intervention. If all of these impoverished children having impoverished children causes a myriad of social problems for you, we will ignore it out of deference to your values and your culture.

Finally, the War in Iraq is on all of our minds. This tragic affair has disturbed all patriotic Americans. Unfortunately, because we are a united nation, we do have to go to war together. This is an area where the Blue States need your help. We beg you to stop electing people who have never served in a war who want to start and operate wars that cost thousands of lives. Knowing that it is only logical that a person who has never been to war cannot possibly understand the trauma, we ask you to please hold these cowards accountable for their actions in future elections.

We need your help so that in the future we no longer send our troops to war unless we have perfect reasons. If you refuse to help us in this area, you must remember that it will be your children who suffer more than ours. As you know, Red States are losing more citizens to the violence of war than Blue States.

On second thought, if Red State culture promotes the election of "chicken-hawks" who like to start wars for suspect reasons, maybe it is a Red State obligation to bear more of the burden.

I also would like to make one last apology. I want you to know that I am sorry for accusing you of blaspheming your Lord and Savior Jesus Christ. Who knows, maybe you are right. Your values and religious convictions are your business. Furthermore, if I am wrong in my interpretation of Christ's message, I accept my eternal punishment. If you are wrong, and Jesus was not a conservative lunatic, I hope that you will willingly accept your punishment of an eternity in Hell. It is the honorable thing to do.

That being said, I still think Paul of Tarsus was a blasphemous asshole, even if everyone else loves him.

I say all of this with complete and utter honesty. I know that I can sometimes be a sarcastic and negative jerk, but I want to assure you that this is truly the way I feel. You should do what you need to do to preserve your culture. Likewise, I need to help preserve mine.

There is no reason to impose our cultures on one another. We are very different, and we have a right to be different without imposing our values on each other. Neither of us will ever change. We are who we are.

I think we will both agree with the late, great, Chinaman and sage Confucius when he said, "You can't polish a turd."

With love and admiration,

John S. Grevstad
Blue State Liberal

Notes

Part I
The Plight of a Blue State Liberal
Chapter 1: Blue State Horror
1. "cnn.com Election Results" 3 November 2004 cnn.com 18 November 2004
<http://www.cnn.com/ELECTION/2004/pages/results/states/US/P/00/epolls.
0.html>

Chapter 2: Red State, Blue State Part I
1. Barry Kosmin and Egon Mayer "American Religious Identification Survey,"
The Graduate School and University Center of the City University of New York,
2001. <http://www.gc.cuny.edu/studies/aris_index.htm>
2. Michael J. Sheridan "A PASTORAL LETTER TO THE CATHOLIC FAITH-
FUL OF THE DIOCESE OF COLORADO SPRINGS ON THE DUTIES OF
CATHOLIC POLITICIANS AND VOTERS," *catholic.org* May 17, 2004.
<http://www.catholic.org/featured/headline.php?ID=967>
3. "cnn.com Election Results"

Chapter 3: Contemplating God
1. Dana Milbank, "Religious Right Finds It's Center in Oval Office: Bush
Emerges as Movement's Leader After Robertson Leaves Christian Coalition,"
The Washington Post, December 24, 2001.
<http://www.washingtonpost.com/ac2/wp-dyn?pagename=article&node=
&contentId=A19253-2001Dec23&notFound=true>
2. Deborah Caldwell Did God Intervene? "Evangelicals are crediting God with
securing re-election victory for George W. Bush," *Beliefnet.com*
<http://www.beliefnet.com/story/156/story_15602_3.html>
3. Frontline: The Jesus Factor March 17, 2000 "The Jesus Day Proclamation:
Reproduced from the holdings of the Texas State Archives," *pbs.com.*
4. "Bush Kills: 152 Executions as Governor of Texas," *bushkills.com.*
<http://www.bushkills.com/>
5. Ibid.

Part II

How in The Hell Did The Liberal Jesus Become a Conservative Icon?

Chapter 4: Blaming Paul

1. "Why Christian Fundamentalist & Many other Conservatives Prefer Paul's teaching to Jesus Christ's," *liberalslikechrist.org*
<http://www.liberalslikechrist.org/about/paulvsall.html>

2. Ibid.

3. Ibid.

4. Ibid.

5. "Thomas Jefferson's letters on Liberty and Religion," *sullivancounty.com.*
<http://www.sullivan-county.com/identity/jeff_letters.htm#jmorality>

Chapter 5: Wolves

1. "Adolf Hitler Quotes," *Brainyquotes.com*:
<http://www.brainyquote.com/quotes/authors/a/adolf_hitler.html>

2. "Bush = God's voice" Burnt Orange Report News, Politics, and Fun From Deep in the Heart of Texas," *burntorangereport.com*, July 17, 2004.
<http://www.burntorangereport.com/archives/001880.html>

3. bin Laden,Osama "The Nuclear Bomb of Islam."

4. "Famous Saddam Hussein Quotes" *allgreatquotes.com.*
<http://www.allgreatquotes.com/saddam_hussein_quotes.shtml>

5. Alan Cooperman "Bush leaves specifics of his faith to speculation. President is openly religious, but his true beliefs remain mystery," *MSNBC.com*, September 16, 2004. <http://msnbc.msn.com/id/6014570/>

6. "Bush says 'God Speaks through Me': But what does he *really* mean," *irregulartimes.com*. <http://www.irregulartimes.com/godspeaksthroughme.html>

7. Deborah Caldwell "Did God Intervene? Evangelicals are crediting God with securing re-election victory for George W. Bush," *beliefnet.com.*
<http://www.beliefnet.com/story/156/story_15602_3.html>

8. Ibid.

9. Ibid.

10. "Pray for George W Bush: Praying for George W Bush and America," *prayforgeorgewbush.com.*
<http://www.prayforgeorgewbush.com/pages/236635/index.htm>

11. George Pataki, "Remarks by Gov. George Pataki at the Republican National Convention," *The Washington Post*, September 2, 2004.

12. Ibid.

13. Bob Sjogren "MEMORANDUM SUBJECT: FAST FOR PRESIDENT BUSH," *breakthechain.org.*
<http://www.breakthechain.org/exclusives/fast4george.html>

14. "Giuliani: 'Thank God that George Bush is our president'" August 31, 2004 CNN.com 20 December 2004 <http://www.cnn.com/2004/ALLPOLITICS/08/30/giuliani.transcript/>
15. Steven Waldman "Heaven Sent: Does God Endorse George Bush?" *slate.com*, September 3, 2004. <http://slate.msn.com/id/2106590/>
16. "Adolf Hitler Quotes" Brainyquotes.com
17. "Adolf Hitler Quotes" *military-quotes.com.* <http://www.military-quotes.com/Hitler.htm>
18. "Adolf Hitler Quotes" *brainyquotes.com.*
19. Ibid
20. "Napoleon Bonaparte quotes" *brainyquotes.com* <http://www.brainyquote.com/quotes/quotes/n/napoleonbo165319.html>

Part III
Conservative Issues and The Message of The Liberal Christ
Chapter 6: The Sanctity of Life

1. "Supreme Court Collection "410 U.S. 113 Roe v. Wade APPEAL FROM THE UNITED STATES DISTRICT COURT FOR THE NORTHERN DISTRICT OF TEXAS No. 70-18 Argued: December 13, 1971—Decided: January 22, 1973," *Legal Information Institute.* <http://supct.law.cornell.edu/supct/search/display.html?terms=abortion&url=/supct/html/historics/USSC_CR_0410_0113_ZO.html>
2. "Dean—Bush Stem cell Decision Based on Religion," *foxnews.com*, January 9, 2004. <http://www.foxnews.com/story/0,2933,107955,00.html>
3. John F. Harris "God Gave U.S. 'What we Deserve' Falwell says," *The Washington Post*, September 14, 2001. <http://www.washingtonpost.com/ac2/wp-dyn?pagename=article&node=&contentId=A28620-2001Sep14&notFound=true>
4. Melanie Hunter "Bush Signs Unborn Victims of Violence Act into Law," *cns-mews.com* April 1, 2004. <http://www.cnsnews.com/ViewPolitics.asp?Page=%5CPolitics%5Carchve%5C200404%5CPOL20040401d.html>
5. "Robertson: U.S. Shouldn't interfere with China's forced abortion policy," *cnn.com*, April 16, 2001. <http://archives.cnn.com/2001/US/04/16/robertson.abortion/>
6. Gary Lainger "Poll: No Role for Government in Schiavo Case," *abcnews.com*, March 21, 2005. <http://abcnews.go.com/Politics/PollVault/story?id=599622&page=1>

7. Stephanie Chavez "Stem Cell Funding is Put in Spotlight," *Los Angeles Times*, May 9, 2004

8. "Bush Sacrifices Stem Cell Research to Radical Right Wing Politics," Democratic National Committee *democrats.org* May 24, 2005. <http://www.democrats.org/news/200505250001.html>

9. Peter Baker "President Vows Veto on Stem Cell Research," *The Washington Post*, May 21, 2005. <http://www.washingtonpost.com/wp-dyn/content/article/2005/05/20/AR2005052000482.html>

Chapter 7 The Defense of Marriage

1. "Hillary GOODRIDGE & others [FN1] vs. DEPARTMENT OF PUBLIC HEALTH & another. [FN2] SJC-08860," *The Massachusetts Court System*, November 18, 2003. <http://www.mass.gov/courts/courtsandjudges/courts/supremejudicialcourt/goodridge.htm>

2. Inside Politics "Bush wants marriage reserved for heterosexuals," *cnn.com*, October 28, 2003. <http://www.cnn.com/2003/ALLPOLITICS/07/30/bush.gay.marriage/>

3. Ibid.

4. "Positive Atheisms Big Scary List of Pat Robertson quotations," *positiveatheism.org*. <http://www.positiveatheism.org/hist/quotes/revpat.htm>

5. "Positive Atheisms Big Scary list of Jerry Falwell quotations," *positiveatheism.org*. <http://www.positiveatheism.org/hist/quotes/foulwell.htm>

6. Henry E. Adams, Ph.D., Lester W.Wright, Jr., Ph.D. and Bethany A. Lohr "Is Homophobia associated with homosexual arousal?" *selfhelpmagazine.com*, March 18, 1999. <http://www.selfhelpmagazine.com/articles/glb/glbtphobia.html>

7. "Pastor convicted of soliciting sex from Teenager," *timesleader.com*, January 15, 2004. <http://www.timesleader.com/mld/timesleader/7717427.htm>

8. "The Propagandist: Neal Horsley, America's leading anti-abortion webmaster, is the profane voice of the extreme Christian right," *splcenter.org* <http://www.splcenter.org/intel/intelreport/article.jsp?aid=136>

9. "Anti-abortion extremist Neal Horsley makes a stunning admission about his farm!" *freerepublic.com*, May 9, 2005. <http://www.freerepublic.com/focus/f-news/1399634/posts>

10. Chris McGann and Cathy Mulady "Gay Sex Scandal Rocks Spokane," *The Seattle Post-Intelligencer*, May 23, 2005.

11. "President Defends Sanctity of Marriage: statement by the President," *whitehouse.gov*, November 18, 2003.

<http://www.whitehouse.gov/news/releases/2003/11/20031118-4.html>
12. "Bush Brother's Divorce Reveals Sex Romp," *cnn.com*, November 25, 2003.
<http://www.cnn.com/2003/ALLPOLITICS/11/25/bush.brother.reut/>
13. Ayelish McGarvey "Dr. Hager's Family Values," *thenation.com*, May 11, 2005 <http://www.thenation.com/doc.mhtml?i=20050530&s=mcgarvey>
14. Ibid
15. "Giuliani accused of 'notorious adultery'" *cbsnews.com*, June 21, 2002.
<http://www.cbsnews.com/stories/2002/06/21/politics/main512992.shtml>
16. Stephanie Salter "A brief history of how marriages have been 'designed'" *polkonline.com*, December 14, 2004.
<http://www.polkonline.com/stories/012300/opi_marriages.shtml>
17. John Iwasaki "Pastor Holds the Line on Gay Unions," *The Seattle Post Intelligencer*, May 2, 2005.
18. Charles Pope "Microsoft Ends Ties with Reed," *The Seattle Post Intelligencer*, May 28, 2005.
19. "Pastor Holds the Line on Gay Unions"

Chapter 8:Money Matters

1. "National Debt Skyrockets Under Bush Administration," *The Washington Dispatch*, November 19, 2004.
<http://www.washingtondispatch.com/spectrum/archives/000731.html>
2. "Heresy: Oral Roberts," *ondoctrine.com*.
<http://www.ondoctrine.com/10robero.htm>
3. Oral Roberts, "How I Learned Jesus Was Not Poor," page 16) "Were Jesus and the Disciples Rich?" *myfortress.org*.
<http://www.myfortress.org/WasJesusRich.html>
the Disciples Rich?" myfortress.org 13 November 2004
<http://www.myfortress.org/WasJesusRich.html>
4. John Hagee, Praise-A-Thon, Trinity Broadcasting Network (TBN), November 5, 2004 "Were Jesus and the Disciples Rich?"*myfortress.org*
<http://www.myfortress.org/WasJesusRich.html>
5. Jesse Duplantis, January 24, 2004, The Church Channel, "The Choke Hold") "Were Jesus and the Disciples Rich?"myfortress.org
<http://www.myfortress.org/WasJesusRich.html>
6. Jesse Duplantis, December 19, 2003 TBN, "The just shall live by faith," "Were Jesus and the Disciples Rich?" *myfortress.org*.
<http://www.myfortress.org/WasJesusRich.html>
7. D.R. McConnell, A Different Gospel, page 174. Fred Price, "Faith, Foolishness, or Presumption?" page 34 "Were Jesus and the Disciples Rich?"*myfortress.org*. <http://www.myfortress.org/WasJesusRich.html>

8. (John Avanzini, "Believer's Voice of Victory" TBN January 20, 1991 "Were Jesus and the Disciples Rich?" *myfortress.org.* <http://www.myfortress.org/WasJesusRich.html>
9. Kenneth Copeland "The Gospel to the Poor" "Were Jesus and the Disciples Rich?"*myfortress.org.* <http://www.myfortress.org/WasJesusRich.html>
10. "Crystal Cathedral Ministries: Books, Gift and Music," cystalcathedral.org <http://store.yahoo.com/cathedral-gifts/aumibo.html>
11. David Brunori "David Brunori's tax talk: Death and No Taxes," *governing.com,* August 2004. <http://governing.com/textbook/estate.htm>

Chapter 9:Moral Crimes and Immoral Punishment
1. "Religious Facts about Adolf Hitler," *The Religious Right: Champions of Intolerance.* <http://metamyth.tripod.com/q-rright.htm>
2. "The Christian Coalition's Fake-Faith Healer," *The Religious Right: Champions of Intolerance.* <http://metamyth.tripod.com/q-rright.htm>
3. Ibid
4. Ibid
5. Ann Coulter "Slander: Liberal Lies About the American Right," *ethicalatheist.com.* <http://www.ethicalatheist.com/docs/ann_coulter.html>
6. "The Christian Coalition's Fake-Faith Healer"
7. "Jerry Falwell is 'newspeak' for The Moral Majority," *The Religious Right: Champions of Intolerance.* <http://metamyth.tripod.com/q-rright.htm>
8. "The Christian Coalition's Fake-Faith Healer"
9. Ibid
10. "Robert E. Lee's Opinion Regarding Slavery," *civilwarhome.com.* <http://www.civilwarhome.com/leepierce.htm>
11. "Strom Watch" *stromwatch.com.* <http://stromwatch.com/>
12. Ibid
13. "Almost Dead, But Not Forgotten: Jesse Helms," *bettybowers.com* <http://www.bettybowers.com/helms.html>
14. Ibid
15. Ibid
16. Ibid
17. Saul Landau "Rush to Judgment: Should Limbaugh do Time?" *Rush Limbaugh TV show (12/8/92) counterpunch.com* October 23, 2003 <http://www.counterpunch.org/landau10252003.html>
18. "E-mails of support pour In to the EIB Network," *rushlimbaugh.com.* <http://www.rushlimbaugh.com/home/letters/emails>
19. "Limbaugh on Drugs: People like Limbaugh should go to jail, says Limbaugh," *fair.org,* November/December 2003.

<http://www.fair.org/extra/0311/limbaugh-drugs.html>
20. "E-mails of support pour In to the EIB Network"
21. Saul Landau "Rush to Judgment: Should Limbaugh do Time?"

Chapter 10: Blind Man's Revenge
1. "The Deck of Chickenhawks" *chickenhawkcards.com,*
<http://www.chickenhawkcards.com/>
3. "Bush vows to defeat Iraqi resistance," *bbc.co.uk,* September 8, 2003
<http://news.bbc.co.uk/2/hi/americas/3088772.stm>
2. "Israeli Study: Iraq War Hurts War On Terror" *foxnews.com,* October 11,
2004. <http://www.tau.ac.il/jcss/foxnews111004.html>
4. "Weapons of Mass Destruction: Who Said What, When," *counterpunch.com,*
May 29, 2003. <http://www.counterpunch.org/wmd05292003.html>
5. Mike Allen "Bush Asserts That Al Qaeda Has Links to Iraq's Hussein," *The
Washington Post,* September 26, 2002.
<http://www.washingtonpost.com/ac2/wp-dyn/A3206-2002Sep25?language
=printer>
6. Dana Millbank "Bush Disavows Hussein-Sept. 11 Link," *The Washington
Post,* September 18, 2003.
<http://www.washingtonpost.com/ac2/wp-dyn/A25571-2003Sep17?language
=printer>
7. "The Downing Street Memos: Seeking the Truth since May 13, 2005," *down-
ingstreetmemo.com.* <http://www.downingstreetmemo.com/>
8. "Report: Tillman's family critical of way Army handled his death" *usatoday,*
May 23, 2005.
<http://www.usatoday.com/sports/football/nfl/2005-05-23-tillman-family_x
.htm>
9. "Reaction to the 2004 State of the Union Address," *American Research Group
Inc.* December 26, 2004 <http://www.americanresearchgroup.com/sotu/>
10. "George W. Bush: Update on the War on Terror," *presidentialrhetoric.com,*
September 7, 2003.
<http://www.presidentialrhetoric.com/speeches/09.07.03.html>
11. Dana Millbank and Mike Allen "U.S.Will Take Action Against Iraq, Bush
Says," *The Washington Post,* March 14, 2002.
<http://www.washingtonpost.com/ac2/wp-dyn?pagename=article&node=&
contentId=A22091-2002Mar13&notFound=true>
12. "George Bush Quotes," *boycottliberalism.com.*
<http://boycottliberalism.com/Bush-quotes.htm>
13. "State of Our Union Has Never Been Stronger," *newsmax.com,* January 29,
2002 <http://www.newsmax.com/archives/articles/2002/1/29/205222.shtml>

14. "George Bush Quotes"

15. "President Bush Discusses Freedom in Iraq and the Middle East," *white-house.gov*, November 6, 2003.
<http://www.whitehouse.gov/news/releases/2003/11/20031106-2.html>

16. "President Bush: Address to the Nation on the Initial Military Operationsin Iraq," *americanrhetoric.com*.
<http://www.americanrhetoric.com/speeches/wariniraq/gwbushiraq31903 .htm>

17. "George Bush Quotes"

18. "Iraq Body Count: Civilians Reported Killed by Military Intervention in Iraq" *iraqbodycount.net* November 5, 2005.
<http://www.iraqbodycount.net/>

19. "McCain: 'No Confidence' in Rumsfeld," *cnn.com*, December 22, 2004
<http://www.cnn.com/2004/ALLPOLITICS/12/14/mccain.ap/>

20. Ibid

21. "Rumsfeld Under Fire From GOP," *cbsnews.com*, December 19, 2004
<http://www.cbsnews.com/stories/2004/12/14/iraq/main660862.shtml

22. "Lott: Rumsfeld Should Go," *foxnews.com*, December 17, 2004.
<http://www.foxnews.com/story/0,2933,141791,00.html>

23. "Bush defends Rumsfeld as 'caring fellow'" *cnn.com*, December 20, 2004.
<http://www.cnn.com/2004/ALLPOLITICS/12/20/rumsfeld.ap/>

Part IV
Blue State Pride, Red State Shame
Chapter 11: Red State, Blue State Part II

1. "Jerry Falwell is 'newspeak' for The Moral Majority," *The Religious Right: Champions of Intolerance.*
<http://metamyth.tripod.com/q-rright.htm>

2. "Martin Luther's 20th Century Soulmate Speaks," *The Religious Right: Champions of Intolerance.*
<http://metamyth.tripod.com/q-rright.htm>

3. "Jerry Falwell is 'newspeak' for The Moral Majority"

4. Jonathan Alter "The Audacity of Hope," *Newsweek,* December 27, 2004.

5. Howard Fineman "Mister Right," *Newsweek,* December 27, 2004

0-595-34484-4

978-0-595-34484-0
0-595-34484-4

www.ingramcontent.com/pod-product-compliance
Lightning Source LLC
Chambersburg PA
CBHW061345280526
45784CB00001B/136

* 9 780595 344840 *